The Sweater Book

The Sweater Book

Edited by Amy Carroll

BALLANTINE BOOKS · NEW YORK

Contents
Everyday

Introduction

The idea of doing The Sweater Book *arose out of a proximity to London's Covent Garden market where craftspeople can be seen displaying and selling hand-made items. Among the chief attractions are the stalls of knitwear designers whose individual sweaters exhibit a flair not usually seen in printed patterns but only in garments for sale from expensive boutiques and shops. By asking the designers to create original designs for use in this book, we hoped to make the best of what's new in fashion knitwear available to the home knitter.*
Though not all the designers are connected with the Covent Garden endeavor, they do share certain characteristics: they are all producing original handknits for sale from home, shops or stalls or for use in publications; and they all have strong ideas about experimenting with shapes, colors, textures, yarns and techniques.

JANE BALL studied fashion and knitted fabric design at school and then began producing knitwear ranges from her workshop for fashion designers as well as selling directly to shops; currently she is designing for industry as well. She uses natural yarns, especially mohair, silk and cotton, mainly because she feels they look good while being comfortable to wear. Her patterns are basically simple ones and rely on stripes and colors for good effect.

BETTY BARNDEN studied and taught knitted textile design but now works from a small studio producing sample garments with instructional patterns for manufacturers' leaflets and magazines as well as selling garments in retail outlets. While her pieces are fashionable, she is most interested in the techniques of knitting and has been experimenting with three-dimensional shapes in her work, such as intarsia picture knitting.

SUE BLACK believes in knitting as a means of artistic expression. Trained in textiles, she later discovered that fabric, form and surface pattern could be constructed as one continuous organic process. Alongside actual knitting techniques, she uses those of appliqué, quilting, embroidery and hand-painting to broaden her approach to design. That she is very successful at it is evidenced by the number of exhibitions she has shown in.

JOAN CHATTERLEY
(*pictured above*) began as a leather designer after studying fashion at college but quickly switched to knitting as it offered more opportunity to experiment with different colors and textures. Starting with machine knitting she now produces handknits in natural yarns only, and her designs contain a profusion of colors, patterns and stitch effects.

JOSE FRANKS worked with Patricia Roberts after leaving art college but now designs and sells her own range of knitwear. She works in natural yarns only, and prefers traditional stitch patterns and sweater shapes. Fair-Isle and "Thirties" styles are primary among the garments she shows.

PIP HUES is a self-taught knitter who studied fashion at college but only began designing at the time when imported sweaters with multiple patterns and colors became popular. She created her own sweater shapes daunted by printed patterns and evolved designs that though simple to do, look "complicated". As well as color, symbols and pattern designs are important to her work and she finds much inspiration from shapes which appear in nature.

ZOË HUNT began earning her living as a knitter by working for Kaffe Fassett. She regards knitting as a form of decoration and not just as a means of keeping the body warm. She approaches a garment as a painter approaches a picture – choosing and using yarns as her colors, mixing different weights and textures. Knowing that knitting is based on a grid formation, she finds that geometric shapes work best for her, and is inspired by things rich in color and theatrical in feel.

NURIT KAYE became disenchanted with the lack of originality in printed patterns when she began knitting for her children and felt impelled to create her own designs. For children especially she feels that yarns must be machine-washable and that garments have simple structures but employ strong colors and motifs. Lately she has begun knitting for adults with the use of more sophisticated styles and designs.

SARA KOTCH first designed handknit patterns for magazines and then went on to create machine knitted designs for children. However, she returned to hand-knitting after studying textiles at college and now tends to regard knitting as fabric. She likes a very rich effect working from a quite structured design and then cancelling it out with random stripes, lines or flashes. While the end result is pleasingly toned down, it does consist of bright, complementary colors.

CLARE ROWLAND AND JOHN ALLEN work as the design team, "John and Clare". He runs the knitting department at London's Royal College of Art and designs garments for their partnership and for other companies; she hand-dyes yarns and has kept a flock of breeding ewes for wool. They create designs together: John contributes to the concept and choice of yarns; Clare makes up the garment adapting the design if the materials make it necessary. As well as employing a wide variety of yarns and trimmings, they also make use of fancy stitch patterns.

FELICITY RUDD applies her knowledge of dressmaking and textiles, learnt at college, to her knitting. Feeling that most people have too many preconceived ideas about color and are too conservative in their approach to clothes, she prefers to create designs incorporating colors and textures not normally found together. She hopes that her garments will be used by people as a way of expressing themselves, not just as a covering.

MAGGIE WHITE studied modern art at college and translated her interest into handknitted garments which she produces from her country workshop. She uses bright primary colors and abstract motifs, like the "Expressionists", to create original designs for both sexes. She keeps her garment shapes very simple – the colors and design are what sets them off. She feels people can look at her garments in the same way they would look at paintings. In keeping with this belief, she has exhibited her sweaters at galleries and shops.

BELINDA WILLIAMSON began designing fabrics for other designers and shops after studying fashion and textiles at college and then went on to found her own company. Recently she began to apply her ideas to handknits. She likes simple but graphic shapes such as batwings and rectangles which she charts out and makes up in brightly colored textured yarns.

Racy Checks

Diamond-studded dropped shoulder pullover with shoulder
fastening looks sporty on both sexes, though males might prefer a
subtler color scheme and plainer buttons.

MATERIALS

Yarn
Main yarn M *20oz* knitting worsted (natural)
1oz each of knitting worsted in 12 different
shades

Needles
1 pair no 3
1 pair no 4 and one spare

Notions
4 buttons $\frac{1}{2}$in in diameter

Stitch gauge
24 sts and 28 rows to 4in over st st on no 4
needles (or size needed to obtain given
tension).

Special note:
In the pattern, both the main yarn and the
second working yarn are carried behind the
knitting when not in use. Secure these by
knitting in at back about every 3 or 4 sts. Do
not secure at every stitch as this results in very
dense knitting.

BACK

With no 3 needles and yarn M cast on 98 sts.
Row 1 K2, *p2, k2; rep from * to end.
Row 2 P2, *k2, p2; rep from * to end.
Repeat these 2 rows until work measures 3¼in.
Increase row: With right side facing k2, *inc in
next st, k2; rep from * to end – 130 sts. Change
to no 4 needles and st st (first row purl). Work
7 rows in yarn M. Now start the diamond pattern, from the chart. Continue adding one more
diamond, 13 sts wide and 13 rows deep at each
color change, one st to the left. After 8 diamond
pattern repeats, add one diamond to the right,
as well as to the left (although it will not be a
complete diamond). Work 3 more diamond
pattern repeats.
Shape neck: After completing 12 diamond
patterns, with right side facing and yarn M knit
47 sts, turn. Next row purl. Next row knit to last
2 sts; k2tog. Repeat the last 2 rows once more.
Put the remaining sts onto a stitch holder. Put
the central 36 sts onto a stitch holder. On the
remaining 47 sts repeat as for the right side
reversing shaping, but before binding off work
6 more rows in st st for the button band.

FRONT

Work the same as back, but reversing the
diamond pattern so that the diamonds begin
on the left side of the front, rather than the
right. Start neck shaping half way through the
11th diamond pattern.
Shape neck: With right side facing, and continuing in diamond pattern, knit 50 sts. Turn
and purl to the end of the row. Next row knit
49 sts, k2tog, turn. Next row purl. Repeat the
last 2 rows decreasing at the neck edge every
alternate row until 44 sts remain, ending with a
purl row. Work 4 more rows in st st to complete
last diamonds. ** Change to no 3 needles and
work 4 rows in k1, p1 rib. Next row rib 6, bind off
2, rib 10, bind off 2, rib 10, bind off 2, rib 10. Next
row rib 10, cast on 2, rib 10, cast on 2, rib 10,
cast on 2, rib 6. Work 3 more rows in rib, then
bind off. Put central 30 sts on a stitch holder.

Work other side to match as far as **, reversing
shaping. Work 6 rows of st st in yarn M.

SLEEVES

Right sleeve
With no 3 needles and yarn M cast on 50 sts.
Work in rib as on the back for 3¼in. Increase
row: Knit and increase in every st to end – 100
sts. Change to no 4 needles and purl one
row. Increase at both ends of every other row
until there are 130 sts, at the same time work
diamonds as follows. Start the first diamond in
the center of the 2nd st st row. Work one more
diamond immediately above it, and then
another one. Then continue in yarn M for
another 38 rows. On the next row work another
diamond in the center of the sleeve, directly
above the first 3 diamonds, but only 11 sts wide
and 11 sts deep. Work another 3 diamonds
above this one, 11 sts wide and 11 sts deep,
one immediately above, one above and to the

left and one above and to the right, separated
by one st. Above these 3 work 5 more diamonds
in the same way, then another 7. Finally above
the 7 start another row of 9 diamonds, but omit
the central one so there are actually only 8.
Work the last diamond pattern in shades to
match the diamonds on the body, and work
just enough rows so that complete diamonds
are formed when the sleeves are sewn in. Work
another one or 2 rows for seam allowance, then
bind off.

Left sleeve
Work the same as the right, with different yarn
changes as illustrated, and omit the 3½
diamonds at the center top.

Chart for back
For the front reverse the
position of the diamonds
so that they start on the
left side of the front,
rather than the right. The
pattern consists of
diamonds 13 sts by 13
rows. At each color
change add one more
diamond to the left on
the back, and to the right
on the front.

NECKBAND

Join shoulders: Transfer the sts from the back shoulder stitch holder onto a needle. With wrong side facing work one st from each needle together until all have been used. Bind off in the normal way. With no 3 needles and yarn M pick up 8 sts along the button band, 42 from the back neck (including those left on stitch holder), 20 along left front, 30 from front stitch holder, 20 along right front, 6 along buttonhole band – 126 sts altogether. Work 3 rows in k2, p2 rib. Next row rib to the last 5 sts, bind off 2, rib 3. Next row rib 3, cast on 2, rib to the end of the row. Work 4 more rows in rib. Bind off loosely, using a no 4 needle.

PUTTING TOGETHER

Sew in the sleeves with back stitch, matching the diamonds to the body. Sew side and sleeve seams. Sew in all ends. Sew on buttons.

designed by **MAGGIE WHITE**

MEASUREMENTS

To fit chest 38–40in (97–102cm)
Back width 21½in (54cm)
Length 27in (68cm)
Sleeve seam 21½in (54cm)

Caterpillar Stripe

Decorative pullover with puffed sleeves and button bands at wrist and waist is knitted up in scraps of earthy-toned shades of classic and novelty yarns.

12 st pattern repeat

Begin motif 2 sts in from the edge on the front, back and sleeves. Introduce colors as you wish, balancing the use of thick and thin yarns.

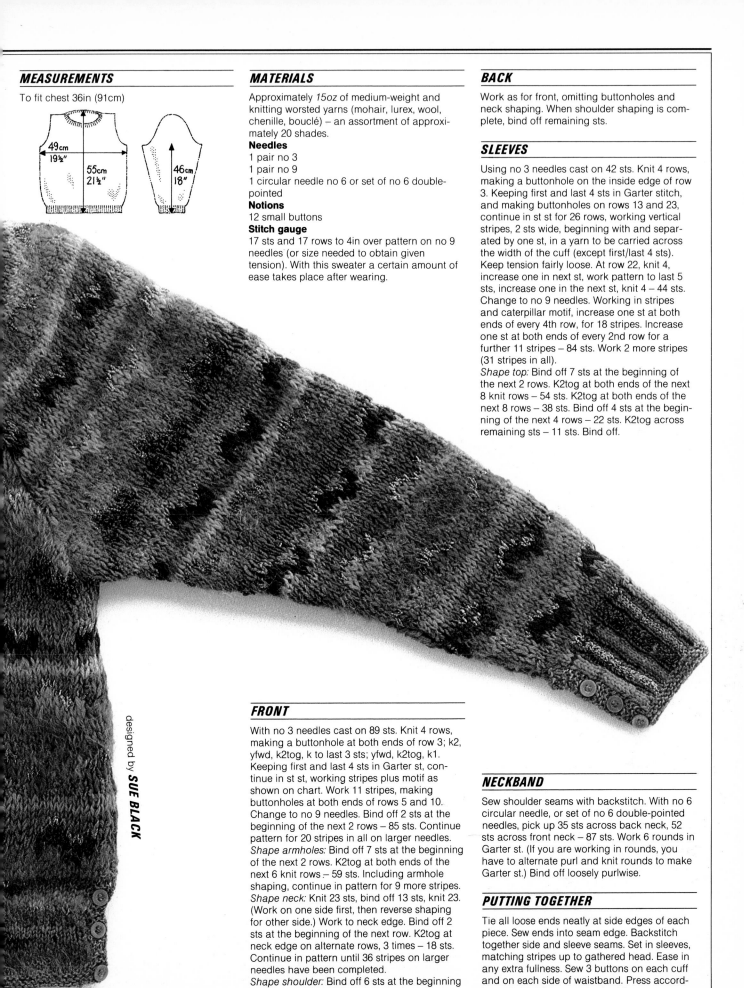

MEASUREMENTS

To fit chest 36in (91cm)

49cm 19½"

55cm 21½"

46cm 18"

designed by *SUE BLACK*

MATERIALS

Approximately *15oz* of medium-weight and knitting worsted yarns (mohair, lurex, wool, chenille, bouclé) – an assortment of approximately 20 shades.

Needles

1 pair no 3

1 pair no 9

1 circular needle no 6 or set of no 6 double-pointed

Notions

12 small buttons

Stitch gauge

17 sts and 17 rows to 4in over pattern on no 9 needles (or size needed to obtain given tension). With this sweater a certain amount of ease takes place after wearing.

FRONT

With no 3 needles cast on 89 sts. Knit 4 rows, making a buttonhole at both ends of row 3; k2, yfwd, k2tog, k to last 3 sts; yfwd, k2tog, k1. Keeping first and last 4 sts in Garter st, continue in st st, working stripes plus motif as shown on chart. Work 11 stripes, making buttonholes at both ends of rows 5 and 10. Change to no 9 needles. Bind off 2 sts at the beginning of the next 2 rows – 85 sts. Continue pattern for 20 stripes in all on larger needles. *Shape armholes:* Bind off 7 sts at the beginning of the next 2 rows. K2tog at both ends of the next 6 knit rows – 59 sts. Including armhole shaping, continue in pattern for 9 more stripes. *Shape neck:* Knit 23 sts, bind off 13 sts, knit 23. (Work on one side first, then reverse shaping for other side.) Work to neck edge. Bind off 2 sts at the beginning of the next row. K2tog at neck edge on alternate rows, 3 times – 18 sts. Continue in pattern until 36 stripes on larger needles have been completed. *Shape shoulder:* Bind off 6 sts at the beginning of the next and following 2 alternate rows.

BACK

Work as for front, omitting buttonholes and neck shaping. When shoulder shaping is complete, bind off remaining sts.

SLEEVES

Using no 3 needles cast on 42 sts. Knit 4 rows, making a buttonhole on the inside edge of row 3. Keeping first and last 4 sts in Garter stitch, and making buttonholes on rows 13 and 23, continue in st st for 26 rows, working vertical stripes, 2 sts wide, beginning with and separated by one st, in a yarn to be carried across the width of the cuff (except first/last 4 sts). Keep tension fairly loose. At row 22, knit 4, increase one in next st, work pattern to last 5 sts, increase one in the next st, knit 4 – 44 sts. Change to no 9 needles. Working in stripes and caterpillar motif, increase one st at both ends of every 4th row, for 18 stripes. Increase one st at both ends of every 2nd row for a further 11 stripes – 84 sts. Work 2 more stripes (31 stripes in all).
Shape top: Bind off 7 sts at the beginning of the next 2 rows. K2tog at both ends of the next 8 knit rows – 54 sts. K2tog at both ends of the next 8 rows – 38 sts. Bind off 4 sts at the beginning of the next 4 rows – 22 sts. K2tog across remaining sts – 11 sts. Bind off.

NECKBAND

Sew shoulder seams with backstitch. With no 6 circular needle, or set of no 6 double-pointed needles, pick up 35 sts across back neck, 52 sts across front neck – 87 sts. Work 6 rounds in Garter st. (If you are working in rounds, you have to alternate purl and knit rounds to make Garter st.) Bind off loosely purlwise.

PUTTING TOGETHER

Tie all loose ends neatly at side edges of each piece. Sew ends into seam edge. Backstitch together side and sleeve seams. Set in sleeves, matching stripes up to gathered head. Ease in any extra fullness. Sew 3 buttons on each cuff and on each side of waistband. Press according to instructions on yarn band.

Random Flashes

A multitude of medium-weight yarns in different colors and textures are knitted on circular needles for ease of construction. Thin metallic thread is wrapped around yarns for sparkle.

MATERIALS

Yarn
8 (9, 10, 11)oz of medium-weight yarns (mohair, lurex, wool, bouclé) – an assortment of approximately 30 shades.

Special note:
Introduce colors as you wish, balancing the use of thick and thin yarns.

Needles
1 pair no 0
1 pair no 3
1 no 0 circular needle
1 no 3 circular needle

Notions
3 buttons

Stitch gauge
28 sts and 36 rows to 4in over st st on no 3 needles (or size needed to obtain given tension).

To make "flashes"
Use a separate ball of yarn for each flash. (In the garment illustrated the flashes were made in the same yarn as the rib run with a fine metallic thread.) See chart for approximate positioning. Work in pattern up to the place where you want to insert a flash. Drop the first yarn and knit 1, 2 or 3 sts with the new yarn. Weave the first yarn round the second to keep holes from appearing in the garment (see p. 121). Drop the second yarn and continue in pattern with the first yarn. Repeat the process, working 1, 2 or 3 more sts with the second yarn as you work back over the next 15–35 rows so that the flash is straight on the diagonal and approximately 4in long.

BODY

With no 0 circular needle cast on 247 (261, 275, 289) sts and work in k1, p1 rib for 10 rows, working the first row into the back of the cast-on stitches for a firmer edge.

1st buttonhole row: Rib 5 sts, bind off 4 sts and rib to end.
2nd buttonhole row: Rib to last 5 sts, cast on 4 sts, rib 5 sts.
Work 16 rows in single rib. Repeat 2 buttonhole rows. Rib 9 rows in single rib. Decrease row: Hold first 14 sts on stitch holder for front band. P4 (2, 9, 6), *p2tog, p9 (10, 10, 11), rep from * 18 times more; p2tog, p4 (1, 8, 6). Put last 14 sts on stitch holder for front band – 199 (213, 227, 241) sts.
Change to no 3 circular needle and st st. Next row k48 (52, 55, 59), make one st by picking up loop between sts and knit into back of it, and mark with thread, k103 (109, 117, 123), make one st and mark with thread, k48 (52, 55, 59) – 201 (215, 229, 243) sts.
Continue increasing in this way on every 4th row keeping increases one above the other until 19 increase rows have been knitted – 237 (251, 265, 279) sts. Continue working straight until there are 94 (100, 106, 112) rows of st st.
Armhole decreases: K48 (51, 54, 57) sts for right front, bind off 19 (20, 21, 22) sts. K103 (109, 115, 121) sts across back. Bind off 19 (20, 21, 22) sts. K48 (51, 54, 57) sts for left front. Continue on left front only with ordinary no 3

needles: Work 2 sts together at armhole edge at the beginning of the next 15 (16, 17, 18) rows – 33 (35, 37, 39) sts. Work straight for another 38 (41, 44, 47) rows. Bind off 7 (7, 7, 7) sts at armhole edge on next and following 3 alternate rows. Bind off remaining 5 (7, 9, 11) sts. Complete the left front reversing the shaping. Complete the back: Work 2 sts together at each end of next 5 rows – 93 (99, 105, 111) sts. Continue straight for another 48 (52, 56, 60) rows. Bind off 7 (7, 7, 7) sts at the beginning of the next 8 rows, then 5 (7, 9, 11) sts at the beginning of the next 2 rows. Bind off remaining 27 (29, 31, 33) sts.

ARMBAND

With ordinary no 0 needles cast on 14 sts and work in k1, p1 rib until band is long enough to reach from under armhole and back again when slightly stretched. Make two.

BUTTON BANDS

Buttonhole border (right front)
Using ordinary no 0 needles, rejoin yarn to 14 sts on stitch holder and make one buttonhole as before keeping spacing even. Continue in rib until it reaches to center back neck when slightly stretched.

Button border (left front)
As buttonhole border leaving out buttonhole.

PUTTING TOGETHER

Join shoulder seams. Stitch the button bands to the fronts and the sleeve bands to the armholes. Sew on 3 buttons.

MEASUREMENTS

To fit chest 32 (34, 36, 38)in (81, 86, 91, 97cm)

44(47,49,52)cm
17½(18½,19½,20½)"
57(60,62,63)cm
22½(23½,24½,25)"

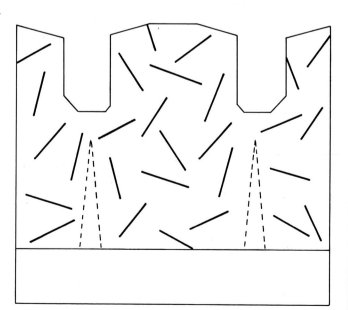

The above chart shows the positioning of the flashes on the garment illustrated. However you can work as many or as few flashes as you wish. The dotted lines indicate the area not knitted when increasing. The chart on the right shows 4 different ways of making the flashes.

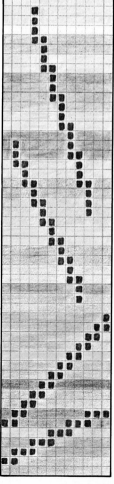

designed by **SARA KOTCH**

Florentines

A duo of unisex Fair-Isles – one slipover, one vest – made up in knitting worsted yarn in different color combinations. Carry the yarns loosely across the back for a good fit.

MATERIALS for slipover

Yarn
Main yarn M 7oz knitting worsted (burgundy)
Yarn A 2oz knitting worsted (natural)
Yarn B 2oz knitting worsted (pale pink)
Yarn C 2oz knitting worsted (dark pink)
Yarn D 5oz knitting worsted (beige)
Yarn E 2oz knitting worsted (pale blue)
Yarn F 2oz knitting worsted (dark blue)

Needles
1 pair no 3
1 pair no 6

stitch gauge
23 sts and 23 rows to 4in over pattern on no 6 needles (or size needed to obtain given tension).

NB Work is Fair-Isle throughout so weave yarn not in use behind work loosely to allow for essential give.

MEASUREMENTS

To fit chest 34 (36, 38, 40)in (86, 91, 97, 102cm)

43(46,49,53)cm
17(18,19½,21)"
64(65,66,67)cm.
25(25½,26,26½)"

Chart for back and front

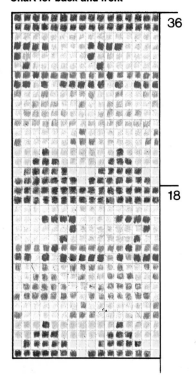

36

18

All sizes start knit rows here and begin purl rows at appropriate points

BACK

With no 3 needles and yarn M cast on 97 (105, 113, 121) sts. Work in k1, p1 rib for 3in. Change to no 6 needles and work 2 rows in st st ending on a purl row. Now follow pattern from chart (36 rows). Work straight until the back measures 15¾in from commencement (should be 2 repeats of the pattern).
Shape armholes: (Knit row) Bind off 5 sts at the beginning of the next 2 rows. K2tog at the beginning and end of every following alternate row until there are 79 (87, 95, 103) sts on the needle. Continue straight in pattern until work measures 8¾ (9, 9½, 10)in from the beginning of armhole shaping – ending on a purl row.
Shape shoulders: Bind off 7 (8, 9, 10) sts at the beginning of the next 6 rows until there are 37 (39, 41, 43) sts on the needle – leave these on a stitch holder for later.

FRONT

Work as for back as far as armhole shaping. Then bind off 5 sts at the beginning of the row and work 43 (47, 51, 55) sts – slip the remaining 49 (53, 57, 61) sts onto a stitch holder – turn and work the left side first.
Shape neck: (Purl row) P2tog, work to the end. K2tog at the beginning and end of the next and every following alternate row until there are 34 (38, 42, 46) sts on the needle. Stop decreases at armhole edge and work straight but continue to k2tog at neck edge until there are 21 (24, 27, 30) sts on the needle – then work straight until front matches back as far as shoulder shaping.
Shape shoulders: (Knit row) Bind off 7 (8, 9, 10) sts at the beginning of the next and following 2 alternate rows; secure yarn.
Work right side to match reversing the shaping and leaving center front st on stitch holder. Sew left shoulder seam.

NECKBAND

With no 3 needles and yarn M and right side facing pick up 37 (39, 41, 43) sts at back neck, 46 (48, 50, 52) sts down left side neck edge, one st at center front, 47 (49, 51, 53) sts up right side neck edge – 131 (137, 143, 149) sts. Work in k1, p1 rib for one row. Now rib to within 2 sts of the center front. Then sl 1, k1, psso, k1, k2tog, rib to end. Repeat the last 2 rows 3 times more. Bind off all sts in rib.

ARMBAND

Sew right shoulder seam. *With no 3 needles and yarn M and right side facing pick up 105 (109, 113, 117) sts and work in k1, p1 rib for 8 rows. Bind off all sts in rib. Repeat from * for left side.**

PUTTING TOGETHER

Use flat, invisible seams. Matching the Fair-Isle carefully sew side and armband seams. Sew neckband seam. Press garment according to instructions on yarn band.

MATERIALS for vest

Yarn
Main yarn M 8oz knitting worsted (black)
Yarn A 2oz knitting worsted (natural)
Yarn B 2oz knitting worsted (pale green)
Yarn C 2oz knitting worsted (dark green)
Yarn D 5oz knitting worsted (beige)
Yarn E 2oz knitting worsted (orange)
Yarn F 2oz knitting worsted (red)

Notions
6 buttons

BACK

Follow instructions for slipover but work only the first 18 rows of the pattern as the repeat, not 36. (There should be 4 repeats of the pattern at 15¾in.)

FRONT

Left front
With no 3 needles and yarn M cast on 45 (49, 53, 57) sts and work in k1, p1 rib for 3in. Change to no 6 needles and work 2 rows ending with a purl row. Now follow the first 18 rows from pattern chart. Work straight repeating the pattern until the front measures 15¾in from the beginning and it matches the back, ending on a purl row.
Shape armholes and neck edge: (Knit row) Bind off 5 sts at the beginning of the row; work to last 2 sts, k2tog. Purl one row in pattern. K2tog at the beginning and end of the next and every following alternate row until there are 31 (35, 39, 43) sts on the needle. Stop decreases at armhole edge but continue to k2tog at neck edge until there are 21 (24, 27, 30) sts on the needle. Work straight until work measures 8¾ (9, 9½, 10)in from armhole shaping and front matches the back.
Shape shoulders: Bind off 7 (8, 9, 10) sts at the beginning of this and the following 2 alternate rows. Secure yarn.

Right front
Work as for left side reversing the shaping.

ARMBAND

Join shoulder seams. Repeat from * to ** as for the slipover armband.

BUTTON BANDS

Buttonhole border (right for women, left front for men)
With right side of work facing, no 3 needles and yarn M, pick up 108 sts between bottom rib border and the beginning of neck shaping. Continue up side neck edge to pick up 59 (61, 63, 65) sts. On all 167 (169, 170, 173) sts work 3 rows in single rib.
Make buttonholes: (right side facing row) Rib 4 sts, *bind off 4 sts, rib 16 sys, rep from * until 6 holes are made; rib the remaining sts. Next row: Rib to point where you previously bound off – *cast on 4 sts, rib 16 sts, rep from * to last 4 sts; rib remaining 4 sts. Work 3 rows more and bind off all sts in rib.

Button border (left front for women, right front for men)

With right side facing, no 3 needles and yarn M, beginning at back neck pick up 37 (39, 41, 43) sts and 58 (60, 62, 64) sts down side neck edge and 108 sts down side front. On all 203 (207, 211, 215) sts rib for 8 rows. Bind off all sts in rib.

PUTTING TOGETHER

As for slipover. Sew on 6 buttons.

designed by **PIP HUES**

Fair-Isle

A modern interpretation of a classic sweater type which is popular with both sexes. The use of a multi-color yarn simplifies the design scheme and so makes the sweater easier to knit up than traditional Fair-Isles.

MATERIALS

Yarn
Main yarn M *6 (6, 7)oz* medium-weight Shetland (gray brown)
Yarn A *6 (6, 7)oz* medium-weight Shetland (dark brown)
Yarn B *6 (6, 7)oz* medium-weight Shetland (pale blue/mid brown mix)
Yarn C *6 (6, 7)oz* medium-weight Shetland (beige)
Yarn D *5 (6, 6)oz* medium-weight Shetland (mid brown)
Yarn E *4 (4, 5)oz* medium-weight Shetland (rust).

Needles
1 pair no 3
1 pair no 5

Stitch gauge
26 sts and 26 rows to 4in over Fair-Isle pattern on no 5 needles (or size needed to obtain given tension).

Chart for back and front

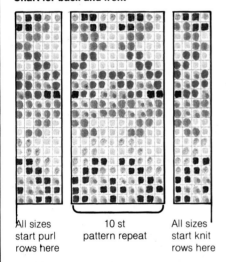

All sizes start purl rows here | 10 st pattern repeat | All sizes start knit rows here

Chart for sleeves

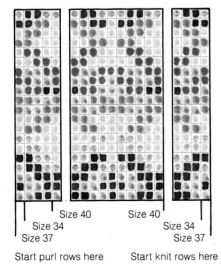

Size 40 · Size 40
Size 34 · Size 34
Size 37 · Size 37

Start purl rows here · Start knit rows here

designed by **JOSE FRANKS**

Special note:
The yarn not in use must be carried loosely at the back of the work and caught every 3rd stitch by the one in use. Read knit rows from right to left and purl rows from left to right.

BACK

With no 3 needles and yarn M cast on 113 (123, 133) sts and work in k1, p1 rib for 2¼in. The right side begins and ends with a knit; the wrong side begins and ends with a purl. Increase row: Rib 9 (9, 11), m1, *rib 19 (21, 22), m1, rep from * 4 times more, rib to end – 119 (129, 139) sts. Change to no 5 needles and joining in and breaking off colors as used, work in the pattern from chart, taking note of the starting and ending positions of the various sizes. Work 4 sts on the right to start and then work 10 sts in pattern 11 (12, 13) times. Work 5 to finish. Continue until back measures 15¾in ending with a wrong side row.
Shape armholes: Keeping to chart, bind off 3 sts at the beginning of the next 2 rows. Decrease one st at each end of the next 5 rows and every following alternate row until 95 (103, 111) sts remain. Work without shaping until the back measures 23 (23¾, 24½)in ending with a purl row.
Shape shoulders: Bind off 9 (10, 11) sts at the beginning of the next 4 rows, then 10 (11, 12) sts at the beginning of the next 2 rows. Leave the remaining 39 (41, 43) sts on a spare needle.

FRONT

Work as for back until the armhole shaping has been worked, continue straight until the front measures 21 (21¼, 22½)in with the right side facing.
Shape neck: On the next row work 36 (39, 42) sts in pattern. K2tog, turn and leave the remaining sts on a spare needle. Continue on these 37 (40, 43) sts, decreasing one st at the

neck edge on the next 9 rows: 28 (31, 34) sts. Continue until the front measures the same as the back to shoulder shaping ending at the armhole edge.
Shape shoulder: Bind off 9 (10, 11) sts at the beginning of the next row and the following alternate row. Work one row back to the armhole. Bind off remaining sts.
With the right side facing, slip the next 19 (21, 23) sts onto a stitch holder, then k2tog and finish the row in pattern. Work the right side by reversing the shaping given for the left.

SLEEVES

With no 3 needles and yarn M cast on 53 (55, 57) sts and work in rib as for the back for 2in.
Increase row: Rib 7, *m1, rib 13 (14, 14), repeat from * twice more, m1, rib to end – 57 (59, 61) sts. Change to no 5 needles and work from chart in pattern, increasing at each end of the 9th row and every following 7th row until there are 77 (83, 87) sts on the needle working all increased stitches into the pattern as they occur. Continue until sleeve measures about 18in ending on the same row as the back at the beginning of the armhole shaping.
Shape top: Bind off 3 sts at the beginning of the next 2 rows. Then decrease one st at each end of the next and every alternate row until 43 (47, 51) sts remain. Work one row. Decrease one st at each end of every row until 29 sts remain. Bind off.

PUTTING TOGETHER

Press all parts except the ribbing, according to instructions on the ball band. Join right shoulder seam then pick up stitches as follows for the neckband: With right side of work facing and using no 3 needles and yarn M knit up 17 (18, 19) sts down the left side of the neck, 19 (21, 23) sts from the center front, 17 (18, 19) sts from the right side of the neck then 39 (41, 43) sts from the back; increase one st in the center of the back – 93 (99, 105) sts.

Work in k1, p1 rib for 2in. Bind off loosely in rib. Join left shoulder seam and neckband seam. Insert sleeves, gathering any excess fabric at the shoulder. Join sleeve and side seams, matching the pattern along the edge. Fold the neckband in half and oversew it down while stretching the band to fit over the head. Press seams.

MEASUREMENTS

To fit chest 34 (37, 40)in (86, 94, 102cm)

46 (51, 55) cm
18 (20, 21½)"
58 (60, 62) cm
23 (23½, 24½)"
46 cm
18"

17

Honeycomb

A high-waisted raglan-sleeved blouson cardigan in multi-color stitch pattern has a crocheted bobble-trimmed yoke and decorative button band.

MATERIALS

Yarn
Main yarn M *8oz* knitting worsted (turquoise)
Yarn A *4oz* knitting worsted (yellow)
Yarn B *4oz* knitting worsted (dark green)
Yarn C *8oz* knitting worsted (blue)
Yarn D *8oz* knitting worsted (rust)

Needles
1 pair no 6
1 pair no 7
1 circular needle no 7
1 crochet hook size C

Notions
10 buttons

Stitch gauge
16 sts and 30 rows to 4in over pattern on no 7 needles (or size needed to obtain given tension).

Abbreviation
Drop 1 Slip st off needle, drop it through 4 rows of st st, pick up st and loops, and knit through them all.

BACK

With no 7 needles and yarn M cast on 64 sts. Change to no 6 needles and work 29 rows in Garter st. Increase row: K2; *inc in next st, k1, inc in next st, k2; rep from * 11 more times; inc in next st, k1 – 89 sts. Change to no 7 needles and join in yarn A. Work in pattern as follows:
Rows 1–4 Work in st st.
Row 5 (With yarn D) k5; *drop 1, k5; rep from * to end.
Row 6 Purl.

Rows 7–10 Do not break off yarn D. Join in yarn B and work 4 rows of st st. Break off yarn B.
Row 11 (With yarn D) k2, *drop 1, k5; rep from * to last 3 sts; drop 1, k2.
Row 12 Purl. Do not break off yarn D.
Rows 13–27 Repeat rows 1 to 12 substituting C for A and M for B.
These 24 rows complete the pattern. Work until 9 color blocks have been completed, ending with 2 rows in D (54 rows of st st).

Shape armholes: (Continue in pattern as above) Bind off 4 sts at the beginning of the next two rows. Then k1, k2tog, tb1, pattern to last 3 sts, k2tog, k1. Purl the next row. Now decrease at both ends of the next and every following 4th row (as above) until 65 sts remain. Next row purl.

There should now be 14 color blocks completed, ending with 2 rows in D (84 rows of st st). Break off yarns and leave these sts on a stitch holder.

SLEEVES

With no 7 needles and yarn M cast on 28 sts. Change to no 6 needles, and work 21 rows in Garter st. Increase row: Increase in first st, *k1, inc in next st; rep from * to last st, inc in last st – 43 sts. Change to no 7 needles and yarn A. Work 4 rows of st st. Join yarn D. Increase row: Increase in first st, k2, drop 1, *k5, drop 1; rep from * to last 3 sts, k2, inc in last st. Purl the next row. Do not break off yarn D. Join yarn B.

designed by *FELICITY RUDD*

Work 4 rows of st st. Next row with yarn D inc in first st, drop 1, *k5, drop 1; rep from * to last st, inc in last st. Working in pattern to match back, and increasing at each end of drop st row using yarn D, work until there are 69 sts. Continue on these sts until 17 color blocks have been worked ending with 2 rows of yarn D. (This should end on same color block as for back up to armhole shaping.) Leave sts on a stitch holder. *Shape top:* (Continue in pattern) Bind off 4 sts at the beginning of the next 2 rows. Then k1, k2tog, tb1, pattern to last 3 sts, k2tog, k1. Purl the next row. Now decrease at both ends of the next and every following 4th row, (as above) until 45 sts remain. (Should end on purl row using yarn D as for back.) Leave remaining sts on a stitch holder.

FRONT

Left front

With no 7 needles and yarn M cast on 32 sts. Change to no 6 needles and work 29 rows of Garter st. Next row k5; *inc once in each of next 2 sts, k1; rep from * 8 more times – 50 sts. Change to no 7 needles and yarn A and work in pattern as follows:

Row 1 With yarn A knit to last 5 sts; with yarn M k5 sts.
Row 2 With yarn M k5; with yarn A purl to end.
Row 3 As row 1.
Row 4 As row 2.
Row 5 With yarn D k2, drop 1, *k5, drop 1; rep from * to last 5 sts, with yarn M k5.
Row 6 With yarn M k5, with yarn D purl to end.
Rows 7–10 As rows 1–4 substituting yarn B for yarn A.
Row 11 With yarn D, *k5, drop 1; rep from * to last 8 sts, k3, with yarn M k5.
Row 12 With yarn M k5, with yarn D purl to end.
Shape armhole: Bind off 4 sts at the beginning of the next row, pattern to end. Then k5, purl to end. On the next row k1, k2tog, tb1, pattern to end. Continue to decrease at armhole edge on the next and every following 4th row until 39 sts remain. Work 5 rows in pattern without shaping. (Should match back and sleeves.) Break off yarn and leave remaining sts on a stitch holder.

Right front

With no 7 needles and yarn M cast on 32 sts. Change to no 6 needles.
Rows 1 and 2 Knit.
Row 3 (Buttonhole) K2, yfwd, k2tog, k to end.
Rows 4–26 Knit.
Row 27 As row 3.
Rows 29 and 30 Knit.
Row 31 *K1, inc once in each of next 2 sts; rep from * 8 more times, k5 – 50 sts.
Change to no 7 needles, and work in pattern below to match left front, reversing Garter st border to beginning of knit row, instead of the end. Work buttonholes on rows 21, 41, and 61.
Rows 1–4 As rows 1–4 on left front.
Row 5 With yarn M k5, with yarn D *drop 1, k5; rep from * to last 3 sts, drop 1, k2.
Rows 6–10 As rows 6–10 on left front.
Row 11 With yarn M k5, with yarn D k3, *drop 1, k5; rep from * to end.
Row 12 As row 12 on left front.
Continue to match left front up to armhole shaping.
Shape armhole: Knit one row in pattern. On the next row bind off 4 sts; purl to last 5 sts, k5. Then k5, pattern to last 3 sts, k2tog, k1. On the next row purl to last 5 sts, k5 with M. Continue decreasing in this manner at the armhole edge on the next row and every following 4th row until 39 sts remain, then work 5 rows. (Remember buttonhole on row 61.)

YOKE

Slip sts onto circular no 7 needle in the following order: left front, then first sleeve, back, second sleeve, then right front.
Row 1 With right side of work facing and yarn M k5, with yarn C k to last 5 sts, with yarn M k5 – 233 sts.
Row 2 With yarn M k5, with yarn C purl to last 5 sts, with yarn M k5.
Using yarn C throughout, with yarn M being used to continue Garter st borders on front edges, work in st st, working buttonholes, decreases and purl sts (for bobble trim positioning) on the following rows:
Row 3 K2, yfwd, k2tog, k to end.
Row 7 K8, *k2tog, k4; rep from * to last 3 sts, k3 – 196 sts.
Row 11 K8, p1, *k19, p1; rep from * to last 7 sts, k7.
Row 13 K2, yfwd, k2tog, k to end.
Row 17 K13, *k2tog, k1, k2tog, k1, k3; rep from * to last 12 sts, k2tog, k10 – 157 sts.
Row 23 K2, yfwd, k2tog, k14, *p1, k16; rep from * to last 19 sts, p1, k18.
Row 27 K7, *k2tog, k1, k2tog, k1, k2tog, k1, k2tog, k1, k3; rep from * to last 15 sts, **k2tog, k1; rep from ** 2 more times, k6 – 118 sts.
Row 33 K2, yfwd, k2tog, k to end.
Row 35 K17, p1, *k11, p1; rep from * to last 16 sts, k16.
Row 37 K7, *k2tog, k1, k3tog; rep from * 16 more times, k2tog, k7 – 66 sts.
Row 38 K5, p to last 5 sts, k5.
Change to no 6 needles with yarn M, work 7 rows in Garter st (working buttonhole on row 43). Bind off using no 7 needles.

PUTTING TOGETHER

Press the st st yoke only. Join sleeve tops to fronts and back, and join side and sleeve seams. Sew on buttons to correspond with buttonholes. Make bobbles through purl sts on the yoke (see below).

EXTRA DETAILS

To make bobbles
Use yarns A, B, and D and a size C crochet hook. Work 10 single crochets through a purl st of yoke, slip stitch through from the last single crochet to the top of the first, cut yarn and pull through remaining loop. Continue in this way until a bobble has been worked on top of every purl st (26 bobbles in all).

MEASUREMENTS

To fit chest 34–36in (81–86cm)

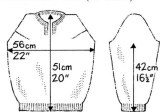

designed by **MAGGIE WHITE**

Chart for back, front and sleeves

The diagonal stripe pattern is worked in the following yarn sequence: 10 rows of yarns M and A; 4 rows of yarn M and a contrast. Or, if you wish, work the entire sweater in just two colors.

Sporty

Unisex winter-weight pullover with tab collar is knitted in stockinette stitch in contrasting horizontal and diagonal stripes. Carrying the yarns across the back makes it extra warm.

MATERIALS

Yarn
Main yarn M *13oz* thick knitting worsted (pink)
Yarn A *13oz* thick knitting worsted (white)
1oz each of 7 contrasts of thick knitting worsted (red, blue, mauve, turquoise, dark pink, mid blue, yellow)
Needles
1 pair no 4
1 pair no 5
1 pair no 6 and 1 spare for shoulders
Notions
3 buttons ½in in diameter
Stitch gauge
20 sts and 20 rows to 4in over st st on no 6 needles (or size needed to obtain given tension).

BACK

With no 4 needles and yarn M cast on 99 sts. Work in k1, p1 rib for 22 rows increasing one st in the last row – 100 sts. Change to no 6 needles. Starting with a knit row, work in st st in pattern of diagonal stripes as on chart.
Work 10 rows of stripes of yarns M and A followed by 4 rows of stripes of yarn M and a contrasting shade, as illustrated. Increase one st at each end of the 7th, 15th, and 23rd rows – 106 sts. Continue straight on these sts for 118 rows from top of rib. Work 2 rows in white. Divide sts onto 3 stitch holders, thus: 38/30/38 for shoulders and back of collar.

FRONT

Work as back until there are 84 rows of st st (ending with a purl row).
Shape neck: Next row work 49 sts in pattern. Turn. Continue working on these 49 sts for a further 23 rows. Decrease one st at neck edge on the next 11 rows. (This should bring in the first of the 2 white rows.) Work one row in white. Leave remaining 38 sts on a stitch holder. Return to sts left on needle. Leave

center 8 sts on a stitch holder. Join yarn to remaining 49 sts and work to match left side reversing shaping. Keep sts on needle.
Join shoulders: Place sts of back right shoulder on needle. With right sides facing, knit together one st from each needle until all have been used. Bind off in normal way. Repeat with other shoulder.

SLEEVES

Count 48 rows down the front and back from shoulder seam and mark. With no 6 needles pick up 96 sts along the edge using yarns M and A to match the body (4 sts M, 4 sts A). Work in st st the same yarn sequence and pattern as the body, 10 rows A and M, followed by 4 rows of M and a contrast, as illustrated. Decrease one st at each end of the 7th and every following 6th row until 72 sts remain. Continue until 80 rows have been worked. Change to no 4 needles. K1, *k2tog; rep from * to last st; k1 – 37 sts. Work 20 rows in k1, p1 rib in yarn M. Bind off loosely in rib (using no 6 needles if binding off is too tight).

BUTTON BANDS

Button border (left side for women, right side for men)
With no 4 needles and yarn A cast on 8 sts. Work in k1, p1 rib until band is the same length as the opening (about 6in). Bind off in rib.

Buttonhole border (right side for women, left side for men)
With no 4 needles and yarn A pick up 8 sts left on stitch holder. Work 6 rows in k1, p1 rib. Make buttonhole in next 2 rows:
Row 1 Rib 3, bind off 2, rib 3.
Row 2 Rib 3, cast on 2, rib 3.
Working approximately 12 rows between, add 2 more buttonholes. Work a further 4 rows. Bind off in rib.

COLLAR

With right side facing, no 4 needles and yarn A pick up and knit 16 sts along right front neck, 30 sts from stitch holder at back, 17 sts along left front neck – 63 sts. Work 6 rows straight in k1, p1 rib. Change to no 5 needles. Increase one st at each end (one st in from edge by picking up horizontal thread and either knitting or purling into the back of it) of next and every alternate row until there are 79 sts. At the same time, after 14 rows from start, change to no 6 needles. Work straight until collar measures 4¾in at center back. Bind off loosely in rib.

PUTTING TOGETHER

Join side and sleeve seams. Sew on button bands and buttons.

MEASUREMENTS

To fit chest 40in (102cm)

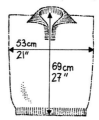

53cm / 21"
69cm / 27"
54cm / 21½"

Cube Crazy

Unisex raglan-sleeved round neck sweater made up of mohair bands formed into color squares. For a varied texture, use knitting worsted for some of the bands.

MATERIALS

Yarn

Main yarn M 7 (8, 8)oz thick knitting worsted (beige)
Yarn A 3oz mohair (pink)
Yarn B 3oz mohair (blue/red mix)
Yarn C 3oz mohair (dark turquoise)
Yarn D 3oz mohair (pale green)
Yarn E 3oz mohair (pale pink)

Needles

1 pair no 3
1 pair no 8

Stitch gauge

17 sts and 25 rows to 4in over pattern on no 8 needles (or size needed to obtain given tension).

Pattern

Rows 1 and 15 P3, *k1 wrapping yarn twice round needle, p5; rep from * to last 4 sts; k1 wrapping yarn twice round needle, p3.

Row 2 K3, *sl next st onto right-hand needle (letting the loops drop), k5; rep from * to last 4 sts; sl 1, k3.

Rows 3, 5, 7, 9, 11, 13 P3, *sl next st, p5; rep from * to last 4 sts; sl 1, p3.

Rows 4, 6, 10, 12, 14 K3, *sl next st, k5; rep from * to last 4 sts; sl 1, k3.

Row 8 K3, *p1, wrapping yarn twice round needle, k5; rep from * to last 4 sts; p1 wrapping yarn twice round needle, k3.

NB Rows 1, 8 and 15 are worked in yarn M.

BACK

With no 3 needles and yarn M cast on 79 (85, 91) sts. Work in k1, p1 rib for 20 rows. Change to no 8 needles and knit one row.
Now begin the pattern: work row 1. Add yarn A and work rows 2–7. Work row 8. Change to yarn B and work rows 9–14. Work row 15. Change to yarn C and work rows 2–7. Work row 8. Change to yarn D and work rows 9–14. Work row 15. Change to yarn E and work rows 2–7. Work row 8. Now begin pattern again and starting with row 9 and yarn A continue to change yarns as set out above until there are 11 complete squares altogether. Now work rows 9–13.
Shape raglan: Bind off 2 (3, 4) sts at the beginning of the next 2 rows**. K2tog at the beginning and end of the next and following alternate rows until there are 29 (31, 31) sts on the needle – leave on a stitch holder for later.

FRONT

Work as for back as far as **. Now k2tog at the beginning and end of the next and following alternate rows until there are 47 (49, 49) sts on the needle.
Shape neck: Next row (purl row) work 29 (31, 31) sts. Slip the last 11 (13, 13) sts onto a stitch holder and continue to work to the end of the row. Continue on the last set of sts as follows: Work 2 tog at raglan edge as before. At the same time decrease one st at the neck edge until there are 5 sts left. Continue to decrease at raglan edge but work straight at neck until there are 2 sts left – work these together and secure yarn. Rejoin yarn at center and work other side to match, reversing the shaping.

SLEEVES

With no 3 needles and yarn M cast on 49 sts. Work in k1, p1 rib for 20 rows. Change to no 8 needles and knit one row.
Now begin the pattern, working the first square with yarn E. On row 8 of the pattern increase as follows: At the beginning and end of this and every following 8th row increase one st until there are 59 (61, 65) sts on the needle, working in the pattern and color sequence as before. Work straight until there are 12 complete squares. Begin the 13th square (yarn B) and work rows 2–5.
Shape raglan: Bind off 2 (3, 4) sts at the beginning of the next 2 rows working pattern. *Work 2 rows.
Next row k2tog at beginning and end of row.

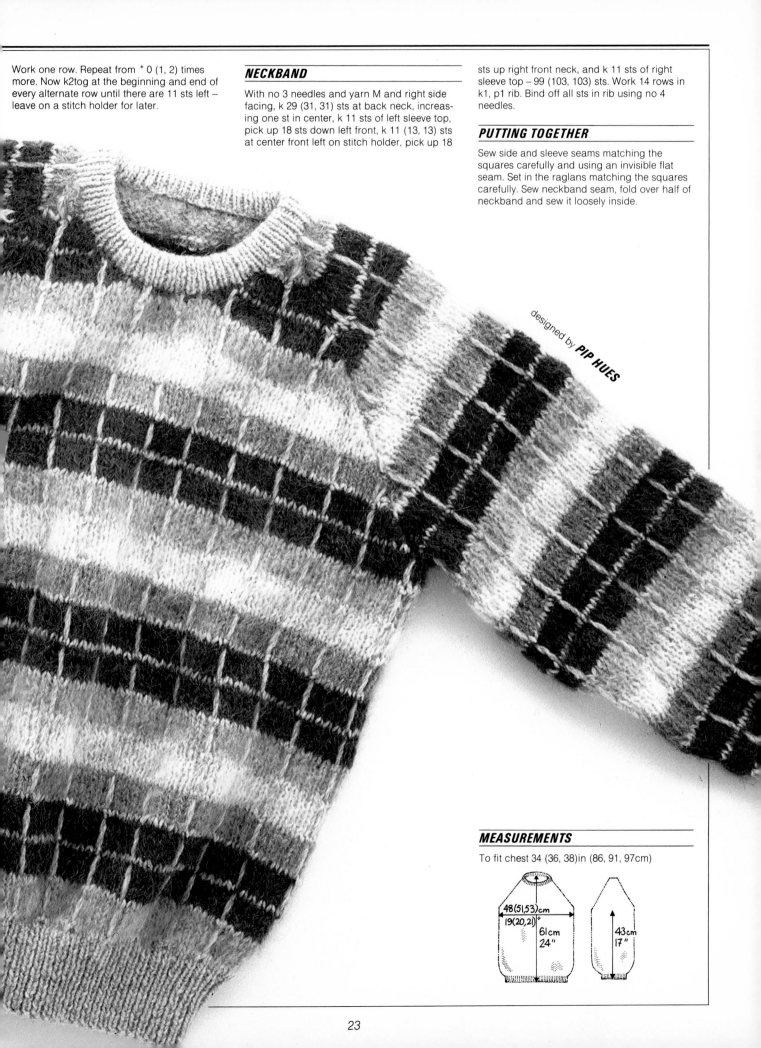

Work one row. Repeat from * 0 (1, 2) times more. Now k2tog at the beginning and end of every alternate row until there are 11 sts left – leave on a stitch holder for later.

NECKBAND

With no 3 needles and yarn M and right side facing, k 29 (31, 31) sts at back neck, increasing one st in center, k 11 sts of left sleeve top, pick up 18 sts down left front, k 11 (13, 13) sts at center front left on stitch holder, pick up 18 sts up right front neck, and k 11 sts of right sleeve top – 99 (103, 103) sts. Work 14 rows in k1, p1 rib. Bind off all sts in rib using no 4 needles.

PUTTING TOGETHER

Sew side and sleeve seams matching the squares carefully and using an invisible flat seam. Set in the raglans matching the squares carefully. Sew neckband seam, fold over half of neckband and sew it loosely inside.

designed by *PIP HUES*

MEASUREMENTS

To fit chest 34 (36, 38)in (86, 91, 97cm)

48(51,53)cm
19(20,21)"
61cm
24"

43cm
17"

designed by **BETTY BARNDEN**

Grid Lines

Man-size pullover in heavy-weight yarn sports a Garter stitch shoulder design. The gridlines are knitted in on the horizontal in Garter stitch and embroidered on the vertical in a modified chain stitch.

MATERIALS

Yarn
Main yarn M 27 (28, 29)oz bulky (caramel)
Yarn A 3oz bulky (blue)
Yarn B 3oz bulky (rust)

Needles
1 pair no 7
1 pair no 9

Stitch gauge

14 sts and 18 rows to 4in over st st on no 9 needles (or size needed to obtain given tension).

NB The horizontal stripes are knitted in Garter stitch as work proceeds and the vertical stripes are embroidered after work is complete.

BACK

With no 7 needles and yarn M cast on 55 (59, 63) sts. Work in k1, p1 rib for 2¾ (3½, 4¼)in ending with a right side row. Increase row: Work in rib, increasing 10 sts evenly across row – 65 (69, 73) sts. Change to no 9 needles, and work in pattern as follows:

Rows 1 and 2 With yarn A knit.
Row 3 With yarn M knit.
Row 4 P2 (4, 6), *k1, p9, rep from * to last 3 (5, 7) sts; k1, p2 (4, 6).
Rows 5–14 Repeat rows 3 and 4 another 5 times.
Rows 15 and 16 With yarn B knit.
Rows 17–28 With yarn M repeat rows 3 and 4 another 6 times.

These 28 rows form the pattern. Repeat them once more, and rows 1–14 once again.
Shape armholes: Keeping pattern correct, bind off 5 sts at the beginning of the next 2 rows, then decrease one st at each end of the next and every following alternate row until 47 (49, 51) sts remain. Continue in pattern until 30 rows have been worked from the beginning of the armhole shaping, ending with 2 rows in yarn B. *** Change to yarn M and work 6 (8, 10) rows in Garter stitch.

Shape shoulders: Bind off 7 sts at the beginning of the next 4 rows. Slip the remaining 19 (21, 23) sts onto a stitch holder.

FRONT

Work as for back until ***. Change to yarn M and work 2 (4, 6) rows in Garter stitch. On the next row knit 18 sts; turn. Work on these sts only, decreasing one st at the neck edge on the next 4 rows – 14 sts remain. Bind off 7 sts at the beginning of the next row. Work one row. Bind off remaining 7 sts. With the right side of the work facing, slip the center 11 (13, 15) sts onto a stitch holder and rejoin yarn to the right of the remaining sts and complete to match the first side, reversing shaping.

SLEEVES

With no 7 needles and yarn M cast on 27 (29, 31) sts. Work in k1, p1 rib for 2¾ (3½, 4¼)in ending with a wrong side row. Change to no 9 needles and work in pattern as for back, except that row 4 reads: P3 (4, 5), *k1, p9; rep from * to the last 4 (5, 6) sts; k1, p3 (4, 5); AND AT THE SAME TIME increase one st at each end of the 5th and every following 6th row until there are 47 (49, 51) sts. Work without shaping until 70 pattern rows are complete, ending with row 14.
Shape top: Keeping pattern correct, bind off 5 sts at the beginning of the next 2 rows. Then decrease one st at each end of the next and every alternate row until 13 (15, 17) sts remain, ending with a wrong side row (a 12th pattern row). Change to yarn B, work 2 rows Garter st decreasing one st each end of both rows. Bind off.

NECKBAND

Join left shoulder seam. With right side of work facing, using no 7 needles and yarn M, knit across 19 (21, 23) sts from the back of the neck, pick up and knit 9 sts from one side of the neck shaping, knit across 11 (13, 15) sts from the front of the neck and pick up and knit 10 sts from the remaining side of the neck – 49 (53, 57) sts. Work in k1, p1 rib for 2in. Change to no 9 needles and bind off in rib.

PUTTING TOGETHER

Join right shoulder seam and neckband. Join side and sleeve seams; set in sleeves. Fold the neckband in half to the inside and sew down neatly ensuring an easy fit over the head. Using yarns A and B as illustrated, embroider vertical lines up each vertical line of purl sts on the right side as follows: Bring yarn up between 2 sts leaving a loop to the left. *Return the needle to the wrong side of the work between the next 2 sts, bringing it up again between the following 2 sts and inside the loop, leaving a loop to the right. Repeat from *. Or, using a crochet hook, work a row of crochet slip sts up each purl st. Press lightly with a warm iron and a damp cloth.

MEASUREMENTS

To fit chest 36 (38, 40)in (91, 97, 102cm)

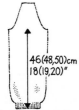

48(51,53)cm
19(20,21)"
70(72,74)cm
27½(28½,29)"
46(48,50)cm
18(19,20)"

Redneck

A unisex winter-weight raglan-sleeved pullover with shawl collar is knitted up in alternating Fair-Isle and stripe patterns in bright shades of thick knitting worsted.

MATERIALS

Yarn
Main yarn M 8 (8, 9, 9)oz thick knitting worsted (dark red)
Yarn A 1oz thick knitting worsted (yellow)
Yarn B 2oz thick knitting worsted (natural)
Yarn C 2oz thick knitting worsted (dark green)
Yarn D 2oz thick knitting worsted (orange)
Yarn E 3oz thick knitting worsted (green)
Yarn F 8 (8, 9, 9)oz thick knitting worsted (dark blue/mauve)
Yarn G 2oz thick knitting worsted (orange/blue mix)

Needles
1 pair no 7
1 pair no 8
1 pair no 10

Stitch gauge 17 sts and 17 rows to 4in over st st on no 10 needles over pattern (or size needed to obtain given tension).

Special note:
On all Fair-Isle rows repeat from * right to the very end of the row even if the row does not end with a complete repeat. On the return row the pattern will match up. There are 3 Fair-Isle sequences as follows:

Fair-Isle sequence (1)
Rows 1 and 3 Knit 1M, *3B, 2M
Row 2 *Purl 2M, 3B
Row 4 *Purl 2C, 3B
Row 5 Knit 1D, *2C, 3D
Row 6 *Purl 4C, 1D
Row 7 Knit 2C, *1D, 4C
Row 8 Purl 1D, *3E, 2D
Row 9 Knit 1D, *3E, 2D
Row 10 Purl 1E, *2D, 3E
Row 11 Knit 3F, *1G, 4F
Row 12 Purl 1F, *3G, 2F
Row 13 Knit 3G, *1A, 4G
Row 14 Purl 1F, *3G, 2F
Row 15 Knit 3F, *1G, 4F

Fair-Isle sequence (2)
Row 1 Purl 1M, *3B, 2M
Row 2 *Knit 2M, 3B
Row 3 *Purl 2M, 3B
Row 4 Knit 1C, *3B, 2C
Row 5 Purl 1D, *2C, 3D
Row 6 *Knit 4C, 1D
Row 7 Purl 2C, *1D, 4C
Row 8 Knit 1D, *3E, 2D
Row 9 Purl 1D, *3E, 2D
Row 10 Knit 1E, *2D, 3E
Row 11 Purl 3F, *1G, 4F
Row 12 Knit 1F, *3G, 2F
Row 13 Purl 3G, *1A, 4G
Row 14 Knit 1F, *3G, 2F
Row 15 Purl 3F, *1G, 4F

Fair-Isle sequence (3)
Row 1 Knit 1M, *3B, 2M
Row 2 *Purl 2M, 3B
Row 3 *Knit 2M, 3B
Row 4 Purl 1C, *3B, 2C
Rows 5–15 As rows 5–15 on sequence (1).

FRONT

With no 7 needles and yarn M cast on 36 (41, 46, 46) sts. Work in k1, p1 rib for 20 rows. Change to no 10 needles and st st.
Increase row: K1 (4, 2, 4) sts, *inc one st (by knitting twice into st); k6 (6, 7, 7) sts; rep from * to the last 2 (4, 2, 5) sts, inc one st, k to end – 76 (81, 86, 91) sts altogether. Work 3 rows in yarn M. Work Fair-Isle sequence (1). Then purl one row F, knit one row E, purl one row C, knit one row M. Work Fair-Isle sequence (2). Then knit one row B, purl one row E, knit one row C, purl one row M. Work Fair-Isle sequence (3). Now work 8 (8, 12, 12) rows of vertical stripes as follows:
Rows 1 and 3 Purl 2F, *1G, 4F
Row 2 Knit 3F, *1G, 4F
Row 4 Knit 3F, *1B, 4F
Row 5 Purl 2F, *1B, 4F
Row 6 Knit 3F, *1E, 4F
Row 7 Purl 2F, *1E, 4F
Row 8 Knit 3F, *1M, 4F
For the two larger sizes only:
Row 9 Purl 2F, *1M, 4F
Row 10 As row 8
Row 11 As row 9
Row 12 As row 8 * *
Shape armholes: Continuing in vertical stripes in yarns F and M bind off 3 sts at the beginning of the next 2 rows. Next row bind off 3 sts at the beginning of the row, work 24 (26, 29, 31) sts, bind off 16 (17, 16, 17) sts § and work the remaining sts. Turn. Next row bind off 3 sts, work to the neck edge leaving the remaining sts on a stitch holder.
Shape neck: (Right side, still in stripes in yarns F and M) decrease one st at the neck edge and work to the end of the row. Decrease 2 sts and work to the end of the row. Decrease one st at the neck edge and work to the end of the row. Repeat the last 2 rows once more. Work one more row. Next row (neck edge) change to no 8 needles and work in k1, p1 rib in yarn M, decreasing one st at the beginning of this and the following alternate row, then continue straight on the neck edge, but continue to decrease one st at the armhole edge until no sts remain. Secure yarn. Work the other side to match, reversing shaping.

BACK

Work as the front as far as **. Then, continuing in vertical stripes in yarns F and M bind off 3 sts at the beginning of the next 4 rows. Bind off 2 sts at the beginning of the next 4 rows, and bind off one st at the beginning of the next row, knitting the last 2 sts of this row together. Change to no 8 needles and with yarn M work in k1, p1 rib, knitting 2 sts together at the beginning and end of every alternate row until 26 (27, 26, 27) sts remain. Bind off.

SLEEVES

With no 7 needles and yarn M cast on 66 (71, 76, 81) sts. Work in k1, p1 rib for 15 rows. Change to no 10 needles and st st.
Increase row: K4 (2, 2, 0) sts; *inc one st in the next st; k2 (3, 4, 4) sts; rep from * to the last 5 (3, 1, 1) sts, inc one st, k4 (2, 0, 0) sts – 46 (51, 56, 56) sts altogether. Work 3 rows in yarn M. Work Fair-Isle sequence (3). Work 39 (39, 43, 43) rows of vertical stripes as on the back with the following yarns: 3 rows F and G; 3 rows E and A; 5 rows E and D; 8 rows E and A; 2 rows E and D; 2 rows E and G; 3 rows F and D; 2 rows F and B; 6 rows F and G; 2 rows F and B; 2 rows F and C; 1 (1, 5, 5) rows F and M. At the same time increase as follows:
Increase one st at the beginning and end of the next and every following 6th row until there are 60 (65, 70, 74) sts.
Shape top: Continuing in stripes in yarns F and M bind off 3 sts at the beginning of the next 2 rows. Bind off 2 sts at the beginning of the next 4 rows. K2tog at the beginning and end of the next and every following alternate row until 40 (43, 46, 48) sts remain. Change to no 8 needles and work in k1, p1 rib in yarn M decreasing one st at the beginning and end of this and every following alternate row until 14 (15, 16, 16) sts remain. Bind off.

PUTTING TOGETHER

Press all pieces according to instructions on yarn band; secure all loose ends. Matching the Fair-Isle carefully, sew side seams with an invisible seam. Insert the sleeves and sew sleeve seams, matching Fair-Isle.

COLLAR

With right side facing, no 8 needles and yarn M pick up sts at bind-off point § increasing 3 or 4 sts to make 20 sts altogether. Work in k1, p1 rib for 2 rows. Next row increase one st at this and every following neck edge row until there are 25 sts. Work straight in k1, p1 rib for approximately 130 rows (measure around the neck as you work). Then decrease one st at every neck edge row until 20 sts remain. Bind off and sew the collar to the sweater.

*designed by **PIP HUES***

MEASUREMENTS

To fit chest 32–34 (34–36, 36–38, 38–40)in (81–86, 86–91, 91–97, 97–102cm)

45(48,51,53)cm
18(19,20,21)"

65(66,69,70)cm
25½(26,27,27½)"

44(44,47,47)cm
17½(17½,18½,18½)"

Diamond Duo

Worsted tapestry wool used to good effect in a thick pullover dotted with gold metal bobbles and matching leg-warmers. This yarn comes in deep-dyed colors and a crinkly texture, but other thick knitting worsted can be used.

designed by *FELICITY RUDD*

MATERIALS

Yarn
Yarn A *4oz* knitting worsted (dark green)
Yarn B *8oz* knitting worsted (dark pink)
Yarn C *8oz* knitting worsted (blue)
Yarn D *8oz* knitting worsted (pale pink)
Yarn E *4oz* knitting worsted (rust)
Yarn F *4oz* knitting worsted (lime green)
Yarn G *8oz* knitting worsted (gray)
Yarn H *4oz* knitting worsted (mauve)
Yarn I *2oz* medium-weight lurex (gold)

Needles
1 pair no 7
1 pair no 8

Stitch gauge
20 sts and 22 rows to 4in over st st on no 8 needles (or size needed to obtain given tension).

MEASUREMENTS

To fit chest 34–36in (86–91cm)

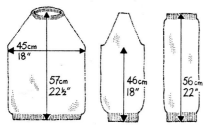

To make bobble (use 4-ply lurex gold)
Knit into the front and back of the stitch twice (making 4 sts). Work 3 rows (starting with p) in st st on these 4 sts; knit one row and lift the first 3 sts over the last (one st left).

BACK

Using no 7 needles cast on 82 sts. K2, p2 to last 2 sts, k2. Work in this k2, p2 rib for 14 rows; increase one st at each end of the last row – 84 sts. Change to no 8 needles. Working in st st and beginning with a knit row, follow the chart for the pattern (see overleaf), working bobbles, if desired, where shown.
Shape armholes: Bind off 6 sts at the beginning of the 77th and 78th row.
Row 79 K1, sl 1, k1, psso, k to last 3 sts, k2tog, k1.
Row 80 Purl.
Continue decreasing as in row 79 on every knit row until 36 sts remain. Purl one row. (38 rows should have been worked from bind-off rows.) Change to no 7 needles. Work in k2, p2 rib for 16 rows as at beginning, increasing one st at each end of the first row. Bind off.

FRONT

Knit the same as the back.

SLEEVES

Using no 7 needles cast on 58 sts. Work in k2, p2 rib as on back for 26 rows, increasing one st at each end of the last row – 60 sts. Change to no 8 needles. Working in st st and beginning with a knit row, follow the chart for the sleeve pattern, working bobbles, if desired, where shown.
Shape top: Bind off 6 sts at beginning of the 77th and 78th row.
Row 79 K1, sl 1, k1, psso, k to last 3 sts, k2tog, k1.
Row 80 Purl.
Continue decreasing as on 79th row on every knit row until 12 sts remain. Purl one row. (38 rows should have been worked from bind-off rows.) Change to no 7 needles. Work in k2, p2 rib for 16 rows increasing one st at each end of the first row. Bind off.

PUTTING TOGETHER

Press pieces lightly, avoiding bobbles and ribbing. Use a flat seam for joining ribbing and a back stitch seam for the other seams. Join the tops of the sleeves (from armhole shaping) to the front and back, and then join the side and sleeve seams. Fold ribbing at neck edge in half, and stitch the bound-off edge to the first row of rib *inside* the garment.

LEG WARMERS

Using no 8 needles for rib as well as for st st, work as for the sleeves, but varying the colors, until top shaping.

At row 77 change to no 7 needles increasing one st at each end of the first row and work k2, p2 rib for 12 rows. Bind off.

Press lightly avoiding ribbing. Use a flat seam to join ribbing and a back stitch seam for st st.

Diamond Duo

Chart for back and front

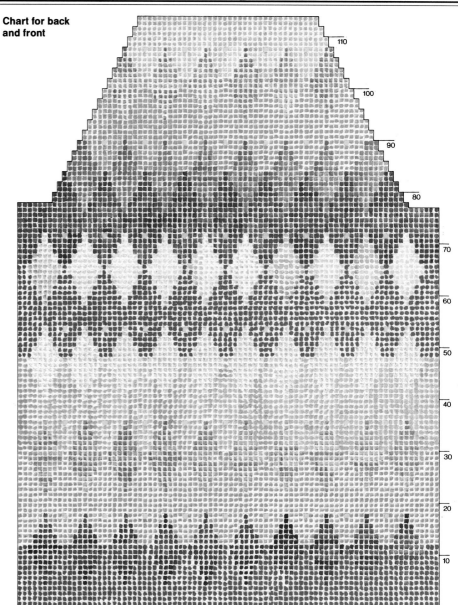

The yellow squares on the chart indicate the positioning of the bobbles. However the working of these is optional – on the garments worn in the illustration above they have been worked on the sweater, but not on the leg-warmers. The instructions for making the bobbles are given at the beginning of the pattern. If you like, you can make the bobbles in knitting worsted yarn instead of lurex.

Chart for sleeves and legwarmers

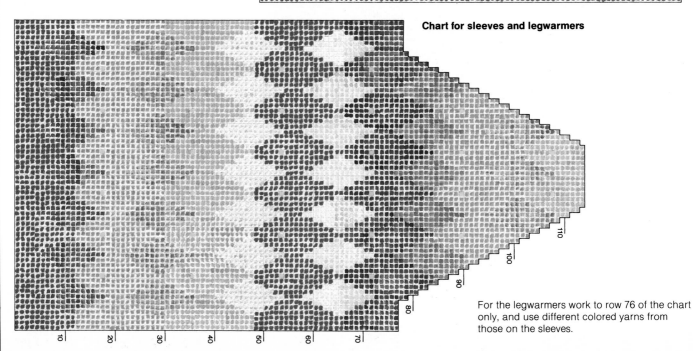

For the legwarmers work to row 76 of the chart only, and use different colored yarns from those on the sleeves.

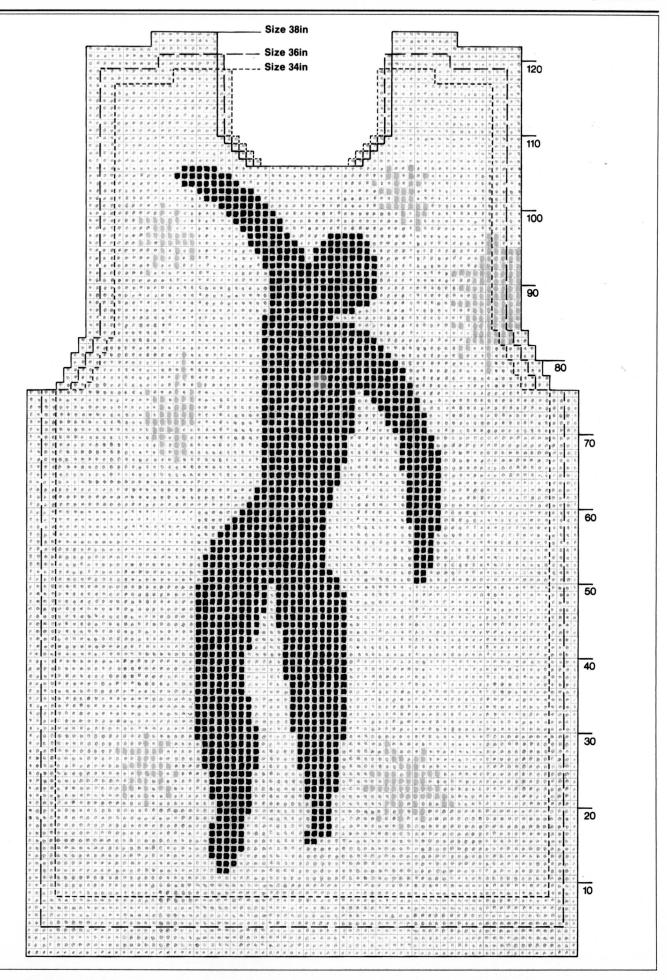

Size 38in
Size 36in
Size 34in

Matisse

Artist's motif traced from a print and knitted in bulky yarns makes up the front panel of a winter-weight pullover. Try your hand at other works of art.

MATERIALS

Yarn
Main yarn M *21 (22, 23)oz* bulky (black)
Yarn A *6 (6, 6)oz* bulky (blue)
Yarn B *2 (2, 2)oz* bulky (yellow)
Yarn C scrap of bulky (red)
Needles
1 pair no 6
1 pair no 8
Stitch gauge
15 sts and 20 rows to 4in over st st on no 8 needles (or size needed to obtain given tension).

BACK

With no 6 needles and yarn M cast on 68 (72, 76) sts. Work in k1, p1 rib for 14 rows. Change to no 8 needles* and work 68 (72, 76) rows in st st beginning with a knit row and ending with a purl row.
Shape armholes: Bind off 4 sts at the beginning of the next 2 rows. Decrease one st at each end of the next and every alternate row until 52 (56, 60) sts remain. Work a further 33 (35, 37) rows in st st thus ending on a purl row.
Shape shoulders: Bind off 8 (8, 9) sts at the beginning of the next 2 rows. Bind off 8 (9, 9) sts at the beginning of the following 2 rows. Slip the remaining 20 (22, 24) sts onto a stitch holder.

FRONT

Work as for back to *. Change to yarn A and work from the chart in st st. Work in the colors as shown and within the outline of the chosen size as indicated on the chart, shaping the armholes as for the back beginning at row 77 of the chart. Work until chart row 106 is completed.
Shape neck (all sizes): Continuing in yarn A, on the next row knit 20 (21, 22) sts; turn. Work on these sts only, decreasing one st at the neck edge on the next 4 rows – 16 (17, 18) sts remain. Work a further 7 (9, 11) rows in st st without shaping thus ending on a purl row.
Shape shoulders: Bind off 8 (8, 9) sts at the beginning of the next row. Work one row. Bind off remaining 8 (9, 9) sts. With right side of work facing, slip the center 12 (14, 16) sts onto a stitch holder and knit to the end. Complete the left side to match, reversing shaping.

SLEEVES

With no 6 needles and yarn M cast on 36 (38, 40) sts. Work in k1, p1 rib for 14 rows. Change to no 8 needles and work in st st increasing one st at each end of the next and every following 6th row until there are 56 (58, 60) sts. Work without shaping until the sleeve measures (17¼ (18, 18¾)in, ending with a purl row.
Shape top: Bind off 4 sts at the beginning of the next 2 rows. Decrease one st at each end of the next and every alternate row until 42 sts remain. Decrease one st at each end of every row until 22 sts remain. Bind off.

NECKBAND

Join left shoulder seam. With the right side of the work facing, using no 6 needles and yarn M knit 20 (22, 24) sts from the back of the neck, pick up and knit 12 (14, 16) sts from the left front neck shaping, knit 12 (14, 16) sts from the center front and pick up and knit 12 (14, 16) sts from the right front neck shaping – 56 (64, 72) sts. Work in k1, p1 rib for 14 rows. Change to no 8 needles and bind off in rib.

PUTTING TOGETHER

Join right shoulder seam and neckband seam. Join side and sleeve seams; set in sleeves. Fold the neckband in half to the inside and sew down neatly ensuring an easy fit over the head. Press lightly with a warm iron and a damp cloth.

MEASUREMENTS

To fit chest 34 (36, 38)in (86, 91, 97cm)

46(48,51)cm
18(19,20)"
62(65,68)cm
24½(25½,26¾)"

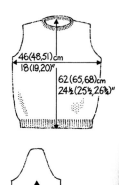

44(46,48)cm
17¼(18,18¾)"

designed by **BETTY BARNDEN**

Banded Blocks

Eye-catching blue and fuchsia blocks banded in black are knitted in panels which can be sewn together when making up or joined as you go along. A stylish short jacket shape, it is knitted in Garter stitch throughout according to the charted design.

MATERIALS

Yarn
Main yarn M *6oz* bulky bouclé (black)
Yarn A *6oz* bulky bouclé (bright pink)
Yarn B *6oz* bulky bouclé (bright blue)

Needles
1 pair no 7

Stitch gauge
12 sts and 19 rows to 4in over Garter stitch on no 7 needles (or size needed to obtain given tension).

designed by *BELINDA WILLIAMSON*

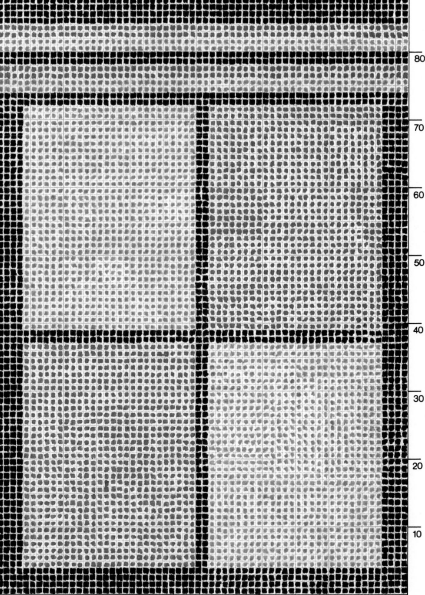

Chart for back and front
For the back, work the entire chart. For the front work 29 sts each side as marked.

80

70

60

50

40

30

20

10

Right front   **Left front**

BACK

With yarn M cast on 62 sts. Work in Garter stitch following the chart. When you begin adding colors, you will have to have three separate balls or bobbins of yarn M. Cross the colors on the back to avoid holes in the fabric (see p. 122). Or, knit panels separately and sew together before joining front band.

FRONT

Left front
With yarn M cast on 29 sts. Work in Garter stitch following the chart.

Right front
With yarn M cast on 29 sts. Work in Garter stitch following the chart.

SLEEVES

Cast on 70 sts in yarn A. Work in Garter st in the following order: 13 rows A, 2 rows M, 2 rows A, 2 rows B, 2 rows M, 2 rows A, 2 rows B, 8 rows M, 2 rows B, 2 rows A, 2 rows M, 2 rows B, 2 rows A, 2 rows M, 14 rows B.
Repeat for the second sleeve but when making up make sure that the front of one sleeve is pink and the front of the other sleeve is blue.

EDGINGS

Front band
With yarn M cast on 8 sts and work 200 rows in Garter stitch. Bind off.

Wristbands
With yarn M cast on 25 sts and work 12 rows in Garter stitch. Bind off. Make two.

PUTTING TOGETHER

If panels were knitted separately, sew together with overcast stitches. Join side and shoulder seams of fronts and back. Sew underarm sleeve seams, i.e. cast on and bound off edges, and sew sleeves into armholes.
Gather the sleeve ends and sew a wrist band on to each end.
Sew on front band.

MEASUREMENTS

To fit chest 32–36in (81–91cm)

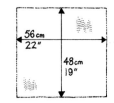

56cm
22"

48cm
19"

44cm
17½"

Flowered Aran

Embroidered lurex daisies contrast well with traditional cabled Aran panels. Both the flowers and snug-fitting jacket style contribute to a very feminine interpretation of traditional masculine motifs.

MATERIALS

Yarn
18 (19, 20)oz knitting worsted (cream)
Scraps of colored lurex for embroidery

Needles
1 pair no 3
1 pair no 5

Notions
7 buttons

Stitch gauge
22 sts and 30 rows to 4in over st st on no 5 needles (or size needed to obtain given tension).

Abbreviations
mb Make bobble by p1, k1, p1, k1 into next stitch, thus making 4 sts into next stitch, turn; k4, turn; p4, slip 2nd, 3rd and 4th sts over 1st st.

tw3 Twist 3. Put right-hand needle behind first 2 sts, k into back of 3rd st, then 2nd st and first st – slip all 3 sts off together.

Panel pattern (31 sts)
Row 1 P1, k3, p1, k1, mb, k6, k2tog, yfwd, k1, yfwd, k2tog, tb1, k6, mb, k1, p1, k3, p1.
Rows 2, 4, 6, 8, 10, 12, 14, 16 P4, k1, p21, k1, p4.
Row 3 P1, tw3, p1, k3, mb, k3, k2tog, yfwd, k3, yfwd, k2tog, tb1, k3, mb, k3, p1, tw3, p1.
Row 5 P1, k3, p1, k1, mb, k4, k2tog, yfwd, k5, yfwd, k2tog, tb1, k4, mb, k1, p1, k3, p1.
Row 7 P1, tw3, p1, k5, k2tog, yfwd, k7, yfwd, k2tog, tb1, k5, p1, tw3, p1.
Row 9 P1, k3, p1, k1, mb, k4, yfwd, k2tog, tb1, k5, k2tog, yfwd, k4, mb, k1, p1, k3, p1.
Row 11 P1, tw3, p1, k3, mb, k3, yfwd, k2tog, tb1, k3, k2tog, yfwd, k3, mb, k3, p1, tw3, p1.
Row 13 P1, k3, p1, k1, mb, k6, yfwd, k2tog, tb1, k1, k2tog, yfwd, k6, mb, k1, p1, k3, p1.
Row 15 P1, tw3, p1, k9, yfwd, sl 1, k2tog, psso, yfwd, k9, p1, tw3, p1.

FRONT

Right front
Using no 3 needles cast on 37 (39, 41) sts. Work 26 rows in k1, p1 rib. Increase row: Rib 3 (4, 5); *up 1, rib 3; repeat from * to last 4 (5, 6) sts, up 1, rib 4 (5, 6) – 48 (50, 52) sts. Change to no 5 needles, and proceed in st st with front panel placed as follows, noting that the 31 sts of the panel are worked as the pattern panel above:
Row 1 K1, patt 31, k16 (18, 20) (1st row of pattern panel).
Row 2 P16 (18, 20), patt 31, p1 (2nd row of pattern panel).
Rows 3–16 Repeat 1st and 2nd rows, working rows 3–16 from pattern panel.
Keeping the pattern correct, repeat rows 1–16, until work measures 10 (10½, 11)in from top of ribbing, finishing at outside edge. (The pattern panel is at the front edge.)

Shape armhole: Bind off 5 (6, 7) sts at beginning of the next row. Decrease one st at armhole edge on next and every alternate row until 37 (38, 39) sts remain. Continue on these sts until work measures 4¾ (5, 5¼)in from beginning of armhole shaping, finishing at front edge.
Shape neck: Bind off 7 sts at the beginning of the next row. Decrease one st at the neck edge of every row until 26 (27, 28) sts remain. Continue on these sts until work measures 7¼ (7¾, 8¼)in from beginning of armhole shaping, finishing at armhole edge.
Shape shoulder: Bind off 8 (9, 9) sts at the beginning of the row and work to end. Work one row in pattern. Bind off 9 sts on next row and work to end. Work one row in pattern. Bind off 9 (9, 10) sts.
NB The pattern as given knits up longer than the sweater shown.

Left front
Work another front to match, placing pattern panel at other side and reversing shaping.

BACK
Using no 3 needles, cast on 83 (87, 91) sts, work 26 rows in k1, p1 rib. Increase row: Rib 1 (3, 5), *up 1, rib 5; rep from * to last 2 (4, 6) sts, up 1, rib 2 (4, 6) – 100 (104, 108) sts. Change to no 5 needles and work in st st with 2 side pattern panels as follows:
Row 1 K16 (18, 20), pattern 31, k6, pattern 31, k16 (18, 20).
Row 2 P16 (18, 20), pattern 31, p6, pattern 31, p16 (18, 20).
Keeping pattern correct, work until back matches front to armhole.
Shape armhole: Bind off 6 (7, 8) sts at beginning of the next 2 rows. Decrease one st at both ends of next and every alternate row until 76 (78, 80) sts remain. Continue on these sts until work matches front to shoulder shaping.
Shape shoulder: Bind off 8 (9, 9) sts at the beginning of the next 2 rows. Bind off 9 sts at the beginning of the next 2 rows. Bind off 9 (9, 10) sts at the beginning of the next 2 rows. Put remaining 24 sts onto a stitch holder.

SLEEVES

Using no 3 needles, cast on 45 sts, and work in k1, p1 rib for 3in. Increase row: *Rib 4, up 1; repeat from * ending rib 5 – 55 sts. Change to no 5 needles. Proceed in st st placing pattern panel as follows:
Row 1 K12, pattern 31, k12.
Row 2 P12, pattern 31, p12.
Continue in pattern from panel, increasing both ends of 3rd and every following 10th row, until there are 73 (75, 77) sts. Continue on these sts until work measures 17 (17½, 18)in from beginning.
Shape top: Bind off 3 sts at the beginning of the next 4 rows; 2 sts at the beginning of the

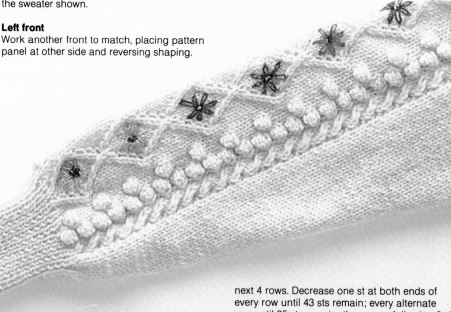

next 4 rows. Decrease one st at both ends of every row until 43 sts remain; every alternate row until 35 sts remain; then every following 3rd row until 23 sts remain. Bind off 4 sts at the beginning of the next 4 rows. Bind off remaining 7 sts.

BUTTON BANDS

Button border (left front)
On no 3 needles, cast on 13 sts, work 130 (136, 142) rows in k1, p1 rib. (Check with the front of the cardigan that this is the correct length – it should be stretched slightly to fit.) Leave sts on waste yarn or stitch holder.

Buttonhole border (right front)
On no 3 needles, cast on 13 sts and work 6 rows in k1, p1 rib.
Make buttonhole: *Rib 6, bind off 2 sts, rib 5. Next row rib 5, cast on 2 sts, rib 6. Rib 19 (20, 21) rows. Repeat from * making 5 more buttonholes, ending last repeat rib 17 (18, 19) rows. Leave sts on waste yarn or stitch holder.

NECKBAND

Join shoulder seams. With right side of work facing and needle holding buttonhole band sts – pick up 26 sts from right front neck, 25 sts from back neck and 26 sts from left front neck. Rib across 13 sts from band – 103 sts. Next row k1, p1 rib. Then rib 6, bind off 2 sts, rib to end. On following row rib, casting on 2 sts over buttonhole. Rib 4 more rows. Bind off in rib.

PUTTING TOGETHER

Press all pieces except rib lightly. Sew rib with flat stitch. Sew seams with back stitch.

EXTRA DETAILS

Embroider flowers inside diamonds on fronts and sleeves using Lazy daisy stitch for petals, and French knots for centers.

MEASUREMENTS

To fit chest 32–34 (34–36, 36–38)in (81–86, 86–91, 91–97cm)

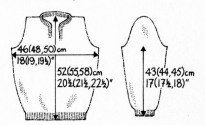

46(48,50)cm
18(19,19½)"

52(55,58)cm
20½(21½,22½)"

43(44,45)cm
17(17½,18)"

designed by *JOAN CHATTERLEY*

Cascade

Rippling waves of medium-weight classic and angora yarns knitted
in alternating plain and lacy triangles give interest to a basic
round-necked sweater shape.

MATERIALS

Yarn
Main yarn M *5oz* medium-weight (dark blue)
Yarn A *3oz* medium-weight (mauve)
Yarn B *3oz* medium-weight (dark pink)
Yarn C *3oz* medium-weight (pale pink)
Yarn D *2oz* medium-weight angora (pale pink)

Needles
1 pair no 1
1 pair no 3

Stitch gauge
28 sts and 20–24 rows to 4in over pattern on
no 3 needles (or size needed to obtain given
tension).

MEASUREMENTS

To fit chest 34–38in (86–97cm)

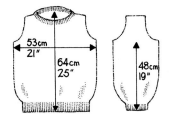

BACK

Using yarn M and no 1 needles cast on 109
sts and work in k1, p1 rib for 37 rows.
Increase row: P2, *up 1, p3; repeat from * to
last 2 sts, up 1, p2 – 145 sts. Change to no 3
needles. Cut off yarn and join in yarn A. (Knot
yarns together and weave up the side of the
work.) Work in following pattern:
Row 1 (right side) – K3, *yfwd, sl 1, k2tog,
  psso, yfwd, k1; rep from * to last 2 sts, k2.
Row 2 Knit.
Row 3 Purl.
Row 4 Knit.
Row 5 K3, *yfwd, k8, sl 1, k2tog, psso, k8,
  yfwd, k1; rep from * to last 2 sts, k2.
Rows 6, 8, 10, 12, 14, 16, 18 and 20 Purl.
Row 7 K4, *yfwd, k7, sl 1, k2tog, psso, k7,
  yfwd, k3; rep from * to last st, k1.
Row 9 K2, k2tog, *yfwd, k1, yfwd, k6, sl 1,
  k2tog, psso, k6, yfwd, k1, yfwd, sl 1, k2tog,
  psso; rep from * ending last repeat yfwd,
  ssk (see p. 132), k2 instead of yfwd, sl 1,
  k2tog, psso.
Row 11 K6, *yfwd, k5, sl 1, k2tog, psso, k5,
  yfwd, k7; rep from * ending last repeat k6
  instead of k7.
Row 13 K3, *yfwd, sl 1, k2tog, psso, yfwd, k1,
  yfwd, k4, sl 1, k2tog, psso, k4, yfwd, k1,
  yfwd, sl 1, k2tog, psso, yfwd, k1; rep from *
  to last 2 sts, k2.
Row 15 K8, *yfwd, k3, sl 1, k2tog, psso, k3,
  yfwd, k11; rep from * ending last repeat k8
  instead of k11.
Row 17 K2, k2tog, *yfwd, k1, yfwd, sl 1, k2tog,
  psso, yfwd, k1, yfwd, k2, sl 1, k2tog, psso, k2
  (yfwd, k1, yfwd, sl 1, k2tog, psso) twice; rep
  from * ending last repeat yfwd, ssk, k2
  instead of yfwd, sl 1, k2tog, psso.

Row 19 K10, *yfwd, k1, sl 1, k2tog, psso, k1, yo,
  k15; rep from * ending last repeat k10
  instead of k15.
At the end of the 20th row cut off the yarn and
join in the next yarn.
These 20 rows form the pattern. Work 4 more
repeats of the pattern in sequence: yarn D, B,
M, C. Then work rows 1–18 of pattern in A.
Shape armholes: (Keeping pattern correct
throughout) bind off 10 sts at the beginning of
the next 2 rows (rows 19 and 20 of pattern).
Join in yarn D and carry on in pattern
decreasing one st at both ends of every row
until there are 105 sts (work in st st at the side
edges if this makes decreasing easier).
Continue on these sts until 4 repeats of the
pattern have been worked from the beginning
of the armhole. (In sequence following yarn D
with B, M, C.)
Shape neck: Join in yarn A and work the 1st
and 2nd rows of pattern. Then bind off 9 sts at
the beginning of the next 6 rows. Cut off yarn
and join in yarn M to work remaining 51 sts.
Using no 1 needles, knit one row, then work
in k1, p1 rib for 7 rows. Bind off loosely in rib.

FRONT

Work as for the back until the armhole shaping
has been completed. Work on 105 sts until the
armhole measures 4¾in from the beginning of
the shaping.
Shape neck: (Keeping pattern correct
throughout) work across 42 sts in pattern; bind
off the next 21 sts loosely, work in pattern
across the remaining 42 sts. Work on these sts
in pattern decreasing one st at the neck edge
on every row until there are 27 sts. Work until
the front matches the back to the shoulder,
ending at the armhole edge. Bind off 9 sts at
the beginning of the next and 2 following
alternate rows. Rejoin appropriate yarn
to work remaining 42 sts and knit
to match.

SLEEVES

Using no 1 needles cast on 53 sts in yarn M
and work in k1, p1 rib for 37 rows. Increase
row: P1, *up 1, p1; rep from * to end – 105 sts.
Change to no 3 needles and work in pattern
as given for the back. Work 6 repeats of the
pattern altogether in sequence beginning with
yarn C, followed by yarns A, D, B, M, C. Then
work rows 1–18 of pattern in yarn A.
Shape top: (Keeping pattern correct) bind off
10 sts at the beginning of the next 2 rows (rows
19 and 20 of pattern). Join in the next yarn (D)
and decrease one st at both ends of the next
and every following alternate row until the
pattern has been completed. Then join in yarn
B and work another whole pattern repeat, still
decreasing each end of every alternate row.
Join in yarn M, work 2 rows in pattern
then bind off the remaining 45 sts.

NECKBAND

Using no 1 needles and yarn M, with the right side of the work facing pick up and knit 81 sts evenly around front neck only (the back has already been worked). Work 7 rows in k1, p1 rib. Bind off in rib.

PUTTING TOGETHER

Join shoulder seams. Sew in sleeves. Join side and sleeve seams.

designed by **JOAN CHATTERLEY**

Clouds

Undulating color bands knitted in contrasting mohair shades are worked in a lacy-looking, reversible pattern. The close-fitting ribbing combined with a generous width produces a fashionable blouson effect.

MATERIALS

Yarn

Main yarn M *6oz* mohair (pink)
Yarn A *3oz* mohair (pale gray)
Yarn B *3oz* mohair (burgundy)
Yarn C *3oz* mohair (gray)
NB A "fine" mohair containing 80% mohair and 20% acrylic was used for model.
Needles
1 pair no 6
1 pair no 9
Stitch gauge
18 sts and 18 rows to 4in over pattern on no 9 needles (or size needed to obtain given tension).
NB This is a very loose, lacy pattern.

BACK

With no 6 needles and yarn M, cast on 71 sts. Work in k1, p1 rib for 4in, beginning alternate rows with p1, and ending with a right side row. Increase row: P3; *up 1, p4; rep from * to end – 88 sts. Break off yarn M and join in yarn A. (Knot yarns together and weave in up the side.) Change to no 9 needles and work in pattern as follows:
Row 1 K2, *yfwd, k2tog; rep from * to end.
Row 2 Purl.
Row 3 Knit.
Row 4 Purl.
Break off yarn A and join in yarn B.
Row 5 K2, *sl 1, k2tog, psso, k4, yfwd, k1, yfwd, k4; rep from * to last 2 sts, k2.
Row 6 P2, *p3tog, p4, yrn, p1, yrn, p4; rep from * to last 2 sts, p2.
Row 7 As row 6.
Row 8 As row 5.
Row 9 As row 6.
These 9 rows form the pattern. Repeat them 5 more times changing the yarns in sequence, i.e., next yarn C, then M, then A, then B, etc.
Shape armholes: (Keeping pattern correct) bind off 9 sts at the beginning of the next 2 rows. Decrease one st at both ends of the next 3 rows – 64 sts. Work on these 64 sts until 4 pattern repeats have been worked from the beginning of the armhole.

Shape shoulder: Do not change the yarn. Bind off 16 sts at the beginning of the next 2 rows.
Shape neck: With size no 6 needles and yarn M work 6 rows in k1, p1 rib, increase one st in the center of the first row – 33 sts. Bind off in rib.

FRONT

Work as for the back until 2 repeats of the pattern have been worked from the beginning of the armhole shaping.
Shape neck: Continuing in the pattern as for the back work as follows: Put 45 sts on one side on a stitch holder and work on the remaining 19 sts. Decrease at the neck edge on every row until 16 sts remain. Work to match the back to the shoulder. Bind off. Work the other side to match, leaving 26 sts in the center.

SLEEVES

With no 6 needles and yarn M cast on 33 sts. Work in k1, p1 rib as on back for 4in; end with a right side row. Increase row: P2, *up 1, p1; rep from * to end – 64 sts. Change to no 9 needles and starting with yarn C work 7 repeats of the pattern. (Color should match the body at armhole shaping.)
Shape top: (Keeping pattern correct) bind off 9 sts at the beginning of the next 2 rows. Decrease one st at both ends of the next 3 rows – 40 sts. Continue on these 40 sts until 2 repeats of the pattern have been worked from the beginning of the armhole shaping. Bind off loosely in yarn already in use (M).

NECKBAND

With no 6 needles and yarn M and with the right side of the work facing, pick up 12 sts from the side of the neck, 26 sts from the center neck, increase one st in center, and 12 sts from the other side of neck – 51 sts. Work 6 rows in k1, p1 rib. Bind off very loosely in rib.

PUTTING TOGETHER

Do not press. Sew rib with a flat stitch. Sew seams with back stitch. Either side can be used for the right side of the sweater. When making up be sure to use the same side for all pieces.

MEASUREMENTS

To fit chest 34–36in (86–91cm) loosely

50cms
20"

57cms.
22½"

46cm
18"

designed by *JOAN CHATTERLEY*

designed by *JANE BALL*

MEASUREMENTS

To fit chest 32–38in (81–97cm)

48cm
19"

64cm
25"

48cm
19"

Lipstick

A simple, one-size roll-neck sweater made memorable by its being knitted in bright cerise mohair with contrasting bands and random color dashes.

MATERIALS

Yarn
Main yarn M *11oz* mohair (dark pink)
Yarn A *1oz* mohair (navy)
Yarn B *1oz* mohair (gray)

Needles
1 pair no 7
1 pair no 9
1 set no 7 double-pointed
Stitch gauge
13 sts and 18 rows to 4in over st st on no 9 needles (or size needed to obtain given tension).

BACK

With no 7 needles cast on 63 sts in yarn M. Work in k1, p1 rib for 14 rows; increase one st at the end of the last row – 64 sts. Change to no 9 needles and work in st st in the following order: 2 rows A, 2 rows B, 2 rows M, 4 rows A, 2 rows B, 2 rows M, 2 rows A, 4 rows B. Continue in M.
To make color dashes in yarns A and B: At random, knit yarn over 4 sts and continue in yarn M.
When work measures 25in, bind off loosely.

FRONT

Knit as for the back until the work measures 20in.
Shape neck: Divide for neck shaping: On knit row k 32 sts. Put remaining stitches on a stitch holder. Turn. Next row: Bind off 2 sts, purl to the end of the row. Then decrease one st at the neck edge on every knit row until 12 sts (14 in all) have been decreased. When work measures 25in bind off. Knit the right neck edge in the same way.

SLEEVES

With no 7 needles cast on 31 sts in yarn M and work in k1, p1 rib for 12 rows. Increase one st at the end of the last row – 32 sts. Change to no 9 needles and work in st st in the following order, and shape the sides by increasing one st at each end of the 3rd and every following 5th row until there are 60 sts: 2 rows A, 2 rows B, 2 rows M, 4 rows A. Continue in M, making dashes at random. Continue knitting straight until sleeve seam measures 19in. Bind off loosely.

PUTTING TOGETHER

Using a flat seam, join the shoulder seams. Place the center of the bound-off edge of the sleeve to the shoulder seam and sew the sleeve top to the side edges of the front and back. Join the side and sleeve seams.
Brush the garment gently with a teasle or nail brush in a downwards direction only.

COLLAR

Starting at the right edge of neck with double-pointed no 7 needles and yarn M pick up evenly 20 sts from the right front and 20 sts from the left front and 26 sts from the back – 66 sts. Increase round: K1, p1 rib increasing one st every 3rd st – 88 sts. Continue in rounds of k1, p1 rib until the work measures 6in. Bind off loosely in rib.

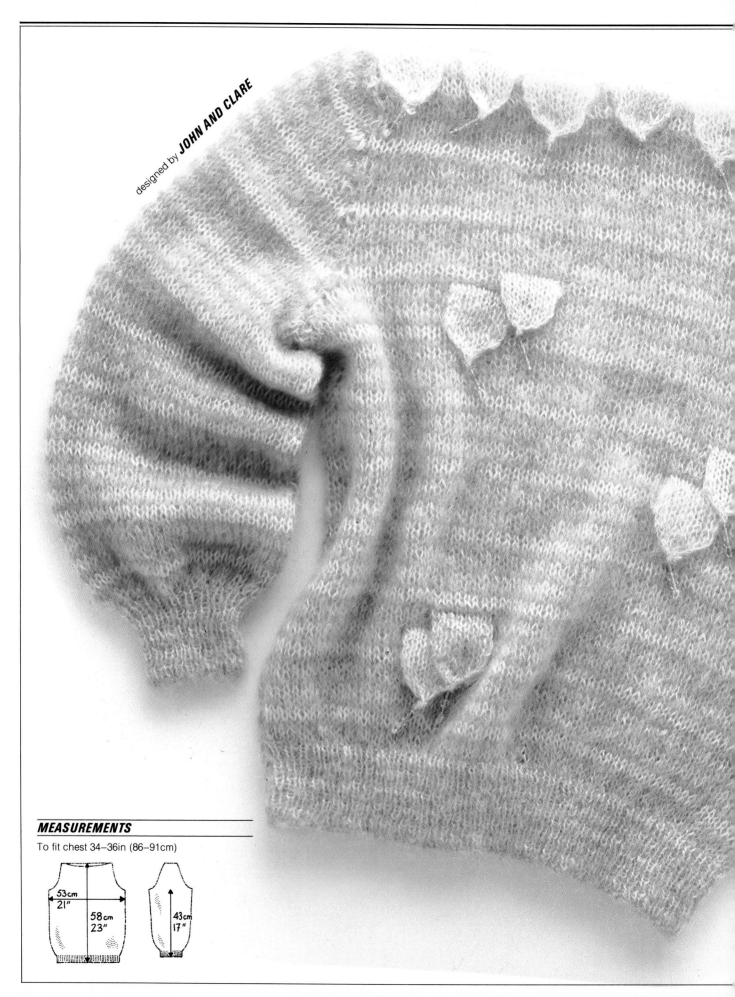

designed by *JOHN AND CLARE*

MEASUREMENTS

To fit chest 34–36in (86–91cm)

53cm
21"

58cm
23"

43cm
17"

Candy Stripes

Baby-soft mohair shades suitable for both daytime and evening wear enliven a simple boat-necked pullover. Extra interest can be given by the addition of knitted "pennants" with beaded tails.

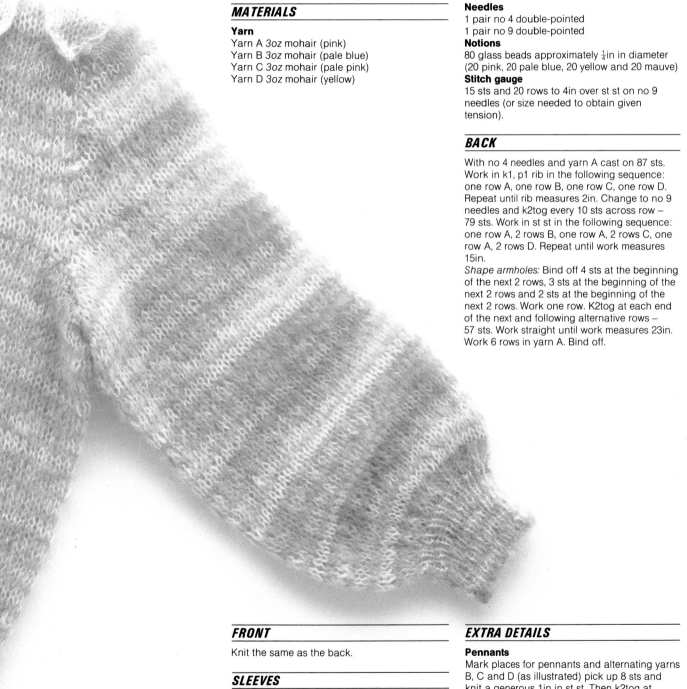

MATERIALS

Yarn
Yarn A *3oz* mohair (pink)
Yarn B *3oz* mohair (pale blue)
Yarn C *3oz* mohair (pale pink)
Yarn D *3oz* mohair (yellow)

Needles
1 pair no 4 double-pointed
1 pair no 9 double-pointed

Notions
80 glass beads approximately $\frac{1}{4}$in in diameter (20 pink, 20 pale blue, 20 yellow and 20 mauve)

Stitch gauge
15 sts and 20 rows to 4in over st st on no 9 needles (or size needed to obtain given tension).

BACK

With no 4 needles and yarn A cast on 87 sts. Work in k1, p1 rib in the following sequence: one row A, one row B, one row C, one row D. Repeat until rib measures 2in. Change to no 9 needles and k2tog every 10 sts across row – 79 sts. Work in st st in the following sequence: one row A, 2 rows B, one row A, 2 rows C, one row A, 2 rows D. Repeat until work measures 15in.
Shape armholes: Bind off 4 sts at the beginning of the next 2 rows, 3 sts at the beginning of the next 2 rows and 2 sts at the beginning of the next 2 rows. Work one row. K2tog at each end of the next and following alternative rows – 57 sts. Work straight until work measures 23in. Work 6 rows in yarn A. Bind off.

FRONT

Knit the same as the back.

SLEEVES

With no 4 needles and yarn A cast on 39 sts. Work in rib as for back for 2in. Change to no 9 needles and increase in every other stitch across row – 58 sts. Work as the body in st st until work measures approximately 17in.
Shape top: (Match stripes to armhole shaping.) Bind off 4 sts at the beginning of the next 2 rows, 3 sts at the beginning of the following 2 rows. Decrease each end of every other row until the sleeve top measures 7in long. Bind off.

EXTRA DETAILS

Pennants
Mark places for pennants and alternating yarns B, C and D (as illustrated) pick up 8 sts and knit a generous 1in in st st. Then k2tog at each end of every row to the end and pull a long strand of yarn through the last stitch.

PUTTING TOGETHER

Turn down the 6 rows of yarn A and stitch securely for neck. Join 3in of front and back for shoulder seams. Sew side and sleeve seams matching all stripes. Thread one bead of each color onto the yarn left at the end of each pennant. Secure the beads to the pennants; catch the back of the pennants to the sweater with a single stitch.

Bandit

A simple dropped-shoulder boat-necked sweater which knits up quickly and makes good use of scraps. Regular medium-weight classic yarn can be substituted for some of the mohair for a more textural appearance.

MATERIALS

Yarn

Main yarn M *3oz* mohair (black)
Yarn A *1oz* mohair (dark pink)
Yarn B *1oz* mohair (green)
Yarn C *1oz* mohair (purple)
Yarn D *1oz* mohair (pale gray)
Yarn E *1oz* mohair (dark gray)
Yarn F *1oz* mohair (pink)
Yarn G *1oz* mohair (red/blue mix)
Yarn H *1oz* mohair (pale blue)
Yarn I *1oz* mohair (mustard)
Yarn J *1oz* mohair (blue)
NB The amount of colored yarns above is approximate: for some shades a whole 1oz ball will not be required; others need slightly more. The total amount of yarn needed is 13oz.

Needles

1 pair no 7
1 pair no 9

Stitch gauge

13 sts and 18 rows to 4in over st st on no 9 needles (or size needed to obtain given tension).

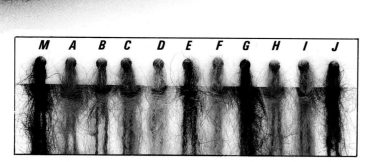

BACK

Using no 7 needles and yarn M cast on 65 sts. K1, p1 rib for 14 rows. Change to no 9 needles and work in st st in the following order: 10 rows A, 10 rows M, 2 rows B, 2 rows C, 10 rows J, 2 rows D, 10 rows E, 4 rows F, 4 rows G, 10 rows H, 10 rows C, 10 rows I, 2 rows G, 2 rows B. Work the last 12 rows in k1, p1 rib in yarn M. Bind off loosely.

FRONT

Knit the same as the back.

SLEEVES

Cast on 33 sts in yarn M on no 7 needles. K1, p1 rib for 12 rows. Change to no 9 needles and, in st st, work the yarns as for the front and the back of the sweater but 4 rows H, not 10, and ending with 2 rows I (instead of 10) and 2 rows of G. At the same time, shape the sides by increasing one st at each end of the 3rd and every following 5th row until there are 61 sts. Bind off loosely.

designed by *JANE BALL*

PUTTING TOGETHER

On both the front and the back fold the top edge of the main color stripe (black) over so that it meets the last row of the previous stripe. Sew down along the neck edge in yarn M on the wrong side. Place the shoulders edge to edge, keeping them flat. Sew flat seams on the shoulder 6in long (on the wrong side).
Find the center of the top of the sleeve edge. Place to the shoulder seam, sew in sleeves. Join side and sleeve seams. (Flat seams must be used at all times.)
Brush the garment gently with a teasel or nail brush in a downward direction only.

MEASUREMENTS

To fit chest 32–38in (81–97cm)

Rose Red

Two different yarns – knitting worsted and mohair – and two different stitches – Moss stitch and Rizotto stitch – combine to good effect in this yoked cardigan. The pretty crocheted collar and an optional silk flower make it versatile enough for evening wear.

MATERIALS

Yarn
Main yarn M *14 (15)oz* knitting worsted (dark red)
Yarn A *6oz* mohair (dark red)
Needles
1 pair no 2
1 pair no 5
1 crochet hook size F
Notions
6 buttons
Stitch gauge
22 sts and 40 rows to 4in over Moss stitch on no 5 needles (or size needed to obtain given tension).

BACK

With no 2 needles and yarn M cast on 101 (107) sts. Work in k1, p1 rib for 2¾in, beginning the 2nd and all alternate rows with p1. Change to no 5 needles and work in Moss stitch as follows:
Every row K1, *p1, k1; rep from * to end.
Continue in Moss stitch until work measures 14¼in.
Shape armholes: Still in Moss stitch bind off 6 (7) sts at the beginning of the next 2 rows, decrease one st at each end of the next 2 rows, then one st at each end of the following 2 alternate rows – 81 (85) sts. Change to yarn A. K2tog at the beginning of the next row only while working Rizotto stitch as follows:
Rows 1 and 3 Knit.
Row 2 K1, *p2tog then without letting the sts fall from the left-hand needle knit the same 2 sts together. Repeat from * ending with k1.
Row 4 K1, p1; rep from * in row 2 to last 2 sts; p1, k1.
Continue in Rizotto stitch until the armhole measures 8 (8¼)in. Bind off 8 (9) sts at the beginning of the next 4 rows, then 9 (9) sts at the beginning of the next 2 rows. Bind off the remaining 30 sts.

FRONT

Left front
With no 2 needles cast on 51 (55) sts and work in rib for 2¾in as on back. Change to no 5 needles and work in Moss stitch until the work measures 14¼in, ending with a wrong side row.
Shape armholes: In Moss stitch bind off 6 (7) sts at the beginning of the next row. Work one row. Decrease one st at the armhole edge of the next 2 rows then one st at the same edge of the next 2 alternate rows – 41 (44) sts.

Change to Rizotto stitch and yarn A as for back but k2tog at the armhole edge of the first row on the first size to give an even number of stitches – 40 (44) sts. Work in Rizotto stitch until the work measures 19¾ (20)in ending at the neck edge.

Bind off 8 sts at the beginning of the next row and one st at the neck edge of the next 7 (9) rows – 25 (27) sts. Continue until the work measures the same as the back to the shoulder shaping ending at the armhole edge.

Shape shoulder: Bind off 8 (9) sts at the beginning of the next and following alternate rows, work one row, bind off the remaining 9 sts.

Right front
Work as for left front reversing shaping.

SLEEVES

With no 2 needles and yarn M cast on 51 (53) sts and work in rib for 2½in, ending with a right side row.
Next row rib 1 (3), *work twice into next st, rib 4; rep from * 9 times more – 61 (63) sts.

Change to no 5 needles and work in Moss stitch as on the back. Work 12 rows in Moss stitch then increase one st at each end of the next row and every following 6th row, keeping the increases in Moss stitch until there are 83 (85) sts on the needle. Continue without shaping until the sleeve measures 17in.
Shape armholes: Bind off 5 (6) sts at the beginning of the next 2 rows. Decrease one st at each end of the following 4th row. Work 2 rows, decreasing one st at the end of the 2nd row – 68 sts. Change to Rizotto stitch and yarn A. Work one row, then decrease one st at each end of the next row. Work 3 rows then decrease one st at each end of the next row and every following alternate row until 36 sts remain. Bind off 2 sts at the beginning of the next 8 rows; bind off the remaining 20 sts.

BUTTON BANDS

Button border (left front)
Using yarn A and an F crochet hook, work 6 rows of double crochet along the left front edge.

Buttonhole border (right front)
Using yarn A and an F crochet hook, work 3 rows in single crochet along the right front edge. Single crochet next row, working 3 single chains for each buttonhole. These

should be positioned ½in from the top and bottom, with 4 more evenly spaced between. (Do this by marking the band with pins.) Next row: Single crochet, working 3 single crochets in the 3 single chains. Work 2 more rows in single crochet.

PUTTING TOGETHER

Press all parts, excluding the ribbing and the mohair, on the wrong side following the instructions on the ball bands. Join shoulder seams. Set in sleeves gathering any excess fabric at the shoulder seam and making sure that the change of stitch seams are joined to match all the way round. Join sleeve and side seams. Sew on buttons.

COLLAR

Work one row of single crochet in yarn M around the neck excluding the button bands. Then turn and *work 5 chains, miss 3 sts, one single crochet into next stitch; rep from * to end. Turn, work 5 single chains as in first row with a single crochet in between, working the single crochet into the 3rd chain of each loop, ending the row as it begins. Break off the yarn. Join in mohair and work 7 doubles into each loop and 1 single crochet into each single crochet. Break off the yarn. Sew in all ends.

designed by **JOSE FRANKS**

MEASUREMENTS

To fit chest 34 (36)in (87, 91cm)

46(48)cm
18(19)"
56(57)cm
22(22½)"
43cm
17"

49

Pretty Plaits

A classic bright blue mohair cardigan is made yet more fashionable by the addition of a contrasting knitted braid which can be worn to suit. The matching cap has its trim sewn to it.

designed by **JANE BALL**

MATERIALS for cardigan

Yarn
Main yarn M *11oz* mohair (blue)
Yarn A *1oz* mohair (rust)
Yarn B *1oz* mohair (green)

Needles
1 pair no 7
1 pair no 9
1 pair no 10½

Notions
5 buttons (or make your own, see p. 123).

Stitch gauge
13 sts and 18 rows to 4in over st st on no 9 needles (or size needed to obtain given tension).

BACK

With no 7 needles cast on 65 sts in yarn M. Work in k1, p1 rib for 14 rows. Change to no 9 needles and work in st st until the work measures 18in.
Shape armholes (set in sleeve): Bind off 3 sts at the beginning of the next 2 rows. Bind off 2 sts at the beginning of the next 2 rows. Decrease one st at the beginning of the next 2 rows. Knit straight until the work measures 25in. Bind off.

FRONT

Left front
With no 7 needles cast on 33 sts. Work in k1, p1 rib for 14 rows. Change to no 9 needles and work in st st until the work measures 18in.
Shape armholes: Repeat shaping as for the back on the left side of the left front only. Continue until the work measures 21¼in, ending with a knit row.
Shape neck: Bind off 2 sts at the beginning of the row. Then decrease one st at the neck edge until 12 sts (14 in all) have been decreased. Continue to knit straight until the work measures 25in (same as for the back). Bind off.

Right front
Repeat as for the left front reversing shaping.

SLEEVES

With no 7 needles cast on 29 sts. Work in k1, p1 rib for 12 rows, increasing one st at the end of the last row – 30 sts. Change to no 9 needles and work in st st, shaping the sides by increasing one st at each end of every 4th row 3 times. Then increase one st each end of every 10th row until there are 46 sts. Knit straight until the sleeve measures 18in.
Shape top: Bind off 2 sts at the beginning of the next 4 rows, then one st at the beginning of the next 2 rows. Decrease one st on both sides every other row until there are 10 sts, ending with a purl row. Bind off.

BUTTON BANDS

Button border (left front)
Join shoulder seams. With no 7 needles cast on 7 sts.
Row 1 K1, p1 to last st, k1.
Row 2 P1, k1 to last st, p1.
Repeat, sewing the band onto the left front as you go along. Knit up to the beginning of the neck. Put sts on a holder.

Buttonhole border (right front)
Repeat as for the left side making 5 buttonholes. The first should be ½in from the lower edge; the last will be on the 3rd row of the neck band.
To make buttonholes: K1, p1, k1, yfwd, k2tog, p1, k1.

NECKBAND

Rib the 7 sts of the right front border. Knit up 18 sts from the right front, 25 sts from the back neck and 18 sts from the left front; then rib sts of left front border – 75 sts. Work in k1, p1 rib for 5 rows, making a buttonhole on the 2nd row. Bind off.

PUTTING TOGETHER

Join side and sleeve seams. Set in sleeves.
Brush with a nail brush in a downward direction only.

EXTRA DETAILS

Braid
With no 10½ needles cast on 8 sts and work in st st until the work measures 50in. Knit 3 strips, one each in M, A and B.
To secure the braid while making, bind the 3 strips together at the top with some yarn. Braid evenly, secure again at the ends. Make pompoms for the ends by wrapping yarn A around 3 fingers 40 times. Wrap yarn around the center to secure – cut ends and fluff up. Sew on to the ends of the braid.

MEASUREMENTS

To fit chest 32–38in (81–97cm)
To fit average size head.

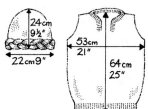

MATERIALS for hat

Yarn
Main yarn M *1oz* mohair (blue)
Yarn A approx ½oz mohair (rust)
Yarn B approx ½oz mohair (green)

Needles
1 pair no 9

Stitch gauge
13 sts and 18 rows to 4in over st st on no 9 needles (or size needed to obtain given tension).

HAT

With no 9 needles and yarn M cast on 56 sts. Work in st st until work measures 9½in. Thread the yarn through the stitches and draw up.

Braid
With no 9 needles and yarn M cast on 5 sts. Work in st st until the strip measures 26in. Bind off. Repeat with yarns A and B. Sew seam. Braid the 3 strips together securing both ends. Sew on to bottom of the hat, with the join of the braid at the seam.

Glitter Bands

Shimmering mohair shades repeat in pattern down the length of this long (to the knee) roll-neck sweater-dress and are echoed in the bobble-topped hat and matching gloves.

MATERIALS for sweater-dress

Yarn
Main yarn M *6oz* mohair (gray glitter)
25oz mohair in scraps of approximately 9 shades, some plain, some with lurex, some multi-colored.

Needles
1 pair no 7
1 pair no 9

Stitch gauge
17 sts and 19 rows to 4in over st st on no 9 needles (or size needed to obtain given tension).

BACK

Using no 7 needles and yarn M cast on 82 sts and work in k2, p2 rib for 19 rows. Increase row: P8, *up 1, p5; rep from * to last 9 sts, up 1, p9 – 96 sts. Change to no 9 needles and work from Chart 1 (overleaf), Rows 1–54. (Cut off yarn, knot together and weave up the side of the work.) Work in st st unless otherwise indicated. Then work rows 1–44 again (approx 24in long).
NB Do *not* work bobbles on body part of sweater.
Shape armholes: Continue working from Chart 1. Bind off 4 sts at the beginning of the next 2 rows, then decrease one st at each end of every row until there are 68 sts, working Rows 1–28 of Chart again (work bobbles on Row 11).
Shape shoulders: Bind off 20 sts at the beginning of the next row, knit to end (do not change yarn). Bind off 20 sts at the beginning of the next row (still using same yarn), purl to end. Bind off remaining sts.

FRONT

Work as for back until Row 18 has been worked after armhole shaping (from Chart 1) – 28 rows altogether from the beginning of the armhole shaping.
Shape neck: Still working from Chart, pattern across 27 sts. Bind off 14 sts, work pattern across the remaining 27 sts. Working on these sts, decrease one st at neck edge until there are 20 sts. Continue on these 20 sts until the front matches the back to shoulder. Bind off. Join appropriate yarn to the remaining 27 sts and work to match.

SLEEVES

Using yarn M and no 7 needles cast on 38 sts. Work in k2, p2 rib for 23 rows. Increase row *P2, up 1, p2, up 1, p1, up 1; rep from * to last 3 sts, p2, up 1, p1 – 60 sts. Change to no 9 needles and work rows 1–38 in pattern from Chart 2. Repeat once more. Then work Row 44 from Chart 1 binding off 4 sts at the beginning of the row. Then work Row 45 from Chart 1 binding off 4 sts at the beginning of the row. Then work Rows 46–54 of Chart 1, decreasing one st at both ends of every alternate row. Still decreasing on every alternate row work rows 1–16

from Chart 1. (Work bobbles on Row 11.) Bind off the remaining sts.

PUTTING TOGETHER

Do not press. Sew rib with a flat stitch. Sew seams with back stitch.

COLLAR

Using yarn M and no 7 needles cast on 118 sts. Work in k2, p2 rib for 7in. Bind off loosely in rib. Attach to neck.

MATERIALS for hat

1oz mohair (gray glitter)
Scraps of other mohair shades.

HAT

Using no 7 needles cast on 70 sts. Work in k2, p2 rib for 4in. Increase row – Increase in first st, p9, *up 1, p10; rep from * to last 10 sts, up 1, p9, increase in last st – 78 sts. Change to no 9 needles and work in pattern from Chart 3 for 22 rows.
Shape crown: Carry on working from Chart 3.
Row 23 *K8, k2tog; rep from * to last 8 sts, k8.
Row 24 *K7, k2tog; rep from * to last 8 sts, k8.
Row 25 K7, k2tog, *k6, k2tog; rep from * to last 7 sts, k7.
Row 26 P6, p2tog, *p5, p2tog; rep from * to end.
Row 27 K5, k2tog, *k4, k2tog; rep from * to end.
Row 28 P4, p2tog, *p3, p2tog; rep from * to end.
Row 29 K3, k2tog, *k2, k2tog; rep from * to end.
Row 30 P2, p2tog, *p1, p2tog; rep from * to end.
Row 31 K1, *k2tog; rep from * across row.
Cut off yarn and draw thread through remaining 9 sts. Fasten off securely.

Do not press. Sew rib with a flat stitch. Sew seam with back stitch.

MATERIALS for gloves

Yarn

1oz mohair (gray glitter)
Scraps of other mohair shades

GLOVES

Left glove

Using no 7 needles cast on 22 sts. Work in k2, p2 rib for 19 rows. Increase row: P5, *up 1, p4;

rep from * to last 5 sts, up 1, p5 – 26 sts. Change to no 9 needles and work in pattern from Chart 4 as follows: Work 4 rows. Next row inc in first st, k2, inc in next st, work to end. Work 3 rows. Next row inc in first st, k3, inc in next st, work to end. Work 3 rows. Next row inc in first st, k4, inc in next st, work to end – 32 sts. Work 4 more rows – 17 rows altogether.

designed by **JOAN CHATTERLEY**

53

Chart 1 Back and front

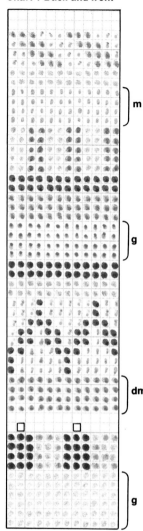

Next row work to last 8 sts, put these 8 sts on stitch holder for thumb. Next row cast on 4 sts at the beginning of the row, work to end – 28 sts. Work 7 more rows (25 rows altogether). Put 14 sts at right side and 8 sts on left side on spare yarn or stitch holder for fingers.

4th finger: (Work in random stripes as you wish for fingers.) Join yarn to remaining 6 sts, with right side of work facing. Cast on 2 sts at the beginning of the row. Work 12 rows on these 8 sts. Cut off yarn and draw yarn through sts. Fasten off securely.

3rd finger: With right side of work facing pick up 4 sts from left side, pick up one st from the base of the 4th finger and pick up 4 sts from the right side (next to 2nd finger). Increase one st at the beginning of the first row. Work 16 rows altogether. Cut off yarn and thread through sts. Fasten off securely.

2nd finger: With right side of work facing pick up 3 sts from left, pick up one st from the base of the 3rd finger, and 4 sts from the right side (next to 3rd finger). Cast on 2 sts at the beginning of the first row. Work 18 rows altogether. Cut off yarn and thread through sts. Fasten off securely.

1st finger: Pick up the remaining 7 sts from the stitch holder, and 3 sts from the base of the 2nd finger. Work 16 rows. Cut off the yarn and thread through sts. Fasten off securely.

Thumb: Pick up 8 sts from the holder and 4 sts from the cast on edge above thumb. Work 12 rows altogether. Cut off the yarn and thread through sts. Fasten off securely.

Right glove
Work as for left glove, reversing all shaping. Do not press. Sew rib with a flat stitch. Sew up seams with back stitch.

MEASUREMENTS

To fit chest 34–40in (86–102cm)

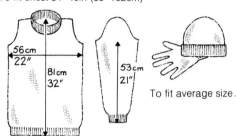

56cm 22"
81cm 32"
53cm 21"

To fit average size.

Chart 3 Hat

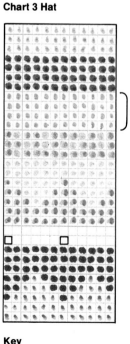

Chart 2 Sleeves

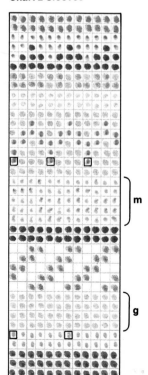

Chart 4 Gloves

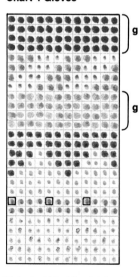

Key
☐ Make bobble
g Garter st
m Moss st
dmv Double Moss variation

Make bobble k1, p1, k1, p1, k1 into next st, turn, purl 5, turn, knit 5, turn, k2tog, k1, k2tog, turn, slip 1, k2tog, psso.

For explanation of other sts see p. 92.

Chart for back

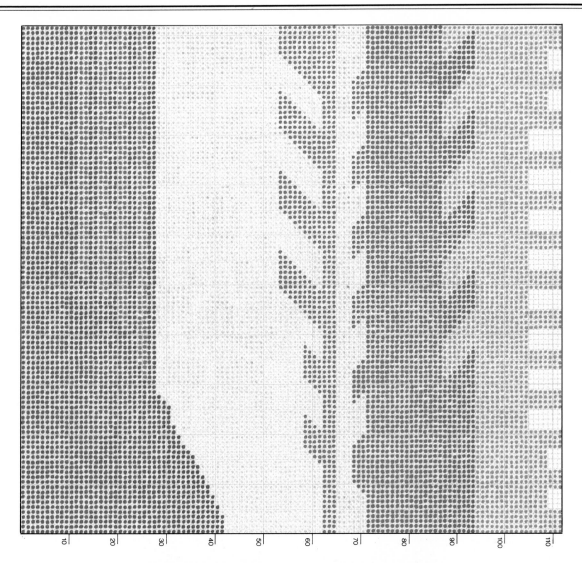

Chart for sleeves

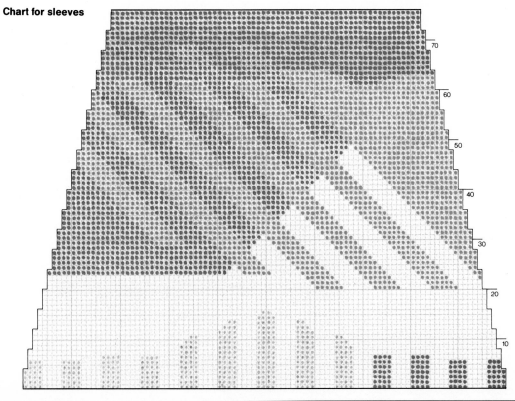

Freestyle

Asymmetrical geometric patterns abound on a high-necked, full-sleeved jacket which is knitted from a charted design in brilliant mohair colors.

MATERIALS

Yarn
Yarn A *5oz* mohair (dark blue)
Yarn B *4oz* mohair (mauve)
Yarn C *4oz* mohair (green)
Yarn D *3oz* mohair (white)
Yarn E *3oz* mohair (cerise)
Yarn F *3oz* mohair (mid blue)

Needles
1 pair no 5
1 pair no 7
1 set no 7 double-pointed

Notions
9 buttons ½in in diameter

Stitch gauge
17 sts and 20 rows to 4in over st st on no 7 needles (or size needed to obtain tension).

BACK

With no 5 needles and yarn A cast on 101 sts and work in k1, p1 rib for 26 rows increasing one st in the center of the last row – 102 sts. Change to no 7 needles and st st. Work in pattern as on chart for 112 rows. When complete leave all stitches on a stitch holder.

FRONT

Left front
With no 5 needles and yarn A cast on 41 sts. Work in k1, p1 rib for 26 rows. Change to no 7 needles and st st and work in pattern as on chart to row 98. Slip first 7 sts onto a stitch holder at the beginning of the row and purl to end. Knit one row. Bind off one st at the begin-

ning of the next row and k2tog at the end of the following row. Now continue straight as chart to row 112 without shaping. Leave sts on a stitch holder.

Right front
Work as for left front reversing shaping at neck edge. Leave stitches on a stitch holder.

NECKBAND

Join shoulders: Transfer sts from stitch holders to double-pointed needles. Place left front against back (right sides together). Knit one row, knitting one st from each needle until all 32 sts have been used. Bind off in the normal way. Repeat for right front. Put the remaining central stitches of back onto a stitch holder. Pick up 7 sts from stitch holder at left front, 12 sts up left side, 38 sts along the back of neck increasing one st in center, 12 sts down right side, and 7 sts from right front stitch holder – 77 sts. With no 7 needles work in k1, p1 rib for 12 rows decreasing one stitch at each end of every alternate row. Bind off loosely.

SLEEVES

With no 7 needles and yarns C, D and E as on chart pick up 100 sts (50 sts each side of shoulder seam). Work in st st, decreasing one st each end of every 4th row. Work 76 rows as on chart – 64 sts.

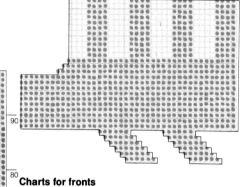

Charts for fronts
For the left front work 82 rows from the chart on the left, reversing the pattern so that the left front is a mirror image of the right front, then work 30 rows as on the chart above. This completes the left front. Work the right front entirely from the chart on the left.

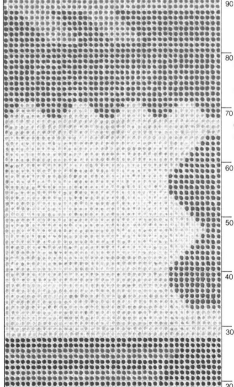

At row 77 k3tog; k2tog to last 3 sts; k3tog – 31 sts. Change to no 5 needles and work in k1, p1 rib for 20 rows in yarn C. Bind off loosely.

BUTTON BANDS

Button border

With no 5 needles and yarn A cast on 16 sts and work in k1, p1 rib in the following yarn sequence: 12 rows A; *5 rows D; 5 rows A; rep from * 3 times more; 6 rows D; 6 rows B; 6 rows D; 6 rows B; 8 rows D; 8 rows B; 8 rows D; 12 rows C; 12 rows E. Bind off all sts.

Buttonhole border

With no 5 needles and yarn A cast on 16 sts and work in k1, p1 rib in the same yarn sequence as the button border, with the addition of 9 buttonholes made in the following way: Rib 6 rows. *Next row rib 8 sts, bind off 2 sts, rib to end. On the following row, rib 8 sts, cast on 2 sts, rib to end. Rib 12 rows. Repeat from * 7 times more, then repeat the 2 buttonhole rows. Rib 4 more rows, then bind off.

PUTTING TOGETHER

Sew side seams and sleeve seams. Sew on button bands and sew buttons in place. Do not press. Brush the garment gently with a nail brush.

MEASUREMENTS

To fit chest 34–40in (86–102cm)
Back width 24in (61cm)
Length 24in (61cm)
Sleeve seam 19in (48cm)

designed by **MAGGIE WHITE**

Shetland and mohair yarns knit up into a warm raglan-sleeved
woolly cardigan with roomy slanting pockets.

MATERIALS

Yarn
Main yarn M *16oz* Shetland thick knitting
worsted (purple)
Yarn A *2oz* mohair (pale mauve)
Yarn B *2oz* mohair (dark green)
Yarn C *2oz* mohair (bright green)
Yarn D *2oz* mohair (pale green)
Needles
1 pair no 3
1 pair no 8
Notions
7 buttons
Stitch gauge
20 sts and 18 rows to 4in over pattern on
no 8 needles (or size needed to obtain given
tension).

BACK

With no 3 needles and yarn M cast on 78 (82,
86, 90) sts. Work in k1, p1 rib for 2¾in. Change
to no 8 needles. Increase row: K3 (5, 7, 9) sts,
*inc in the next st, k13; rep from * to last 5 (7,
9, 11) sts, inc in the next st, k4 (6, 8, 10) – 84
(88, 92, 96) sts altogether. Purl one row. With
yarns M and B work 6 rows of the pattern as
follows:

Row 1 *K3 M, 1 B; rep from * to the end of the
row.
Row 2 *P1 B, 3 M; rep from * to the end of the
row.
Row 3 *K1 M, 3 B; rep from * to the end of the
row.
Row 4 P2 M, *1 B, 3 M; rep from * to last st;
p1 M.
Row 5 K1 M, *1 B, 3 M; rep from * to last 2 sts;
k2 M.
Row 6 P1 B, *1 M, 3 B; rep from * to the last 2
sts; p2 B.

Repeat the 6 rows of the pattern 6 more times,
substituting yarns C, D, A, D, C for yarn B.
Repeat the pattern again, starting with B and
following the same yarn changes, until the
pattern has been worked 9½ times. (Work
should measure approximately 16¼in from the
beginning.) Work 0 (2, 4, 6) more rows of
pattern.
Shape armholes: Continuing with the same
yarn sequence, decrease as follows: Bind off 3
sts at the beginning of the next 2 rows. Bind off
2 sts at the beginning of the next 2 rows. K2tog
at the beginning and end of the next and every
following knit row until there are 30 (32, 34, 36)
sts on the needle. Leave on a stitch holder.

Pocket backs (make 2)
With no 8 needles and yarn M cast on 22 sts
and work in st st for 18 rows, ending on a purl
row. Leave sts on a stitch holder.

FRONT

Left front
With no 3 needles and yarn M cast on 37 (39,
41, 43) sts. Work in k1, p1 rib for 2¾in. Change
to no 8 needles and increase 3 sts as follows:
K 4 (6, 8, 10) sts, *inc in the next st, k13 sts; rep
from * to last 5 sts; inc in next st, k4 – 40 (42,
44, 46) sts altogether. Purl one row. Now begin
the pattern and work it 3 times altogether. Work

rows 1–4 of pattern. Divide for pocket: Work 7
(8, 9, 10) sts in pattern. Leave these on a stitch
holder. Knit the next 2 sts together and work to
the end of the row. *Pattern to the last 2 sts;
p2tog, turn, k2tog, work to end of row; rep
from * until there are 11 (12, 13, 14) sts on the
needle, finishing on a knit row. Leave on a
stitch holder. Go back to 7 (8, 9, 10) sts on
stitch holder (knit row) and continue in pattern
across 22 sts of pocket back – 29 (30, 31,
32) sts. Work straight in the pattern to the same
point as piece just worked ending on a knit
row. Now pick up 11 (12, 13, 14) sts left on
stitch holder and purl in pattern across these
and 29 (30, 31, 32) sts just worked – 40 (42,
44, 46) sts. Continue in the pattern changing the yarns as before until pattern has been
worked 9½ times. Work 0 (2, 4, 6) more rows of
pattern.
Shape armholes: (Knit row) Bind off 3 sts, work
to the end of the row. Work one row. Bind off 2
sts, work to the end of the row. Work one row.
K2tog at the beginning of the next row and
every alternate row until there are 20 (21, 22,
23) sts on the needle. K2tog, work to end of the
row. Next row bind off 6 (7, 8, 9) sts and pattern
to the end of the row. Now k2tog at the beginning and end of the next and every following
knit row until there are no sts left – secure yarn.

Right front
Follow instructions for left front as far as divide
for pocket. Then work as follows: K in pattern
on 33 (35, 37, 39) sts and leave the remaining
7 (8, 9, 10) sts on a stitch holder. Turn. *P2tog
work to the end. Knit next row to the last 2 sts,
k2tog; rep from * until there are 11 (12, 13, 14)
sts on the needle ending on a knit row. Leave
sts on a stitch holder. Now go back to 7 (8, 9,
10) sts left on stitch holder (knit row) and knit
in pattern. Turn. Purl in pattern across these
and 22 sts of pocket back. Continue straight on
all 29 (30, 31, 32) sts until piece is worked to
the same point as piece just worked. Now purl
across 29 (30, 31, 32) sts in pattern and continue across 11 (12, 13, 14) sts left on stitch
holder; on all 40 (42, 44, 46) sts work as for left
front reversing all the shaping.

SLEEVES

With no 3 needles and yarn M cast on 42 (45,
48, 51) sts and work in k1, p1 rib for 2¾in.
Change to no 8 needles and increase 14 sts
as follows: K1 (3, 4, 5) sts; *inc in the next st,
k2 sts; rep from * to last 2 (3, 5, 7) sts; inc in
next st, k1 (2, 4, 6) – 56 (60, 62, 64) sts altogether. Purl one row. Now begin the pattern
(changing the yarns as for back and front).
Work 2 repeats of the pattern, then increase as
follows: (knit row) at the beginning and end of
this row inc one st and repeat this increase on
every following 6th row until there are 64 (68,
72, 76) sts on the needle. Work straight until
the pattern has been repeated 9½ times altogether. Work 0 (2, 4, 6) more rows of the
pattern.
Shape top: (knit row) Bind off 3 sts at the
beginning of the next 2 rows. Bind off 2 sts at
the beginning of the next 2 rows. K2tog at the
beginning and end of the next and every
following knit row until there are 10 (12, 14, 16)

sts on the needle – leave these on a stitch
holder. Work second sleeve to match.

NECKBAND

With no 3 needles and yarn M and right side
facing, pick up 6 (7, 8, 9) sts at right front neck,
12 sts from right side neck edge, k10 (12, 14,
16) sts from sleeve top, 30 (32, 34, 36) sts from
back neck, inc one st in center, 10 (12, 14, 16)
sts from 2nd sleeve top, pick up 12 sts down
left side neck edge and 6 (7, 8, 9) sts at left
front – 87 (95, 103, 111) sts. Rib for 9 rows. Bind
off in rib.

BUTTON BANDS

Button border (left front)
With right side facing, no 3 needles and yarn
M pick up 123 (127, 131, 135) sts evenly beginning at the top of the neckband. Work in k1, p1
rib for 9 rows. Bind off all sts in rib.

Buttonhole border (right front)
With right side facing, no 3 needles and yarn
M pick up 123 (127, 131, 135) sts evenly beginning from bottom border and work 3 rows in
single rib. Now make 7 buttonholes: Rib 3 (2, 4,
3) sts, *bind off 3 sts, rib 16 (17, 17, 18) sts, rep
from * to last 6 (5, 7, 6) sts; bind off 3, rib 3 (2,
4, 3). On return row cast on 3 sts where previously bound off. Now rib for another 4 rows –
bind off all sts in rib.

PUTTING TOGETHER

Use an invisible flat seam. Sew side and sleeve
seams matching the zig-zags carefully. Sew in
raglans and sew down pocket backs.

MEASUREMENTS

To fit chest 32–34 (34–36, 36–38, 38–40)in
(81–86, 86–91, 91–97, 97–102cm)

43(45,47,49)cm
17(17½,18½,19)"
68(71,74,76)cm
27(28,29,30)"

43(44,46,47)cm
17(17½,18,18½)"

MATERIALS

Yarn
Main yarn M *4oz* mohair (black)
11oz in scraps of approximately 12 shades of mohair
Needles
1 pair no 7
1 pair no 9
Notions
6 buttons
Stitch gauge
14 sts and 16–18 rows to 4in over st st on no 9 needles (or size needed to obtain given tension).

Crazy Paving

Panels of varying color blocks made up of mohair scraps are
sewn together to form a loose-fitting dropped-shoulder jacket.
Roll back the cuffs for a high fashion look and finish with a
number of handmade buttons.

designed by *JANE BALL*

BACK

With no 7 needles and yarn M cast on 81 sts.
Work in k1, p1 rib for 12 rows; decrease one st
at the end of the last row – 80 sts. Change to
no 9 needles. To knit panels of color divide
into 4 sections. Knit the first 20 sts with one
color. Put remaining sts on stitch holder. Work
the first panel in st st for 20 rows altogether.
Then continue but vary the blocks of color as
you knit up, using 10 or 20 rows. To give
interest to the design k 4 rows using 2 different
colors at different places. Bind off when the
length of the panel measures 31½in.
Starting again at the bottom, pick up 20 more
sts from the stitch holder. Work as above.
varying the colors and making sure that the
same color does not appear in
adjacent panels.
Repeat for remaining two panels.

FRONT

Right front
With no 7 needles and yarn M cast on 41 sts.
Work in k1, p1 rib for 12 rows; decrease one st
at the end of the last row – 40 sts. Change to
no 9 needles. Knit 20 sts. Put remaining 20 sts
on a stitch holder.
1st Panel: Knit as for the back panel. When
work measures 26½in start shaping neck.
Shape neck: On a knit row bind off 2 sts at the
beginning; then bind off one st at the edge of
every knit row until 12 sts (14 in all) have been
decreased. Continue to knit straight until work
measures 31½in. Bind off.
2nd Panel: Knit as for back without shaping.

Left front
Repeat as for right front reversing shaping.

SLEEVES

With no 9 needles cast on 60 sts. Work in st st
in stripes of color varying width in 2, 4 and
10 row combinations until the work measures
22in. Bind off loosely.

BUTTON BAND

With no 7 needles and yarn M cast on 7 sts.
Row 1 K1, p1 to last st; k1.
Row 2 P1, k1 to last st; p1.
Repeat and sew band onto the left front as you
go along, pulling it gently around the neck
edge. When you reach the center of the right
front neck edge make the first buttonhole:

K1, p1, k1, bind off 2, p1, k1. On the next row,
p1, k1, p1, cast on 2, k1, p1. Continue border
as before.
Make 6 buttonholes in all, spacing them evenly,
with the last one ½in from the lower edge.
Sew the border to the right front.

PUTTING TOGETHER

Sew all panels, back and front by laying
garment pieces flat. Pin sections then oversew
neatly in medium shade yarn. Join shoulder
seams (flat). Find the center top of the sleeve.
Place this to the shoulder seam and sew
together (dropped shoulder). Join side and
sleeve seams. Sew on buttons.
Brush the garment gently with a nail brush in a
downward direction only.

MEASUREMENTS

To fit chest 34–40in (86–102cm)

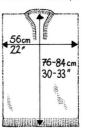

56cm
22"

76-84cm
30-33"

56cm
22"

Jacob's Delight

Fair-Isle bordered coat (or shorter jacket) with warm shawl collar
suits both sexes. Worked in heavy-weight yarn on large needles,
it is knitted in two main pieces.

MATERIALS for coat

Yarn
Main yarn M *8oz* thick knitting worsted (blue gray)
Yarn A *3oz* thick knitting worsted (brown)
Yarn B *3oz* thick knitting worsted (natural)
Yarn C *3oz* thick knitting worsted (green)
Yarn D *4oz* thick knitting worsted (yellow)
Yarn E *3oz* thick knitting worsted (blue)
Yarn F *3oz* thick knitting worsted (purple)
Yarn G *1oz* thick knitting worsted (orange)

Needles
1 pair no 7
1 pair no 9
1 pair no 10

Notions
4 buttons

Stitch gauge
16 sts and 20 rows to 4in over st st on no 10
needles (or size needed to obtain given
tension).

MATERIALS for jacket

Main yarn M *6oz* thick knitting worsted
Yarns A–G, needles and buttons – the same as
the cardigan

Special note:
On all Fair-Isle rows: repeat from * right to the
end of the row even if the row does not end
with a complete repeat. On the return row, the
pattern will match up. Do this unless otherwise
stated.
There are two stripe sequences in the pattern
as follows:
Stripe sequence (1): one row st st E; one row
st st C; one row st st B; one row st st M.
Stripe sequence (2): one row st st B; one row
st st A; one row st st D; one row st st G.

MEASUREMENTS

To fit chest 34–36 (36–38, 38–40)in (86–91,
91–97, 97–102cm)

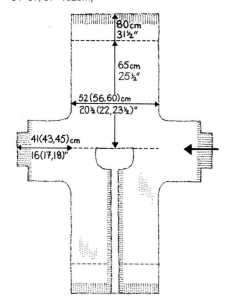

LEFT SLEEVE

With no 10 needles and yarn M, cast on 28 sts.
Work in Garter stitch for 22 rows. Increase row:
Increase one st into every stitch – 56 sts altogether. Beginning with a purl row, work 4 rows
in st st. Increase row: With purl side facing and
yarn A, increase one st at the beginning and
end of the row, and knit 58 sts altogether. (By
knitting the row instead of purling it, a ridge is
formed around the cuff.) †† Next row purl 58
sts A. Then work in pattern as follows:
Row 1 Knit 4A, *2B, 10A.
Row 2 Purl 3A, *4B, 8A.
Row 3 Increase one st at the beginning and
end of the row using A – 60 sts.
Row 4 Purl 2B, *2A, 4B.
Row 5 Knit 1B, *2A, 2B.
Row 6 Purl 2C, *2B, 4C.
Row 7 Knit 2C, *1B, 2C, 2B, 2C, 2B, 3C.
Row 8 *Purl 2B, 2C, 1B, 1C, 1B, 2C, 1B, 2C.
Row 9 Knit 1B, *2C, 1B, 3C, 1B, 2C, 3B.
Row 10 Purl 3B, *2C, 1B, 1C, 1B, 2C, 5B.
Row 11 Knit 1C, *2B, 2C, 1B, 2C, 3B, 2C.
Row 12 Purl 2C, *3B, 3C, 2B, 4C.
Row 13 Knit 2M, *8B, 4M.
Row 14 Purl 2C, *2D, 3C, 3D, 4C.
Row 15 Knit 1C, *3D, 2C, 1D, 2C, 2D, 2C.
Row 16 Purl 2D, *2E, 1D, 1E, 1D, 2E, 5D.
Row 17 Knit 2D, *2E, 1D, 3E, 1D, 2E, 3D.
Row 18 *Purl 2E, 1D, 2E, 1D, 1E, 1D, 2E, 2D.
Row 19 Knit 1F, *2D, 2F, 2D 2F, 1D, 3F.
Row 20 Purl 2F, *2D, 4F.
Row 21 Knit 3F, *2G, 2F, 2G, 6F.
Row 22 Purl 4F, *4G, 8F.
Row 23 Knit 60F.
Row 24 Purl 4F, *4G, 8F.
Row 25 Knit 5F, *2D, 10F.
Work 4 (5, 6) rows F. Follow stripe sequence
(1). Work 2 (3, 4) rows F. Then purl 2M, *8F,
4M. On the next row knit 1A, *10F, 2B; rep from
* to next-to-last st, k1A. Work 3 (4, 5) rows F.
Follow stripe sequence (2).† Work 2 (3, 4)
rows F.
Increase for underarms: Knit 1F; inc into next
st; 2F, *4G, 8F; rep from * to last 2 sts; inc into
next st, k1F. Purl 6F, *2D, 10F. Work the next 3
rows in F, inc 2 sts at the beginning and end of
every row – 74 sts. Then follow stripe sequence
(1) and inc 2 sts at the beginning and end of
rows 2 and 4 – 82 sts.

FRONT

Purl 41F; turn (leave remaining 41 sts on a
stitch holder for back). Slip one st and k40F. At
the end of the row cast on 78 sts in F. (For the
jacket, cast on 54 sts.) ‡ Purl 119 (95 for
jacket) F. Knit 119 (95 for jacket) F. Purl 3F,
*4M, 8F. Knit 5F, *2A, 10F. Work 3 (4, 5) rows
F. Follow stripe sequence (2). ‡ Work one (2, 3)
rows F. Make pocket: Purl 30 (6 for jacket) F;
put next 20 sts on a stitch holder; cast on 20
sts F; purl remaining 69F.
*** Knit 2G, *8F, 4G;

rep from * to last 9 sts; k9F. *Purl 10F, 2D; rep
from * to last st; p1D. Work 3 (4, 5) rows F.
Follow stripe sequence (1). ** Work 2 (3, 4)
rows F. Then work as follows:
Row 1 Purl 4F, *2D, 10F.
Row 2 Knit 4F, *4G, 8F.
Row 3 Purl in F.
Row 4 Knit 4F, *4G, 8F.
Row 5 Purl 2F, *2G, 2F, 2G, 6F.
Shape neck:
Row 6 Bind off 15F. *K4F, 2D.
Row 7 Purl 1F, *1D, 2F, 2D, 2F, 2D, 3F.
Row 8 Knit 2tog D, *1F, 1D, 2F, 1D, 2F, 2D,
2F, 1D.
Row 9 *Purl 2E, 1D, 3E, 1D, 2E, 3D.
Row 10 Knit 2tog D, 1E, *1D, 2E, 5D, 2E, 1D, 1E.
Row 11 *Purl 2F, 2C, 1D, 2C, 3D, 2C.
Row 12 Knit 2tog C, 1C, *2D, 4C, 3D, 3C.
Row 13 Purl 9B, *4M, 8B.
Row 14 Knit 2tog B, 2B, *4C, 8B; rep from * to
last 9 sts; k9B.
Row 15 *Purl 10B, 2C.
Row 16 Knit 2tog B; knit rem sts in B.
Work next 3 rows in A, k2tog at the beginning
of rows 1 and 3. Change to no 9 needles and
with yarn M, work Garter stitch for 5 rows.
Change to no 7 needles and work Garter
stitch for another 5 rows. Bind off all sts firmly.

BACK

Pick up the 41 sts left on the stitch holder at the shoulder and knit across all sts in F. Purl 41F then cast on 78 (54 for jacket) F – 119 (95 for jacket) sts. Work next 2 rows in F. § Knit 3F,

*4M, 8F. Purl 5F, *2A, 10F. Work next 3 (4, 5) rows in F. Follow stripe sequence (2). Work next 2 (3, 4) rows in F. Purl 2G, *8F, 4G; rep from * to last 9 sts; p9F. *Knit 10F, 2D; rep from * to last st; k1D. Work next 3 (4, 5) rows in F. Follow stripe sequence (1). Work next 2

(3, 4) rows in F. Then work as follows:
Row 1 Knit 4F, *2D, 10F.
Row 2 Purl 4F, *4G, 8F.
Row 3 Knit all in F.
Row 4 Purl 4F, *4G, 8F.
Row 5 Knit 2F, *2G, 2F, 2G, 6F.
Row 6 Purl 2F, *2D, 4F; rep from * to last st. Purl 1F.
Row 7 *Knit 2D, 2F, 2D, 2F, 1D, 3F.
Row 8 *Purl 2F, 1D, 2F, 1D, 1F, 1D, 2F, 2D.
Row 9 Knit 1D, *2E, 1D, 3E, 1D, 2E, 3D; rep from * to last st; k1D.
Row 10 Purl 2D, *2E, 1D, 1E, 1D, 2E, 5D.

Row 11 Knit 3D, *2C, 1D, 2C, 7D.

Row 12 *Purl 4D, 3C, 3D, 2C; rep from * to last st; p1C.

Row 13 Knit 2C, *8D, 4C; rep from * to last 9 sts; k9D.

Row 14 Purl 9B, *4M, 8B.

Row 15 Knit 2C, *8B, 4C; rep from * to last 9 sts; k9B.

Row 16 *Purl 10B, 2C; rep from * to last st, p1C. §§ Knit one row B; purl one row E; knit one row C; §§§ purl one row A. Work the next 3 rows in M. Then repeat the stripes but work from §§§ to §§. Now complete the second half of the back, but work backwards in pattern from §§ to § (i.e. work row 16, then 15, then 14, etc.). Work next 2 rows in F. Now purl 41 sts in F and bind off 78 (54 for jacket) in F. Leave the remaining 41 sts on a stitch holder.

Pocket back (right side only): With no 10 needles and yarn F cast on 20 sts. Work 23 rows. Leave these sts on a stitch holder.

FRONT

Right front

With no 7 needles and yarn M cast on 98 (74 for jacket) sts and work in Garter stitch for 3 rows. Change to no 9 needles and continue in Garter stitch for 2 more rows.

Make buttonholes: Knit 4, *bind off 3, k17. Rep from * twice more. Now bind off 3 and knit the remaining 31 (7 for jacket) sts (4 buttonholes altogether). Knit 31 (7 for jacket) and *cast on 3, k17. Rep from * twice more then cast on 3 and knit the remaining 4 sts. Work next 3 rows in Garter stitch. Change to no 10 needles and purl one row in A.

Shape neck: K1; inc into the next st; knit remaining sts in A. Purl one row A. Knit 1B; inc into the next st; knit remaining sts in B. *Purl 10B, 2C. Knit 1B; inc into the next st; k1B, *4C, 8B; rep from * to last 9 sts; k9B. Purl 9B, *4M, 8B. Knit 1C; inc into the next st; *knit 2D, 4C, 3D, 3C. *Purl 2D, 2C, 1D, 2C, 3D, 2C. Knit 1E, inc into next st (first part of the st in D, second part in E). *Knit 1D, 2E, 5D, 2E, 1D, 1E. *Purl 2E, 1D, 3E, 1D, 2E, 3D. Knit 1F; inc into the next st (first part of st in D, second part in F); *knit 1D, 2F, 1D, 2F, 2D, 2F, 1D, 1F. Purl 1F, *1D, 2F, 2D, 2F, 2D, 3F. Knit 1D; inc into the next st (first part of st in D, second part in F); knit 3F; *2D, 4F. Purl 2F, *2G, 2F, 2G, 6F; now cast on 14 sts in F – 119 (95 for jacket) sts. Knit 4F, *4G, 8F; rep from * to last 3 sts; k3F. Purl one row in F. Knit 4F, *4G, 8F. Purl 4F, *2D, 10F. Now repeat the first side working backwards from ** to ***.

Pocket front: Purl 30 (6 for jacket) in F. Now put the next 20 sts on a stitch holder and purl across the 20 sts of the pocket back left on a stitch holder, and continue purling across the 69 sts in F.

Now follow pattern on first side from ‡ to ‡‡. Knit 41F; bind off 78 (54 for jacket) in F; re-attach yarn at the end of 41 sts and purl 41F and across 41 sts (at back shoulder) left on stitch holder.

SLEEVE

Decrease for underarms: Using yarn M, decrease one st at the beginning and end of the row. Purl 80A. Using yarn C, decrease 2 sts at the beginning and end of the row. Purl 76E. Using yarn F, decrease 2 sts at the beginning and end of the row. Purl 72F. Using yarn F, decrease 2 sts at the beginning and end of the row. Purl 68F. Using yarn F, decrease 2 sts at the beginning and end of the row. Purl 7F, *2D,

10F. Using yarn F, decrease 2 sts at the beginning of the row; knit 2F, *4G, 8F; rep from * to last 4 sts; k2togF (twice).

Now on 60 sts repeat instructions for the sleeve working backwards from † to ††. **NB** at every inc row dec instead – 58 sts. Using yarn F, decrease one st at the beginning and end of the row. Purl 56A. With right side facing purl one row in M (this raises the cuff to match the first side). Knit 56M. Purl 56M.

Decrease for cuffs: Using yarn M, knit 2tog to end of row – 28 sts. On the next and following 20 rows work in Garter stitch with yarn M. Bind off all sts.

Sew in all loose ends and secure them. Press garment according to instructions on the yarn band. Join shoulder seam with an invisible stitch matching the stripes and Fair-Isle carefully. Join the side and sleeve seams.

COLLAR

(Garter stitch throughout): With no 10 needles and yarn M and right side facing, pick up 18 sts beginning at the top of the buttonhole band and the first 7 rows of the neck front edge. Knit one row. Increase row: knit 15; inc into the next and following st, k1. Repeat this double increase at the end of every right side row until there are 26 sts on the needle. Knit one row. With right side facing k1; inc into the next st; knit 24. Knit 3 rows. On the next right side row and every following 4th row until there are 31 sts on the needle, k1; inc into the next st; knit to the end of the row. Next row (wrong side at the neck edge) k31. Then *k17; turn; knit back along 17 sts; turn; knit all 31 sts. Knit one more row. Repeat from * 4 more times. Knit 30 rows. Repeat from * 5 more times. Next row at collar edge with right side facing, k1, k2tog at the beginning of this and every following 4th row until 26 sts remain. Next row at neck edge with wrong side facing k2tog (twice), k22. Next row knit 24. On the following row k2tog (3 times), k18. Bind off sts. Sew around neck to match the first side.

HEM BORDER AND POCKET BANDS

Hem border

Using no 10 needles and yarn M, with right side facing, pick up 170 (180, 200) sts. Work in Garter stitch for 8 rows. Bind off all stitches. Left side pocket back: With no 10 needles and yarn F, pick up 20 sts of first side pocket left on stitch holder. Work in st st for 22 rows. Bind off all sts.

Pocket bands

Use no 9 needles and yarn F. Right side: Pick up 20 sts on stitch holder and beginning with a purl row work 4 rows of st st. Next row make holes for turn-in as follows: p1, *p2tog, M1; rep from * to last st; p1. Work 3 rows of st st. Bind off. Left side: Pick up 20 sts where previously cast on and work 2 rows of st st. Next row work row of holes (as above) and complete to match right side.

Fold back pocket bands to inside (like a hem), and sew into place. Sew down the pocket backs. Sew on buttons and press, if yarn band permits.

MATERIALS

Yarn

Yarn A *4oz* fine-weight cotton (pink)

Yarn B *3oz* fine-weight cotton (blue)

Yarn C *3oz* fine-weight cotton (yellow)

Yarn D *3oz* fine-weight cotton (green)

Needles

1 pair no 1

1 pair no 3

Notions

1 button

Stitch gauge

28 sts and 48 rows to 4in over pattern on no 3 needles (or size needed to obtain given tension).

designed by *JOHN AND CLARE*

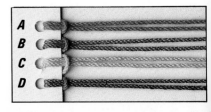

Live-Wire

Bright colored cottons are knitted up in an openwork pattern, formed by decreasing on one row and picking up stitches the next, to produce a firm, knobbly texture.

BACK

With no 1 needles and yarn A cast on 121 sts. Work in k1, p1 rib for 2in. Change to no 3 needles and work in the following pattern and yarn sequence:

Row 1 Knit.
Row 2 Purl.
Row 3 K2tog across row to last st, k1.
Row 4 *K1, pick up horizontal thread before next stitch and knit it; repeat from * to last st, k1.

Yarn sequence

2 rows B; 2 rows C; 2 rows D; 4 rows A;** 2 rows B; 2 rows C; 2 rows D; 2 rows A; 4 rows B; 2 rows C; 2 rows D; 2 rows A; 2 rows B; 4 rows C; 2 rows D; 2 rows A; 2 rows B; 2 rows C; 4 rows D; 2 rows A; 2 rows B; 2 rows C; 2 rows D; 4 rows A. Repeat from ** until work measures 11in (118 pattern rows).

Shape armholes: Bind off 6 sts at the beginning of the next 2 rows being careful to keep pattern correct. Decrease one st at each end of the next 4 rows. Decrease one st at each end of every alternate row 4 times. Continue straight until work measures 13in (142 pattern rows) then divide work and knit side separately. Bind off when work measures 16½in (180 pattern rows).

FRONT

Work as the back until the front measures 14¼in (160 pattern rows) omitting back opening.
Shape neck: Bind off 11 sts at center and work on, knitting 2 together at neck edge until 29 sts remain. Continue in pattern until work measures 16½in (180 pattern rows). Bind off. Work other side to match.

SLEEVES

With no 1 needles and yarn A cast on 81 sts. Work in k1, p1 rib for 6 rows. Change to no 3 needles and hold the rib onto the body of knitting exactly 3½in down from the armhole bind-off point. Check the position in the color change sequence and start the sleeve at that point. This ensures the sleeve and body stripes match. Work straight for 3½in in pattern.
Shape top: Bind off 6 sts at the beginning of the next 2 rows. Decrease one st at each end of every 4th row for 4in (48 pattern rows). Decrease every alternate row until sleeve top measures 6in (58 pattern rows). Bind off.

NECKBAND

Join shoulder seams. With no 1 needles and yarn A pick up 18 sts from each side of the back and 51 sts from the front – 87 sts. Work in k1, p1 rib for 6 rows making one buttonhole in the neckband. Bind off in rib.

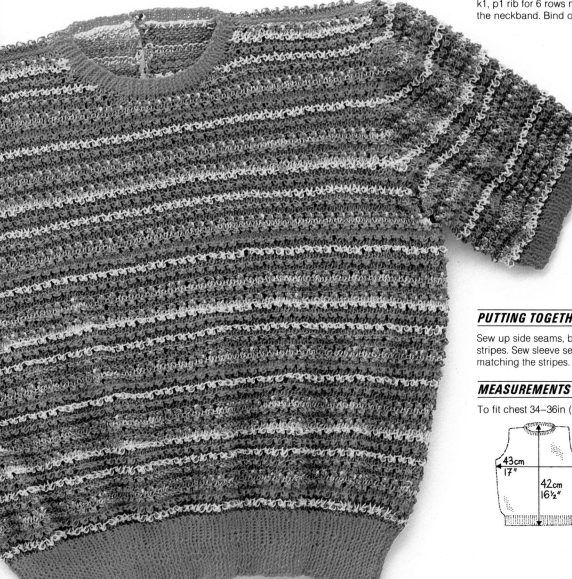

PUTTING TOGETHER

Sew up side seams, being careful to match the stripes. Sew sleeve seams and set in sleeves, matching the stripes. Sew on button.

MEASUREMENTS

To fit chest 34–36in (86–91cm)

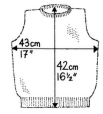

43cm 17"
42cm 16½"
11cm 4½"

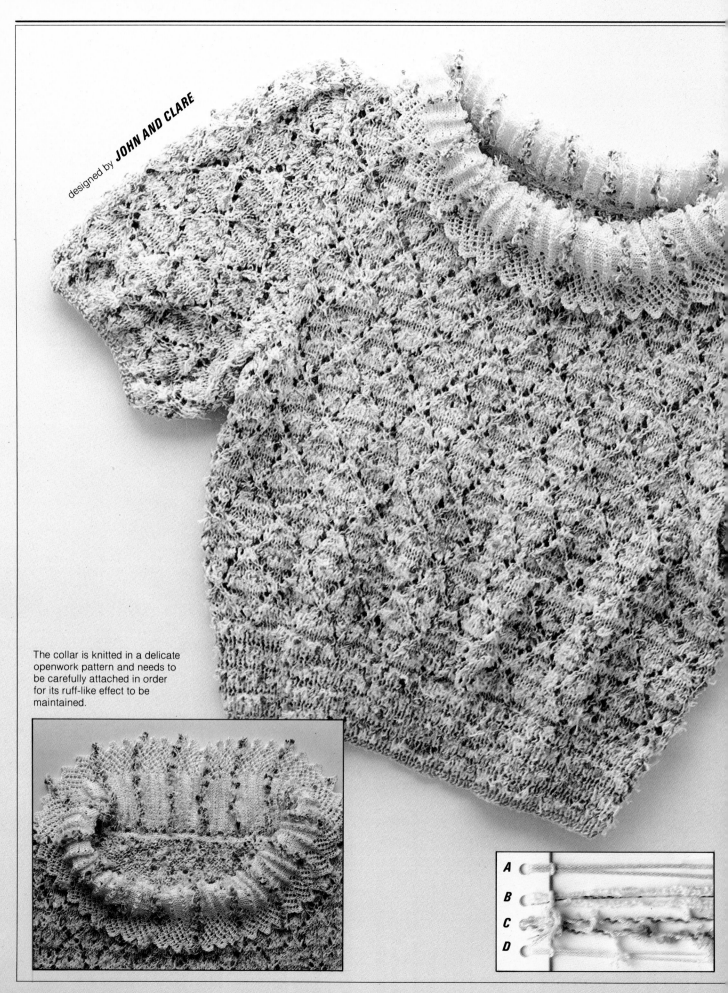

designed by *JOHN AND CLARE*

The collar is knitted in a delicate openwork pattern and needs to be carefully attached in order for its ruff-like effect to be maintained.

A
B
C
D

Diamond Lace

Knitted lace collar decorates a short-waisted summery top made up of a combination of cotton, chenille and lurex mix and a raggy-textured yarn knitted in delicate open-work diamonds.

MATERIALS

Yarn
Yarn A *6oz* fine-weight cotton (pale blue)
Yarn B *4oz* medium-weight chenille run with a very fine metallic thread (white/silver)
Yarn C *4oz* medium-weight multi-color terry-look mix (blue)
Yarn D *1oz* very fine (crochet) cotton (white)

Needles
1 pair no 1
1 pair no 4

Stitch gauge
22 sts and 32 rows to 4in over pattern on no 4 needles (or size needed to obtain given tension).

BACK

With no 1 needles and yarn A, cast on 87 (93, 97) sts loosely. Work in k1, p1 rib in the following yarn sequence: 2 rows A, 2 rows B, 2 rows C, until work measures 2½in. (Continue this yarn change sequence throughout the sweater.) Change to no 4 needles and knit across the row, increasing to 91 (101, 111) sts. Purl one row. Then work in pattern as follows (multiple of 10 plus 1):
Row 1 K1; *yfwd, sl 1, k1, psso, k5, k2tog, yfwd, k1; rep from * to end.
Rows 2, 4, 6, 8, 10, 12, 14, 16 Purl.
Row 3 K1; *k1, yfwd, sl 1, k1, psso, k3, k2tog, yfwd, k2; rep from * to end.
Row 5 K1; *k2, yfwd, sl 1, k1, psso, k1, k2tog, yfwd, k3; rep from * to end.
Row 7 K1; *k3, yfwd, sl 1, k2tog, psso, yfwd, k4; rep from * to end.
Row 9 K1; *k2, k2tog, yfwd, k1, yfwd, sl 1, k1, psso, k3; rep from * to end.
Row 11 K1; *k1, k2tog, yfwd, k3, yfwd, sl 1, k1, psso, k2; rep from * to end.
Row 13 K1; *k2tog, yfwd, k5, yfwd, sl 1, k1, psso, k1; rep from * to end.
Row 15 K2tog; *yfwd, k7, yfwd, sl 1, k2tog, psso; rep from * to last 9 sts; yfwd, k7, yfwd, sl 1, k1, psso.
Work 3½ repeats of pattern.
Shape armholes: Bind off 4 sts at the beginning of the next 2 rows. Bind off 3 sts at the beginning of the next 2 rows. Bind off 2 sts at the beginning of the next 2 rows. K2tog at each end of the next row – 71 (81, 91) sts. Continue straight until 6½ repeats of the pattern have been worked altogether. Divide for neck.
Shape neck: Bind off 19 (25, 31) sts in the center of work. Work to the end of the row. Work back to the neck edge. Bind off 5 sts working away from the neck edge. Bind off 2 sts working away from the neck edge. K2tog at neck edge every row until 12 (14, 16) sts remain. Continue straight until 7½ repeats of pattern have been worked altogether. Work other side to match.

FRONT

Knit the same as the back.

SLEEVES

With no 1 needles and yarn A cast on 61 sts. Work in k1, p1 rib for 2 rows. Change to no 4 needles and yarn B and increase in every 3rd st – 81 sts. Purl one row.
Work 2 repeats of the pattern, using the same yarn sequence as the body.
Shape top: Bind off 4 sts at beginning of the next 2 rows. Bind off 3 sts at beginning of the next 2 rows. K2tog every other row for 2½ patterns. Work straight for ½ pattern. Bind off.

COLLAR

Yarn sequence: On the 1st and 2nd repeats of the pattern run a fine metallic thread with yarn D on rows 9 and 10; on the third repeat use yarn C on rows 9 and 10. Repeat this yarn sequence throughout the collar.
With no 1 needles and yarn D cast on 31 sts.
Row 1 Knit into back across row.
Row 2 Knit.
Row 3 K3, p20, yo, k2tog; (yfwd, k2tog) 2 times; yfwd, k2.
Row 4 K29, turn (leave 3).
Row 5 P21, yo, k2tog; (yfwd, k2tog) 2 times; yfwd, k2.
Row 6 K30, leave 3.
Row 7 P22, yo, k2tog; (yfwd, k2tog) 2 times; yfwd, k2.
Row 8 K31, leave 3.
Row 9 (Yarn D + fine metallic thread or yarn C) Sl first st; (yfwd, k2tog) 14 times; yfwd, k2.
Row 10 (Yarn as row 9) K9, p23, k3.
Row 11 K35.
Row 12 Bind off 4, knit to end.
Repeat from row 3 another 50 times, or until the collar when unstretched fits inside the neck edge. Bind off.

PUTTING TOGETHER

Join the shoulder seams, side seams and sleeve seams. Set in the sleeves, taking any fullness to the sleeve top. Join the collar to make a circle and mark in four places (the join being one of them). Mark the center front and center back of the sweater. Pin the collar join to the center back and the other marks to the shoulder seams and center front, inside the sweater. With yarn D using diagonal stitches and from the front of the sweater, sew the edge of the collar (3 slip sts) inside the neck edge of the sweater, keeping the stitches near the edge of the sweater to prevent it rolling over. Now sew the very edge of the collar, from the inside of the sweater, just below the other stitches.

MEASUREMENTS

To fit chest 34–36 (36–38, 38–40)in (86–91, 91–97, 97–102cm)

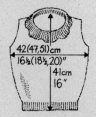

42(47,51)cm
16½(18½,20)"
41cm
16"
10cm
4"

Lacey Vee

Delicate cotton, slub linen, and chenille and lurex bands incorporating oblique openwork patterns are finished with a hand knitted lace collar.

MATERIALS

Yarn

Yarn A *4oz* fine-weight cotton (white)
Yarn B *4oz* medium-weight chenille run with a very fine metallic thread (white/silver)
Yarn C *4oz* medium-weight slub linen or cotton (natural)
Yarn D *1oz* very fine (crochet) cotton (white)
Yarn E scrap of medium-weight terry-look cotton (natural)

Needles

1 pair no 1
1 set no 1 double-pointed
1 pair no 7

Stitch gauge

18 sts and 24 rows to 4in over pattern using yarns as in pattern on no 7 needles (or size needed to obtain given tension).

BACK

With no 1 needles and yarn A cast on 81 sts. Work 16 rows of k1, p1 rib in the following yarn sequence: 4 rows A, 2 rows B, 4 rows C, 2 rows B. Change to no 7 needles and increase 9 sts across row – 90 sts. Work in pattern, below, for 80 rows (back should measure about 15in from the beginning), changing yarn as on rib throughout sweater.

Pattern (multiple of 9)
Row 1 *K4, yfwd, k2tog, pass the "made" st over the k2tog, yfwd, k3; rep from * to the end of the row.
Row 2 Purl.
Row 3 *K3, yfwd, k2tog, pass the "made" st over k2tog, yfwd, k4; rep from * to the end of the row.
Continue in this way, working pattern one st further to the right every alternate row.
Shape armholes: Bind off 4 sts at the beginning of the next 2 rows. Bind off 3 sts at the beginning of the next two rows. Bind off 2 sts at the beginning of the next 2 rows. K2tog at the beginning and end of the next 2 rows – 68 sts. ** Continue straight until work measures 23in. Bind off, but not with yarn B.

FRONT

Work as back until **.
Next row pattern 32, k2tog, turn and leave remaining 34 sts on a spare needle. Work 3 rows. K2tog at neck edge on next row. Repeat last 4 rows until there are 27 sts. Continue straight until work measures 23in. Bind off, but not with yarn B.
Return to other 34 sts and work to match.

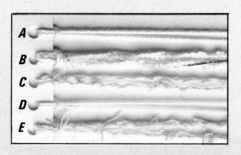

SLEEVES

With no 1 needles and yarn A cast on 41 sts loosely. Work in k1, p1 rib for 16 rows as body. Change to no 7 needles and increase to 63 sts by knitting twice into every other stitch.
Work in the same pattern and yarn sequence as body but start with 2 rows B, 4 rows A, 2 rows B, 4 rows C. Work straight until the sleeve measures about 16in and the stripes match the body at the beginning of the armhole shaping (86 pattern rows).
Shape armhole: Bind off 4 sts at the beginning of the next 2 rows, 3 sts at the beginning of the next 2 rows, 2 sts at the beginning of the next 2 rows – 45 sts. Work straight for 24 rows. K2tog each end of every row for 18 rows. Bind off.

NECKBAND

Join shoulder seams. With no 1 double-pointed needles and yarn A pick up 48 sts along each side of the front neck edge and 34 sts along the back neck edge – 130 sts. Mark the stitch at the center front with yarn. Work 14 rows of k1, p1 rib in the following yarn sequence: 4 rows A; 2 rows B; 2 rows C; 2 rows B; 4 rows A, decreasing on each row as follows: 2 sts before marked point sl 1, psso, k1 (center st), k2tog. Continue in rib. Repeat this sequence at the center front on each row. Bind off in rib.

COLLAR

With no 1 needles and yarn D cast on 10 sts.
Row 1 Knit into back across row.
Row 2 K2, *yfwd twice, k2tog; rep from * to last 2 sts, yfwd twice, k2 – 15 sts.
Row 3 K3, p1, *k2, p1; rep from * to last 2 sts, k2.
Rows 4, 5 and 6 Knit.
Row 7 Bind off 5, knit to end.
Rows 2–7 form the pattern. Work 2 patterns in yarn D and one pattern in yarn E. Continue until the collar is the same measurement as the neckband. Bind off.

MAKING UP

Sew side and sleeve seams, taking care to match the stripes. Turn under and sew the front edges of the collar, and sew it in place.

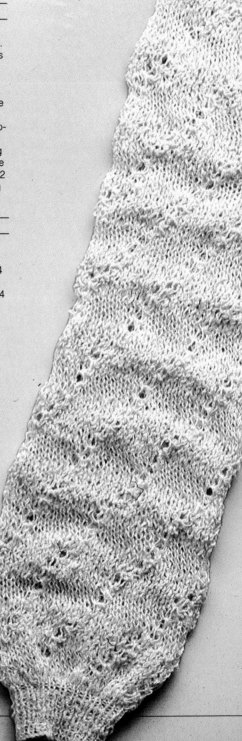

designed by *JOHN AND CLARE*

MEASUREMENTS

To fit chest 34–36in (86–91cm)

46cm
18"

58cm
23"

41cm
16"

Sparkle Stripes

Mohair, chenille and bouclé yarns in soft, sparkly colors make up
into a short-sleeved round-neck cardigan and a long-sleeved
pullover with optional soft shirt collar. Use double-pointed needles
throughout.

MATERIALS for pullover

Yarn
Yarn A *6oz* mohair (pink)
Yarn B *4oz* mohair (random dyed mauve, yellow and turquoise)
Yarn C *7oz* medium-weight chenille run with a very fine metallic thread (white/silver)
Yarn D *3oz* multi-ply cotton bouclé, thick knitting worsted (natural)

Needles
1 pair no 1 double-pointed
1 pair no 7 double-pointed

Stitch gauge
17 sts and 25 rows to 4in over st st, using yarns as in pattern on no 7 needles (or size needed to obtain given tension).

BACK

With no 1 needles and yarn A cast on 75 (79, 83) sts.
Row 1 K1, p1 in C.
Row 2 Start again without turning the work, and rib as before using yarn A.
Repeat rows 1 and 2 until the rib measures 2in. Change to no 7 needles and st st. Work in the following yarn sequence, carrying yarns not in use up the side of the work, being careful not to pull them too tightly. Knit these loose yarns into the edge stitch every few rows.
Yarn sequence
8 rows C; 1 row D; 2 rows B; 1 row D; 2 rows B; 2 rows C; 1 row D; 2 rows C; 1 row A; 1 row C; 1 row A; 1 row C; 1 row A; 1 row D.
Work 68 rows of st st (work should measure 12¾in from the beginning).
Shape armholes: Bind off 5 sts at the beginning of the next 2 rows. Bind off 2 sts at the beginning of the next 4 rows – 57 (61, 65) sts. Work straight for another 44 rows. Bind off loosely.

FRONT

Work as the back until there are 104 rows of st st. Work 24 (26, 28) sts, bind off 9 sts and work to the end of the row. Work one row. *K2tog at the start of the next and every other row (as you work away from the neck edge) until there are 21 (22, 23) sts left. Work straight until the front is the same length as the back. Bind off loosely. Work the other side as before from *.

SLEEVES

With no 1 needles and yarn A cast on 41 sts. Work in k1, p1 rib for 2in as on back. Change to no 7 needles and st st and with yarn C knit twice into every alternate stitch on the next row – 61 sts. Work one row in D then continue in st st using the same yarn sequence as the back (8 rows C; 1 row D etc). When the 25 row yarn sequence has been repeated one more time than the body at the beginning of the armhole shaping (so that the sleeve striping matches the body striping) shape sleeve top.
Shape top: Bind off 5 sts at the beginning of the next 2 rows. K2tog at each end of this and every alternate row 15 times, then every row 10 times. Bind off loosely (do not use yarn D).

NECKBAND AND COLLAR

Sew left shoulder seam. With no 1 needles and yarn C pick up and knit 35 sts across the back to the other shoulder seam. Continue to pick up 60 sts round the front neck edge (30 sts to center front, 30 sts to other shoulder seam) – 95 sts. Change to yarn A for one row as body ribbing and work 5 rows of k1, p1 rib as on the body. Bind off loosely in yarn A.

Collar
With no 1 needles and yarn A cast on 85 sts and work in k1, p1 rib as the back for 3in. Bind off loosely.

PUTTING TOGETHER

Sew side seams, sleeve seams and the remaining shoulder seam, matching stripes exactly. Pin sleeves in position to match stripes and sew from underarm seam up to shoulder seam on the front. Sew from underarm seam to shoulder seam on the back. Mark the center back of the neck with a pin. Pin the center of the collar to the center of neck back on the wrong side of the sweater under the rib. Ease in the collar and pin until there is a gap of about 5½in at the center front. Sew in place without restricting the elasticity of the knitting.

MATERIALS for cardigan

Yarn
Yarn A *6oz* mohair (pale green)
Yarns B, C and D as sweater.

BACK

Knit the same as the pullover.

FRONT

Left front
With no 1 needles and yarn A cast on 41 (43, 45) sts and rib as on sweater. Leave 5 sts on stitch holder for button band and work straight for 68 rows (about 12¾in from the beginning). Shape armhole as on back. When 104 rows of st st have been worked, shape neck.
Shape neck: Bind off 5 sts and work to the end of the row. Work one row. K2tog at the beginning of the next and every other row as you work away from the neck edge until 17 (18, 19) sts remain. Work until the front is the same length as the back. Bind off.

Right front
Repeat as for left front, reversing all shaping, and with the addition of 2 buttonholes (see p. 124). Work one buttonhole two rows from the beginning, and one at the top of the rib. Put 5 sts on a stitch holder for button band.

SLEEVES

With no 1 needles and yarn A cast on 59 (61, 63) sts. Work rib as body for 1in.
Increase row: Increase in every 4th stitch across the row – 73 (76, 78) sts. Change to no 7 needles and st st. Work in yarn sequence as on body for 18 rows.
Shape top: (stripes should match body at armhole shaping) Bind off 5 sts from the beginning of the next 2 rows. K2tog at each end of this and every alternate row 15 times and then every row 10 times. Bind off loosely.
NB Do not use yarn D at the very top of the sleeve.

BUTTON BANDS

Button border (left front)
With no 1 needles and yarn A pick up 5 sts from stitch holder and work in k1, p1 rib as on back until the band reaches to the top of the front when slightly stretched. Leave sts on a stitch holder.

Buttonhole border (right front)
Work as button border with the addition of 4

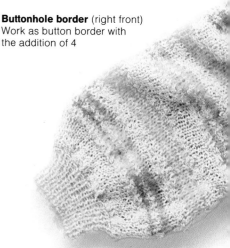

evenly spaced buttonholes (see p. 124), the top one being worked about 2¾in from the neck edge.

NECKBAND

Sew shoulder seams and sew on button bands. With no 1 needles and yarn A pick up 30 sts from each front (including sts left on holders) and 35 sts across back. Work in k1, p1 rib for 6 rows, making one buttonhole in the 4th row. Bind off in rib very loosely.

PUTTING TOGETHER

Sew side seams and sleeve seams, matching stripes exactly. Pin sleeves in position to match stripes and sew from underarm seam to shoulder seam on the front, and from underarm seam to shoulder seam on the back. Sew on buttons.

MEASUREMENTS

To fit chest 34–36 (36–38, 38–40)in (86–91, 91–97, 97–102cm)
Back width 17½ (18½, 19½)in (45, 47, 49cm)
Length 21in (53cm)
Sweater sleeve seam 17in (43cm)
Cardigan sleeve seam 4in (10cm)

designed by **JOHN AND CLARE**

Contrasting Cottons

A new look for the twin-set: a turquoise tank top with multi-color banding and ribbon trim at shoulder and waist is matched with a lemon yellow cardigan. The vertical dashes common to both are embroidered on afterwards.

designed by **JANE BALL**

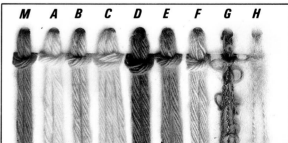

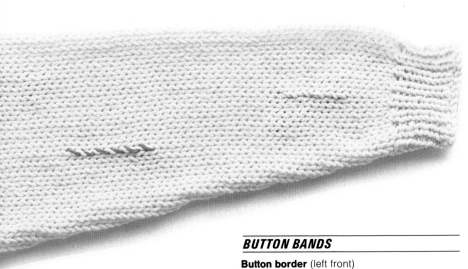

MATERIALS for cardigan

Yarn

14oz bulky-weight cotton (lemon)
Scraps of bulky-weight cotton in three contrasting shades (fawn, pale blue and turquoise)

Needles

1 pair no 5
1 pair no 7

Notions

5 buttons (or make your own, see p. 123).

Stitch gauge

13 sts and 18 rows to 4in over st st on no 7 needles (or size needed to obtain given tension).

BACK

Cast on 61 sts with no 5 needles. K1, p1 for 12 rows. Change to no 7 needles and continue in st st. Work straight until the work measures 20in. Bind off.

FRONT

Left front

Cast on 31 sts with no 5 needles. K1, p1 for 12 rows. Change to no 7 needles and continue in st st until the work measures 15¾in.
Shape neck: Bind off 2 sts at the beginning of the row. Then decrease one st at the beginning of the neck edge until 12 sts (14 in all) have been decreased. Continue straight until the work measures 20in. Bind off.

Right front

Knit as for the left front reversing shaping.

SLEEVES

Using no 5 needles cast on 31 sts and work in k1, p1 rib for 10 rows, increasing one st at the end of the last row – 32 sts. Change to no 7 needles, work in st st and shape the sides by increasing one st at each end of the 3rd and every following 5th row until there are 58 sts. Continue to knit straight until the sleeve measures 19in. Bind off loosely.

BUTTON BANDS

Button border (left front)
Join shoulders with flat seams. With no 5 needles cast on 6 sts. Work in k1, p1 rib, sewing band onto left front as you go along. Knit to the beginning of the neck. Put sts on a stitch holder.

Buttonhole border (right front)
Repeat as for the left side making 5 button-holes. The first should be ½in from the lower edge, the last will be on the 3rd row of the neckband.
To make buttonholes: Rib 3, yfwd, k2tog, p1.

NECKBAND

Rib sts of the right front border. Knit up 18 sts from the right front, 25 sts from the back neck and 18 sts from the left front, then rib 6 sts of the left front border. K1, p1 rib for 5 rows making a buttonhole on 2nd row. Bind off tightly in rib.

PUTTING TOGETHER

(Use flat seams.) Find the center of the top of the sleeve edge. Place to shoulder seam. Sew in sleeves. Join side and sleeve seams. Press according to instructions on the ball band.

EXTRA DETAILS

Embroidering vertical dashes
Using a blunt embroidery needle and scraps of yarn, work duplicate stitch over every other vertical loop of each knitted stitch across 6–10 rows. To secure, sew back into stitch on inside. Make about 20 dashes over garment.

MEASUREMENTS

To fit chest 32–38in (81–97cm)

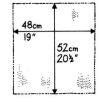

MATERIALS for tank top

Yarn

Main yarn M *7oz* bulky-weight cotton (turquoise)
Yarn A *1oz* bulky-weight cotton (lemon)
Yarn B scrap of bulky-weight cotton (fawn)
Yarn C scrap of bulky-weight cotton (orangey-yellow)
Yarn D scrap of bulky-weight cotton (dark brown)
Yarn E scrap of bulky-weight cotton (brown)
Yarn F scrap of bulky-weight cotton (blue)
Yarn G scrap of knitting worsted bouclé (brown) mixed with lurex (copper)
Yarn H scrap of mohair (pale blue)

Needles

1 pair no 7

Notions

4 yards of ¼in wide ribbon (lemon)

Stitch gauge

13 sts and 18 rows to 4in over st st on no 7 needles (or size needed to obtain given tension).

BACK

With no 7 needles and yarn B cast on 60 sts.
On the first row k1, *yfwd, k2tog, rep from * to last st, k1.
Purl the next row.
Continue in st st in the following yarns until the work measures 20½in ending with a purl row:
4 rows A, 2 rows C, 2 rows D, 2 rows E, 2 rows A, 2 rows F, 2 rows B, 2 rows G, 2 rows H, 4 rows F, 2 rows M, 2 rows H. Continue in M.
Slotting row: K1, *yfwd, k2tog, rep from * to last st, k1.
Next row purl. Bind off loosely.

FRONT

Knit the same as the back.

PUTTING TOGETHER

Sew shoulder seams using a flat seam. Sew 4in from shoulder edge towards neck. Sew side seams.
Thread ribbon evenly in and out of holes at the hem and shoulder/neck edges.
Leave approximately 10in of ribbon hanging on both sides. Tie bows on shoulders.
Draw up at hem and tie in a bow at either side.

EXTRA DETAILS

Embroidering vertical dashes
See instructions for these on Cardigan.

Pineapple

Simple summer top in bulky-weight cotton is finished with a crochet edging and decorated with a seasonal sequin and embroidery motif.

MATERIALS

Yarn
7oz bulky-weight cotton (tan)
Scraps of thick embroidery thread (green, yellow and natural)

Yarn
7oz bulky-weight cotton (tan)
Oddments of thick embroidery thread (green, yellow and natural)

Needles
1 pair no 7
1 size B crochet hook

Notions
9 sequins $\frac{1}{2}$in in diameter
10 sequins $\frac{3}{8}$in in diameter

Stitch gauge
16 sts and 20 rows to 4in over st st on no 7 needles (or size needed to obtain given tension).

FRONT

Cast on 61 sts. Work in k1, p1 rib for 2½in. Continue in st st until work measures 14¼in.
Shape armholes: Bind off 3 sts from each side. Knit the first and last 3 sts in Garter stitch and decrease one st each side inside the Garter st border every alternate row 4 times. On the second decrease row, bind off the center 7 sts and work each side separately. Continue to knit the 3 sts at the armhole edge and neck edge in Garter stitch, decreasing one st at each end of every alternate row until 9 sts remain. Work straight until the front measures 21in from the beginning. Bind off. Work the other side to match, reversing shaping.

BACK

Work the same as the front but cast off the 7 center stitches after you have decreased one st each side (from the armholes) 4 times.

PUTTING TOGETHER

Join side and shoulder seams. Work one row of single crochet around the neckline and armholes. Embroider pineapples as on chart, using stem stitch. Sew on sequins.

MEASUREMENTS

To fit chest 32–34in (81–86cm)

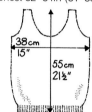

38cm
15"
55cm
21½"

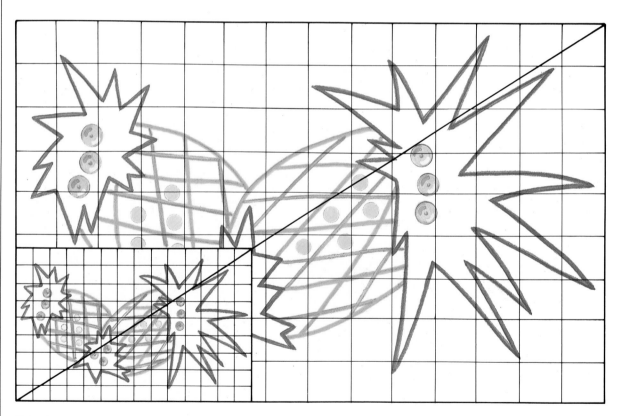

Enlarging designs

Any motif can be made bigger by using the following method. First outline the motif in a square or rectangle and place this at the bottom left-hand corner of a larger piece of paper. Draw a diagonal line from the bottom left-hand corner of the design through the top right-hand corner and onwards to the margin of the paper piece. Determine the desired height of the design from bottom left and mark this point. Then draw a line between it and the opposite point making sure you cross the diagonal line. Where the lines cross at the top right-hand corner draw a vertical line to the base and a corresponding one at the left side. You now have the enlarged outline.

To transfer the motif to the larger piece of paper, divide both the motif and the enlarged outline into an identical number of squares. Draw the motif freehand on the outline, square by square.

designed by **NURIT KAYE**

designed by *JANE BALL*

Ribbons & Bands

Soft silky yarn banded with pastel-colored mohair and random color bars give a simple cardigan a very feminine "look". Thread pink or blue baby ribbon at the shoulders and add handmade buttons in keeping with the color scheme.

MATERIALS

Yarn
Main yarn M *16oz* bulky-weight silk (white)
Yarn A *1oz* mohair (blue)
Yarn B *1oz* mohair (dark pink)
Yarn C *1oz* mohair (pale pink)
Yarn D *1oz* mohair (white)
Yarn E *1oz* lurex (silver)
Yarn F *1oz* bulky-weight cotton (pale blue)

Needles
1 pair no 6
1 pair no 8

Notions
5 buttons (or make your own, see p. 123)
2 yards of $\frac{1}{4}$in wide ribbon (pale blue)

Stitch gauge
12 sts and 16 rows to 4in over st st on no 8 needles (or size needed to obtain given tension).

MEASUREMENTS

To fit chest 32–38in (81–97cm)

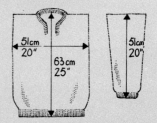

BACK

With no 6 needles and yarn M cast on 61 sts. Work in k1, p1 rib for 14 rows, beginning 2nd and alternate rows with p1. Change to no 8 needles and starting with a k row work in st st in the following yarns: 2 rows M, 2 rows B, 2 rows C, 2 rows M, 2 rows D, 2 rows A, 2 rows F, 2 rows M, 2 rows E with D, 2 rows C, 2 rows M, 2 rows D. Continue to knit in yarn M. At approximately every 15 rows or 3½in knit a color bar* randomly in the fabric.
*Color bar: Knit part of the row in yarn M. At your chosen spot, introduce a new yarn (any of the colors used for striping) and knit over 6–10 sts. Break off the yarn and continue to knit in yarn M to the end of the row.
Bind off loosely when the work measures 25in.

FRONT

Left front
With no 6 needles and yarn M cast on 29 sts and work in k1, p1 rib as on the back for 14 rows. Change to no 8 needles and starting

with a k row work in st st following the instructions for the back until the front measures 23½in ending with a p row.
Shape neck: Knit to the last 4 sts then k2tog twice. Decrease one stitch at the neck edge on every row until 18 sts remain. Knit 6 rows or until the work measures 25in. Bind off loosely.

Right front
Work as for left front reversing shaping.

Right front
Work as for left front reversing shaping.

SLEEVES

With no 6 needles and yarn M cast on 31 sts and work in k1, p1 rib as for the back for 10 rows. Change to no 8 needles and starting with a k row work striping in st st using only the first 16 rows of striping and then continue in yarn M. To shape the sleeve sides increase one st at each end of the 3rd and then every following 5th row until there are 61 sts. Continue straight until the sleeve seam measures 20in. Bind off loosely.

BUTTON BANDS

Button border (left front)
With no 6 needles and yarn M cast on 7 sts and work in rib as on the back until the strip measures ½in less than the length of the left front. Put the stitches onto a holder. Sew the band in position.

Buttonhole border (right front)
Work as for the button border with the addition of 5 buttonholes. The first buttonhole is made ½in up from the lower edge; the last buttonhole should be made after sts have been picked up on the neck band. First, mark the position of the buttons on the button border with pins to ensure even spacing, then work the buttonholes to correspond.
To make buttonhole: k1, p1, k1, yfwd, k2tog, p1, k1.
Leave stitches on needle but sew into position.

NECKBAND

With sts still on the needle at buttonhole border, pick up 18 sts at right front, 25 sts at back, 18 sts at left front and 7 sts from stitch holder – 75 sts. K1, p1 for 5 rows, remembering to make a buttonhole near the top right neck edge of the border. Bind off.

PUTTING TOGETHER

Press garment pieces flat by using a cool iron and a damp cloth. Pull into shape. Leave to dry. Using a flat seam, join shoulder seams. Place the center of the bound-off edge of each sleeve at the shoulder seam then sew the sleeve top to the side edges of the front and back. Join side and sleeve seams.
Add ribbon trimming: Thread ribbon through holes at the shoulder seam – make a bow.
Brush mohair using a nail brush.

Night & Day

A very contemporary Fair-Isle in Shetland wool with lurex contrasts, we've shown it in two colorways. Suitable for both women and men, you can use all medium-weight classic yarns for a more traditional interpretation.

MATERIALS

Yarn

Main yarn M 5 (6, 7)oz medium-weight Shetland (black or white)
Yarn A *1oz* medium-weight lurex (red)
Yarn B *1oz* medium-weight lurex (green)
Yarn C *1oz* medium-weight lurex (mauve)
Yarn D *1oz* medium-weight lurex (blue)
Yarn E *1oz* medium-weight lurex (turquoise)
NB The same yarns A–E are used on the black slipover, but in a different order.

Needles

1 pair no 1
1 pair no 4
1 set no 1 double-pointed

Stitch gauge

32 sts and 32 rows to 4in over Fair-Isle pattern on no 4 needles (or size needed to obtain given tension).

Chart for back and front

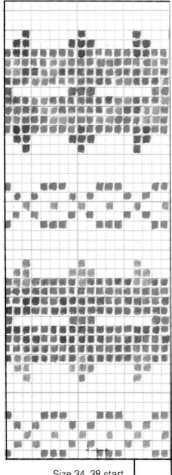

Size 34, 38 start
k rows here

Size 36 start
k rows here

Note on chart: Chart is worked from right to left on knit rows, left to right on purl rows. Observe starting point for each size and begin purl rows at appropriate point.

BACK

With no 1 needles and yarn M, cast on 137 (145, 155) sts and work in k1, p1 rib for 3in, beginning 2nd and alternate rows with p1. Change to no 4 needles and st st and work 4 rows. Then work in pattern from the chart, until the back measures 11 (11½, 12)in.
Shape armholes: Bind off 12 sts at the beginning of the next 2 rows, then decrease one st at each end of the next 6 (6, 7) rows – 101 (109, 117) sts. Continue in pattern until the work measures 18½ (19¾, 21)in.
Shape shoulders: Bind off 10 (12, 13) sts at the beginning of the next 4 rows. Bind off 12 (12, 14) sts at the beginning of the next 2 rows – 37 sts. Put the remaining 37 sts on a holder.

FRONT

Work as for the back until the armhole shaping has been completed. Work a further 8 rows in pattern. Divide for the neck. In pattern work 50 (54, 58) sts. Slip the remaining 51 (55, 59) sts onto a holder. Turn and proceed on the first set of sts. Continue in pattern but work 2 sts together at the neck edge on every alternate row until 32 (36, 40) sts remain. Continue until the front measures the same as the back to the shoulder shaping, finishing at the armhole edge. Bind off 10 (12, 13) sts at the beginning of the next and following alternate row. Work one row. Bind off the remaining 12 (12, 14) sts. Rejoin yarn to the remaining stitches left on the holder. Slip the first stitch onto a safety pin, then work the remaining stitches to match the other side, reversing shaping.

NECKBAND

Join shoulder seams. Using double-pointed no 1 needles and yarn M, with the right side facing, start at the left front shoulder and pick up 64 (67, 70) sts along the left front edge, then knit up the center stitch, which always remains a knit stitch, then 64 (67, 70) sts along the right

front edge and 37 sts from the back neck – 166 (172, 178) sts. Proceed to work in rounds as follows:

Work in k1, p1 rib to within 2 sts of the center front stitch, sl 1, k1, psso; knit the center stitch, k2tog, continue in rib to the end of the round.

Repeat the round 7 more times. Bind off in rib, still decreasing at the front.

ARMBAND

With the right side of the work facing, using no 1 needles and yarn M, knit up 173 (181, 189) sts along the armhole edge. Beginning the first row with p1, proceed in rib for 8 rows. Bind off in rib. Work the other band in the same way.

PUTTING TOGETHER

Press all parts except the ribbing according to the instructions on the ball band. Sew in all ends. Join side seams. Press all seams.

MEASUREMENTS

To fit chest 34 (36, 38)in (86, 91, 97cm)

43(46,48)cm
17(18,19)"

49(52,55)cm
19½(20½,22)"

designed by *JOSE FRANKS*

Harlequin

A multitude of different yarns of varying weights and textures are knitted into separate diamonds to form a jacket with a flared waist and optional padded shoulders. For adventurous knitters only!

designed by ZOË HUNT

MATERIALS

Yarn
Approximately *23oz* of medium-weight and knitting worsted yarns (lurex, mohair, bouclé, chenille, wool, crepe) – an assortment of 25 different shades. (Thinner yarns can be stranded with other thin yarns to bring them up to a suitable weight)

Needles
1 pair no 2
1 pair no 4
1 crochet hook size C

Notions
9 buttons ⅜in in diameter

Stitch gauge
21 sts and 32 rows to 4in over st st on no 4 needles (or size needed to obtain given tension).

Special note:
Each diamond is worked with a separate piece of yarn, none of the yarns are carried across the back of the work. Many of the diamonds have several different yarns within them. To get rid of the yarn ends, knit in the first and last 2in by catching in to every alternate stitch on the back of the work for about 6 sts leaving a small amount on the inside of the work.

BACK

With no 4 needles cast on 81 sts. In st st, work diamonds as on chart. Work straight in pattern for 40 rows ending with a purl row. Inc one st at each side on rows 41, 49, 57 – 87 sts. Continue straight in pattern until there are 68 rows altogether ending with a purl row.
Shape armholes: Bind off 6 sts at the beginning of the next 2 rows, then one st at each end of the next and every alternate row, 5 times in all – 65 sts – ending with a purl row. Continue straight for 44 more rows.
Shape shoulders: Next row bind off 7, knit 20, bind off 11 for back neck, knit to the end of the row. Finish left side first as follows: next row (purl side facing) bind off 7 sts, purl to end. Next row bind off 4 sts, knit to end. Next row bind off 6 sts, purl to end. Next row bind off 4 sts, knit to end. Bind off remaining 6 sts. Finish right side to match reversing shaping.

FRONT

Left front
With no 4 needles cast on 41 sts. In st st work diamonds as on chart. Work straight in pattern for 30 rows. Increase one st at side edge on rows 31, 39, 47, 55, 63 (every 8th row) – 46 sts. Continue straight until there are 68 rows altogether ending with a purl row.
Shape armhole: Bind off 6 sts at the beginning of the next row, then decrease one st at side edge on the next knit row and every alternate row 5 times in all – 35 sts. Knit 23 more rows ending with a knit row.
Shape neck: Bind off 3 sts at the beginning of the next and every alternate row 4 times, 2 sts once and one st twice, leaving 19 sts. Continue until the front is the same length as the back at shoulders.
Shape shoulder: Bind off 7 sts at the beginning of the next row. Purl one row. Bind off 6 sts at the beginning of the next and following alternate row.

Right front
Work the same as the left front reversing all shaping. The diamonds are worked as a mirror image of the left front.

SLEEVES

With no 2 needles cast on 45 sts. Work 10 rows of st st, ending with a knit row. Knit one row to form hemline. Change to no 4 needles. Continue in pattern from chart. Work straight for 16 rows. Inc one st at each end of the next and every following 8th row until there are 57 sts. Inc one st at each end of every 4th row until there are 83 sts. Inc one st at each end of every 2nd row until there are 105 sts – 132 rows altogether.
Shape top: Bind off 6 sts at the beginning of the next 2 rows. Dec one st at each end of the next and every following alternate row until there are 85 sts. Dec one st at each end of every 4th row until there are 65 sts. Dec one st at each end of every 2nd row until there are 51 sts. Next row k2tog to last st, k1, then bind off. (This gives a slight gather to the head of the sleeve and helps the sleeve to stay puffed.) Work the second sleeve as a mirror image of the first.

Chart for back
Continue this diamond pattern, 9 sts by 16 rows throughout the back.

PUTTING TOGETHER

Press lightly according to yarns used. Sew shoulder seams using a fine back stitch. Set in sleeves making 3 pleats either side of shoulder. Sew sleeve and underarm seams. Turn up cuff hems and catch down lightly.

PEPLUM

With no 4 needles, pick up 161 sts round lower edge of garment – 40 sts from right front, one st at side seam, 79 sts from back, one st at side seam, 40 sts from left front. Work in st st in the same color sequence as waist as follows:

Rows 1 to 4 Alternate working 1 of a color followed by 9 of a color.

Row 5 Increase row: Keeping colors as in row 1, begin with 2 sts; *work 7 of a color then k1, m1, k1, m1, k1 in the next color; rep from * to last 2 sts; work 2 sts. (There will be sections of 7 and 5 sts.)

Rows 6 to 8 Work 2 sts; then alternate working 7 of a color followed by 5 of a color to last 2 sts; work 2 sts.

Row 9 Increase row: Begin with 2 sts; *work 7 of a color then k1, m1, k3, m1, k1 in the next color; rep from * to last 2 sts; work 2

sts. (There will be sections of 7 sts.)

Rows 10 to 12 Work 2 sts; then alternate working 7 of a color to last 2 sts; work 2 sts.

Row 13 Increase row: Begin with 3 sts; *work 5 of a color then k1, m1, k7, m1, k1 in the next color; rep from * to last 3 sts; work 3 sts. (There will be sections of 5 and 11 sts.)

Rows 14 to 16 Work 3 sts; then alternate working 5 of a color followed by 11 of a color to last 3 sts; work 3 sts.

Row 17 Increase row: Begin with 3 sts; *work 5 of a color then k1, m1, k9, m1, k1 in the next color; rep from * to last 3 sts; work 3 sts. (There will be sections of 5 and 13 sts.)

81

Rows 18 to 20 Work 3 sts; then alternate working 5 of a color followed by 13 of a color to last 3 sts; work 3 sts.

Row 21 Increase row: Begin with 4 sts; *work 3 of a color then k1, m1, k13, m1, k1 in the next color; rep from * to last 4 sts; work 4 sts. (There will be sections of 3 and 17 sts.)

Rows 22 to 24 Work 4 sts; then alternate working 3 of a color followed by 17 of a color to last 4 sts; work 4 sts.

Row 25 Increase row: Begin with 4 sts; *work 3 of a color then k1, m1, k7 of the next color and introduce a new color as k1, before continuing to k7, m1, k1 in the original color; rep from * to the last 4 sts, work 4 sts. (There will be sections of 3, 9, 1, 9 sts.)

Rows 26 and 27 Work 4 sts; then alternate working 3 of a color followed by 8 of a color to last 4 sts; work 4 sts.

Row 28 Work 4 sts; then alternate working 3 of a color followed by 7 of a color, followed by 5 of a color, followed by 7 of a color to last 4 sts; work 4 sts.

Row 29 Work 5 sts; then alternate working 1 of a color, followed by 8 of a color, followed by 5 of a color, followed by 8 of a color to last 5 sts; work 5 sts.

Rows 30 and 31 Work 5 sts; then alternate working 1 of a color, followed by 3 groups of 7 of a color to last 5 sts; work 5 sts.

Row 32 Work 5 sts; then alternate working 1 of a color, followed by 6 of a color, followed by 9 of a color, followed by 6 of a color to last 5 sts; work 5 sts.

Row 33 Change to no 2 needles. Using a medium-weight yarn knit across the row.

Row 34 Knit across the row to form hemline. Beginning with a knit row, work 8 more rows in st st. Cast off. Press peplum lightly according to yarns used. Turn back hem. With no 2 needles and medium-weight yarn pick up 28 sts along the right front edge. With wrong side facing knit one row to form hemline. Then, beginning with a knit row, work 8 more rows in st st. Bind off. Repeat on the left front edge.

BUTTON BANDS

Button border (left front)
With no 2 needles, medium-weight lurex and right side facing, pick up 102 sts down front edge to waist. Work 3 rows in st st ending with a knit row. Next row knit to form hemline. Then, beginning with a knit row work 10 more rows of st st. Bind off.

Buttonhole border (right front)
Pick up sts as for left side. Work buttonholes as follows. On first row k2, *bind off 2, k10; rep from * to last 4 sts, bind off 2, k2. On following row p2, *cast on 2, p10; rep from * to last 4 sts, cast on 2, p2. Knit 3 rows. Then make buttonholes in facing as follows. On next row p2, *bind off 2, p10; rep from * to last 4 sts, bind off 2, p2. On following row k2, *cast on 2, k10; rep from * to last 4 sts, cast on 2, k2. Work 7 more rows of st st. Bind off.
Turn back hems and stitch in place. Sew on buttons.

EDGINGS

Using medium-weight lurex work 2 rows of single crochet around the neck edge, down the left front edge of the peplum, round the lower edge of the peplum, up the right front edge to the waist, and round the cuffs.

EXTRA DETAILS

If required shoulder pads may be made as follows: With no 4 needles cast on 40 sts. Work in Garter st, decreasing one st at each end of every 4th row until 20 sts remain. Bind off. Roll up like a croissant and stitch into the head of the sleeve.

MEASUREMENTS

To fit chest 34in (86cm)

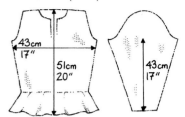

Chart for front
Continue this diamond pattern, 9 sts by 16 rows throughout the front.

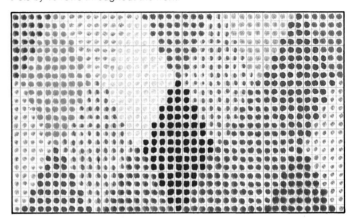

Chart for sleeves

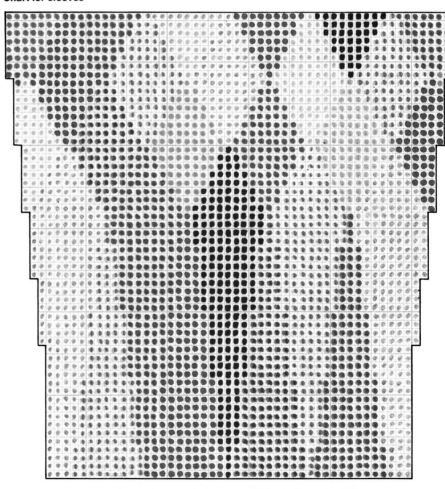

After working 40 rows in the elongated diamond shapes as shown on the chart above, work the rest of the sleeve in diamonds 9 sts by 16 rows.

The chart shows only half of the back and half of the front. The other side is worked as a mirror image of the side shown.

Chart for front   **Chart for back**

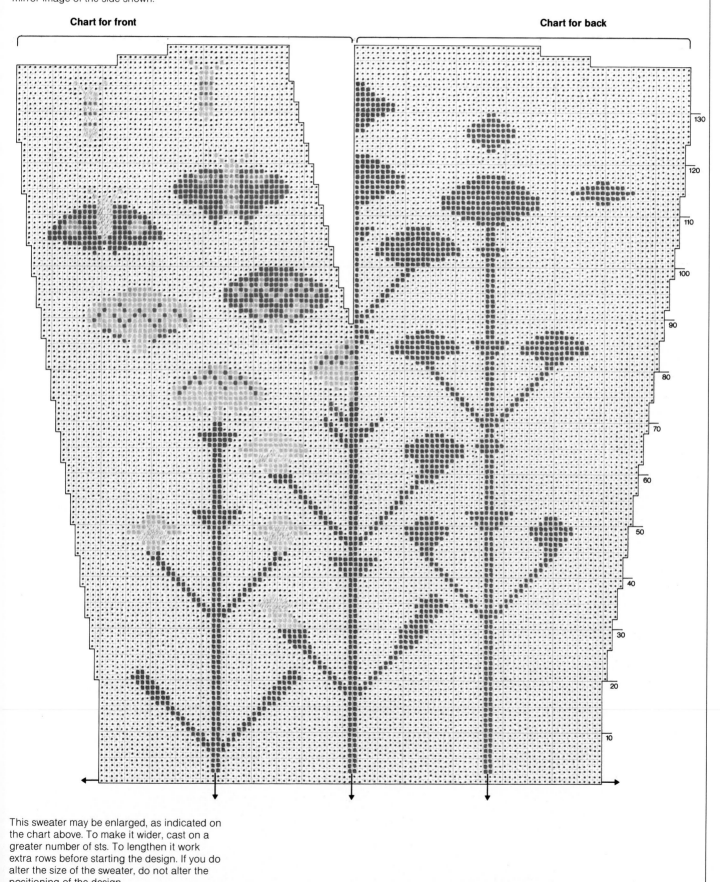

130
120
110
100
90
80
70
60
50
40
30
20
10

This sweater may be enlarged, as indicated on the chart above. To make it wider, cast on a greater number of sts. To lengthen it work extra rows before starting the design. If you do alter the size of the sweater, do not alter the positioning of the design.

Butterflies

Highwaisted vee-necked evening top incorporating
complementary motifs on front and back and knitted butterfly
appliqués is knitted in medium-weight classic yarn and scraps
of various novelties.

MATERIALS

Yarn
Main yarn M approximately *8oz* medium-weight (black)
Yarn A *2oz* medium-weight random dyed bouclé (blue/green)
Scraps of various shades of medium-weight angora (red, pink, magenta, pale green) and chenille (speckled)

Needles
1 pair no 3
1 crochet hook size E

Notions
14 small buttons

Stitch gauge
28 sts and 33 rows to 4in over pattern on no 3 needles (or size needed to obtain given tension).

FRONT

With yarn M cast on 100 sts. Purl one row. The design starts on the next row. Divide yarn A into three fairly equal parts. Knit 22 with yarn M; join in the first ball of yarn A, k2; k25 M; join in the second ball of yarn A, k2; k25 M; join in the third ball of yarn A, k2; k22 M. Continue in pattern as on chart. Increase one st at both ends of the 21st and every following 6th row until 88 rows have been worked from the beginning.

Shape neck: Knit to center 6 sts; k2tog, tb1, k2, k2tog, k to end – 122 sts. Next row purl 61, turn, work on this side whilst leaving sts for other side on a stitch holder. Continue to increase at side edge on every 6th row three times more.

then every 10th row twice, and at the same time k1, k2tog on neck edge every 4th row, until 53 sts remain, ending at side edge (work should measure 16½in from the beginning). *Shape shoulder:* Bind off 10 sts at the beginning of the next and following three alternate rows. Work one row, then bind off remaining 13 sts. Work other side to match, reversing shaping.

BACK

Work the same as the front, omitting neck shaping and following chart for back design. Bind off remaining 28 sts at back neck.

PUTTING TOGETHER

Join shoulders. Work 4 rows of single crochet evenly around side and bottom edges, making 7 buttonholes on the third row of the front sides, 5 single crochets apart. Work 2 rows of single crochet around the neck edge. Press according to instructions on yarn band.

Butterfly wings

Upper wings: *Cast on 10 sts. Purl one row. Next row k2tog, k to last st, increase in last st. Next row purl to last 2 sts; p2tog. Continue to k2tog at the beginning of every knit row and p2tog at the end of every purl row until 4 sts remain. Bind off. Repeat from * 3 more times, then repeat another 4 times, reversing shaping.

Lower wings: *Cast on 7 sts. Purl one row. Increase one st at both ends of the next row. Purl one row. K2tog at both ends of every knit

row until 3 sts remain. Next row sl 1, k2tog, psso. Cut yarn and pull through last stitch. Make 7 more wings by repeating from * 7 more times.

Stitch the wings neatly onto the butterfly bodies. Catch the edges of each wing down with one or 2 sts to stop them curling.

MEASUREMENTS

To fit chest 34in (86cm)

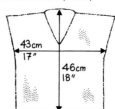

Dragonflies

Embroidered shoulder panel is incorporated into an asymmetrical lurex evening top knitted in a lacy pattern with triangular shaped ribbing at waist.

MATERIALS

Yarn

Main yarn M approximately 7oz medium-weight lurex (blue)
Yarn A 2oz medium-weight (black)
Scraps of various shades of angora and lurex for embroidery

Needles

1 pair no 1
1 pair no 3
1 crochet hook size E

Notions

6 small buttons (black)

Stitch gauge

28 sts and 34 rows to 4in over pattern on no 3 needles (or size needed to obtain given tension).

FRONT

With no 1 needles and yarn M cast on 3 sts. Working in k1, p1 rib, cast on 2 sts at the beginning of every row until there are 101 sts. Continue in k1, p1 rib for a further 14 rows. Increase row: With right side of work facing *k2, k twice into next st; rep from * to last 2 sts, k2 – 134 sts. Purl next row. Change to no 3 needles. Work in lace pattern (as directed below), increasing one st at both sides on the 12th pattern row, and every following 12th row, 5 times – 144 sts. Continue to increase one st at side edge opposite to shoulder-inset every 12th row.

Pattern

With right side of work facing
Row 1 K3, *k2tog, yfwd, k6; rep from * to last 3 sts; k2tog, yfwd, k1.

Rows 2, 4, 6 and 8 Purl.
Row 3 K4; rep from * on row 1 to last 2 sts; k2.
Row 5 K5; rep from * on row 1 to last st; k1.
Row 7 K6; rep from * on row 1 to end.
Rows 9–12 St st.
These 12 rows (8 rows forming diagonal holes and 4 plain rows) form the pattern. Start the first hole of the next pattern one stitch over, in the direction of the diagonal, and so on. Remember to work pattern sequence in at the beginning of rows as appropriate. At 145 sts bind off 4 sts at side edge on shoulder inset side. Then k2tog on every row this side. Continue until 54 sts remain. Bind off.
Shoulder inset: *With no 3 needles and yarn A, make one st. Working in st st increase one st on inside edge, every row. Increase one st on outside edge every 16th row until there are 60 sts, ending with a knit row.**
Shape neck: Whilst continuing to increase one st on outside edge every 16th row, bind off 6 sts at neck edge, then bind off 3 sts at neck edge on following alternate row. Decrease one st every row at neck edge 10 times. Decrease one st every alternate row at neck edge 3 times. Work 4 more rows, ending at armhole edge – 39 sts.
Shape shoulder: Bind off 10 sts at the beginning of the next and following alternate 2 rows. Bind off remaining 9 sts.

BACK

Work as for front, reversing all shaping.
Shoulder inset: Work as for front from * to ** but reversing shaping. Continue to increase one st on inside edge every row and increase one st on outside edge every 16th row until there are 81 sts.
Shape neck and shoulder: Next row bind off 36 sts, purl to end. Next row bind off 10 sts, knit to last 3 sts; k2tog, k1. Next row p2tog, purl to end. Repeat the last 2 rows twice more. Bind off remaining 9 sts.

PUTTING TOGETHER

Back stitch together side seams to armhole on both sides. Join right shoulder with a flat seam. With neck edge point of front shoulder inset in line with center front of front, ease diagonal line onto shoulder inset; overlapping about 2mm. Sew neatly with yarn M. Repeat for back shoulder inset but with seam running from back neck edge, diagonally to armhole. Turn in and press a hem 5 st wide at shoulder inset top armhole, running off to nothing, at underarm.
Edgings: Using yarn A, work 4 rows of single crochet across left front shoulder, starting at neck edge and working 6 buttonholes on the 2nd row. At the end of the 4th row continue round the neck with one row of crochet as follows: 3 chains, miss 2 sts, one single crochet into next st, 3 chains, miss 2 sts, one double into next st. Work 4 rows of single crochet across left back shoulder. Using yarn M, work a crochet edge around the right armhole as follows: make one double, make 3 chains, miss 2 sts, make 3 doubles into the next st, make 3 chains, miss 2 sts. Using yarn M, work one row of crochet across the join of the body and the shoulder inset using the same pattern as around the neck edge.
Sew 6 buttons onto back shoulder inset.

The above chart shows the dragonfly motif that is embroidered on the front shoulder inset in satin stitch. This can be enlarged as desired using the grid (see p. 74).

EXTRA DETAILS

Embroider 3 dragonflies on the front shoulder inset in satin stitch, using scraps of angora and lurex as illustrated.

MEASUREMENTS

To fit chest 34–38in (86–97cm)

51cm
20"

54cm
21"

designed by *SUE BLACK*

87

Petal Pink

Metallic pink thread wrapped around pink mohair produces a sparkly finish on a short evening jacket. The flower motif is outlined on the surface first then filled in with the various yarns.

The flower motif for the shoulder embroidery shown above can easily be enlarged to any size you desire. For an explanation of the enlarging technique using a grid, see p. 74.

MATERIALS

Yarn
Main yarn M *11oz* mohair type bulky (pink) run with very metallic thread
Yarn A *1oz* medium-weight (pink)
Yarn B scrap of medium-weight (green)
Yarn C scrap of lurex (pink)
Yarn D scrap of lurex (green)

Needles
1 pair no 7
1 pair no 8
1 crochet hook size F

Notions
7 buttons

Stitch gauge
13 sts and 15 rows to 4in over st st on no 8 needles (or size needed to obtain given tension).

designed by **NURIT KAYE**

BACK

With no 7 needles and yarn M cast on 59 sts. Work in k1, p1 rib for 1¾in. Change to no 8 needles and continue in st st until the work measures 13½in.
Shape armholes: Bind off 2 sts at the beginning of the next 4 rows – 51 sts. Then bind off one st at the beginning of the next 4 rows – 47 sts. Continue straight until the work measures 21¾in from the beginning, ending with a purl row. Knit 13 sts then bind off center 21 sts, then knit remaining 13 sts. On the following row, bind off 13 sts for shoulder. Re-attach yarn and bind off remaining 13 sts.

FRONT

Left front
With no 7 needles and yarn M cast on 29 sts. Work in k1, p1 rib for 1¾in. Change to no 8 needles and continue in st st. Work until front measures 13½in.
Shape armholes: Bind off 2 sts at the beginning of the next and the following alternate row – 25 sts. Then bind off one st at the beginning of the following 2 alternate rows – 23 sts. Continue straight until work measures 17½in.
Shape neck: Bind off 2 sts at neck edge then one st every alternate row until 13 sts remain. Continue straight until the work measures 21¾in. Bind off.

Right front
Knit the other side to match reversing shaping and with the addition of 7 evenly spaced buttonholes (see p. 124).

SLEEVES

With no 7 needles and yarn M cast on 31 sts and work in k1, p1 rib for 2in. Change to no 8 needles and work in st st, increasing one st each side every 2in 7 times – 45 sts. Work straight until sleeve measures 17¾in from the beginning.
Shape top: Decrease for armhole by binding off 2 sts at the beginning of the next 4 rows – 37 sts, then one st at each end of every alternate row until 21 sts remain. Bind off.

PUTTING TOGETHER

Sew all seams. Work one row of single crochet round front edges and neck. Sew on buttons to correspond with buttonholes.

EXTRA DETAILS

Shoulder embroidery

Embroider the outline as on chart with yarns C and D. (The top of the flower extends about 1¼in over the shoulder seam.) Fill in with yarns A, B and C, making sure your stitch does not go right through the garment.

MEASUREMENTS

To fit chest 34in (86cm)

designed by **JOHN AND CLARE**

M

A

Silky Tassels

A thick fluffy yarn is alternated with a loopy mohair and threaded with silken bands and tassels. Gather up the sleeves so that the tassels overlap down the arms.

MEASUREMENTS

To fit chest 34–38in (86–97cm)

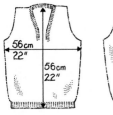

MATERIALS

Yarn

Main yarn M *11oz* mohair-type bouclé (black)
Yarn A *4oz* very thick tasselled yarn or thick chenille used double (black)
Scraps of 3 or 4 colors of thick shiny yarn or several strands of finer yarn

Needles

1 pair no 4
1 pair no 9

Notions

2 buttons

Stitch gauge

14 sts and 22 rows to 4in over st st on no 9 needles, using yarns as in pattern: 8 rows M, one row A (or size needed to obtain given tension).

BACK

With no 4 needles and yarn M cast on 61 sts and work in k1, p1 rib for 2in. Change to no 9 needles and *work in st st for 8 rows. Join yarn A and work one row of Reverse st st. Repeat from * throughout garment. Work straight until the back measures 14¼in.
Shape armholes: Bind off 4 sts at the beginning of the next 2 rows. Bind off 3 sts at the begin-

ning of the next 2 rows. Bind off 2 sts at the beginning of the next 2 rows. Work straight until work measures 22in. Bind off.

FRONT

Left front

With no 4 needles and yarn M cast on 31 sts and work in k1, p1 rib for 2in. Leave 5 sts on a stitch holder for front band. Change to no 9 needles and work remaining 26 sts as for back until piece measures 6in. Then decrease at center front once every pattern (about 7 times) until the width of the front is 3in; at the same time, shape the armhole so that it matches the back. Bind off when work measures 22in.

Right front

Work as for left front except that on row 2 of rib make one buttonhole at the center front: rib one, bind off one, then continue in rib; on the following row replace the bound-off stitch. Additionally, at the top of the rib make another buttonhole, in the same way, at the center front.

SLEEVES

With no 4 needles and yarn M cast on 41 sts and work in k1, p1 rib for 2in. Change to no 9 needles and work pattern as for back increasing one stitch at both ends of a row once every pattern until there are 61 sts. Work straight until sleeve measures 18in.
Shape top: Bind off 5 sts at the beginning of the next 2 rows. K2tog at each end of every

other row for 5in. Then k2tog at each end of every row for 2in. Bind off all remaining stitches.

FRONT BANDS

Pick up stitches from holders and work each in k1, p1 rib to reach the center back.

PUTTING TOGETHER

Join shoulder and side seams. Set in sleeves. Sew front bands to cardigan, joining the ends at the center back. Sew on buttons.

EXTRA DETAILS

To add color bands

Using several strands of the chosen yarn (depending on its thickness), measure out enough to go all around the cardigan at its widest extent, when fully stretched. Thread the strands through just underneath the first thick row taking them along over about 4 stitches and then under one, and so on. You may find using a needle makes this easier. Fasten off the threads securely at the opposite end, first stretching the garment to make the stitches stand out. Continue to thread color bands as desired.

To make tassels

Cut a piece of card the length you want the tassels to be. Wind the colored yarn (and some yarn M) around it to the required thickness. Slip the yarn off the card holding firmly onto it. Thread a needle with yarn M and take it through the loop twice holding both ends tightly (use this thread later to fasten tassel). Wind yarn M around the tassel several times about ¼in from the top. Cut the tassel at the bottom. Sew the tassels below the bands onto the cardigan where illustrated.

Razzle-Dazzle

Leftover Shetland, angora and lurex yarns knitted in a variety of stitches and patterns end up as a cardigan of dazzling dimension. If your yarn basket is less eclectically stocked, any medium-weight yarns can be used.

MATERIALS

Yarn
Main yarn M *4oz* medium-weight Shetland (dark mauve)

6oz of assorted medium-weight yarns (Shetland, angora, lurex)

Needles
1 pair no 2
1 pair no 4

Notions
5 buttons

Stitch gauge
28 sts and 32 rows to 4in over st st on no 4 needles (or size needed to obtain given tension).

Patterns
Make bobble:
  K1, p1, k1, p1, k1 into next st. Turn. K5, turn, p5, turn, k2tog, k1, k2tog; turn, sl 1, k2tog, psso.
Garter stitch:
  Knit or purl every row.
Moss stitch:
  Row 1 K1, p1.
  Row 2 P1, k1 on even number of sts.
Double moss stitch:
  Rows 1 and 2 K2, p2.
  Rows 3 and 4 P2, k2 on number of sts divisible by 4.
Double moss variation:
  Row 1 K2, p2.
  Row 2 P2, k2 on number of sts divisible by 4.

NB Work in st st unless otherwise indicated. When working in patterns work the first row of a new color in st st so as not to get an ugly change of color on the right side.

BACK

Using yarn M and no 2 needles cast on 106 sts and work 35 rows in k2, p2 rib, beginning the 2nd and each alternate row with p2. Increase row: P2, *up 1, p4; repeat from * to end – 132 sts. Change to no 4 needles and work in pattern from Chart 1. Knot yarns together and weave up the side of the work. Do not pull yarns tightly when working in two-color patterns. Work 80 rows altogether, ending after a wrong side row.
Shape armholes: Continue working from chart and bind off 6 sts at the beginning of the next 2 rows. Then decrease one st at each end of every row until 84 sts remain. Continue on these 26 sts until 64 rows have been worked from the beginning of the armhole shaping. Without changing colors bind off 26 sts at the beginning of the next 2 rows. Bind off the remaining sts.

FRONT

Left front
Using yarn M and no 2 needles cast on 54 sts, and work 35 rows in k2, p2 rib as on the back. Increase row: P6, *up 1, p8; repeat from * to end – 60 sts.

designed by JOAN CHATTERLEY

Change to no 4 needles and work in pattern from Chart 1 to match the back. Work 80 rows altogether, ending at the side edge.
Shape armholes and neck: Still working from chart, bind off 6 sts at beginning and decrease one st at the end of the next row. Decrease one st at the armhole edge of the next 14 rows; at the same time decrease one st at the front edge of every following 4th row until 26 sts remain. Continue on these 26 sts until 64 rows have been worked from the beginning of the armhole shaping working to match the back. Without changing colors, bind off stitches.

Right front

Work another front to match; reverse shaping. (You will have to knit 81 rows to end at the side edge.)

SLEEVES

Using yarn M and no 2 needles cast on 54 sts and work 35 rows in k2, p2 rib as on the back.

Increase row: *P2, up 1; repeat from * to last 2 sts, p2 – 80 sts. Change to no 4 needles and work in pattern from Chart 2 for 122 rows.
Shape top: Still working in pattern, bind off 6 sts at the beginning of the next 2 rows. Then decrease one st at each end of the next and every following alternate row until 40 rows have been worked from the beginning of the shaping. Bind off the remaining 28 sts.

BUTTON BAND

Using yarn M and no 2 needles cast on 10 sts. Work in k1, p1 rib for 5 rows.
To make buttonhole: *Rib 4, bind off 2, rib 4.
   Next row – Rib 4, cast on 2, rib 4.
   Rib 18 rows.
Repeat from * working 5 buttonholes altogether.
Work in rib for approximately 45in. (The band should be slightly stretched to fit around the front edge of the cardigan.)

PUTTING TOGETHER

Press all pieces very lightly avoiding ribbing. (Use a flat stitch for rib seams and a back stitch for all other seams.) Join shoulder and side seams. Join sleeve seams and set in sleeves. Sew the button band around the cardigan edge making sure that the stripes match evenly across the fronts.
Sew on buttons.

MEASUREMENTS

To fit chest 34–36in (86–91cm)

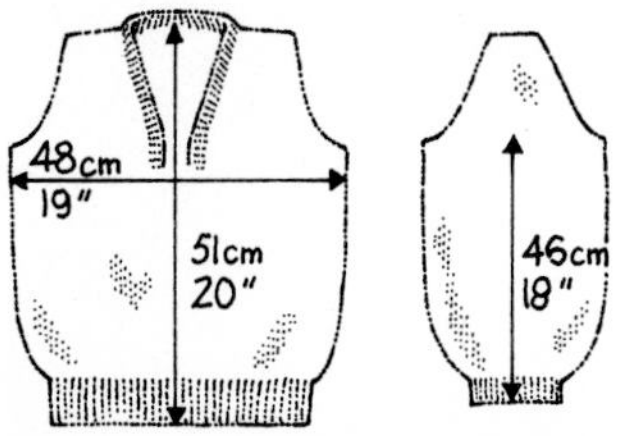

48cm 19"
51cm 20"
46cm 18"

Chart 1 Back and front

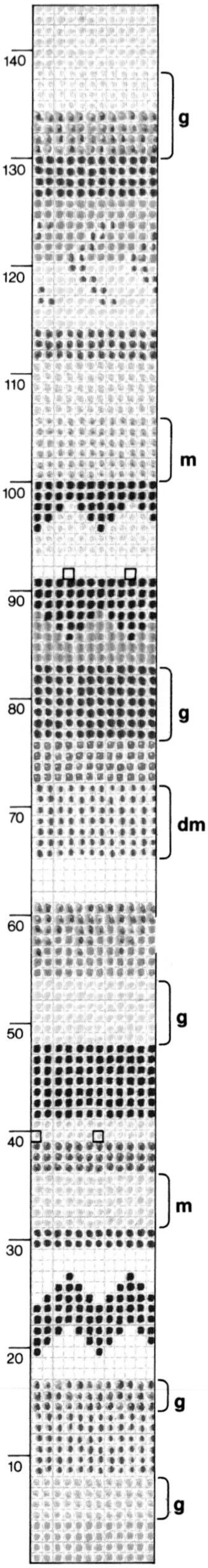

Chart 2 Sleeves

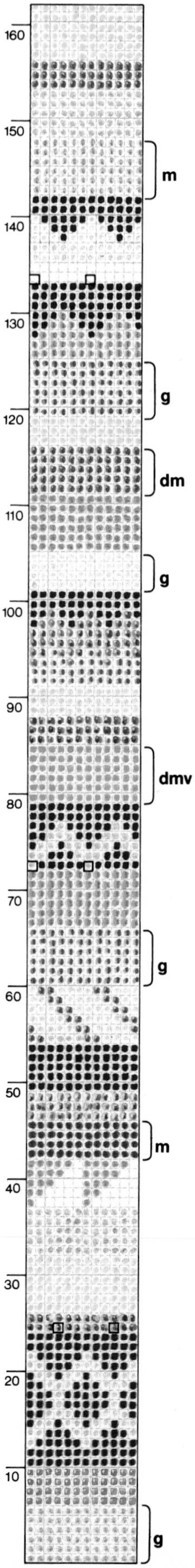

Key
☐ Make Bobble
g Garter st
m Moss st
dm Double Moss st
dmv Double Moss variation

Bobble Stripes

Square-shouldered round-necked pullover is knitted in the round
using an assortment of brightly colored, varied textured yarns
and stitch patterns.

designed by **SARA KOTCH**

MATERIALS

Yarn

*12 (14)*oz of assorted medium-weight yarns –
approximately 25 different shades.

Special note:
Introduce colors as you wish, balancing the
use of thick and thin yarns.

Needles

1 pair no 1 and no 3
1 circular needle no 1
1 circular needle no 3

Stitch gauge

28 sts and 38 rows to 4in over pattern
on no 3 needles (or size needed to
obtain given tension).

Abbreviation

mb K1, p1, k1, p1, k1 into next st; turn;
k5 bobble sts; turn; bind off 4 sts.

SLEEVE

With ordinary no 1 needles cast on 58
(60) sts. Work in k1, p1 rib for 30 (35) rows
working the first row into the back of
the cast-on sts for a neater edge.
Increase row: Inc 1, *p4, inc 1; rep
from * to last 2 sts; p2 – 70 (72) sts.
Change to ordinary no 3 needles
and work in the following pattern:
Row 1 *K1, p4; rep from * to end
(p3, *k1, p4; rep from * to last 4 sts;
k1, p3).
Row 2 K4, *p1, k4; rep from * to last
st; p1 (k3, *p1, k4; rep from * to last 4 sts,
p1, k3).
Row 3 *Mb, p4, k1, p4; rep from * to end (p3,
*mb, p4, k1, p4; rep from * to last 9 sts; mb,
p4, k1, p3).
Row 4 As row 2.

Rows 5 to 20 Repeat rows 1 to 4 four
   more times.
Row 21 As row 1.
Row 22 As row 2.
Row 23 *K1, p4, mb, p4; rep from * to end (p3,
   *k1, p4, mb, p4; rep from * to last 9 sts, k1,
   p4, mb, p3).
Row 24 As row 2.
Rows 25–40 Repeat rows 21–24 four more
   times.
These 40 rows complete the pattern.
Work rows 1–10 again. Working in pattern,
increase one st at both ends of the next and
every following 6th row until 10 (12) increase
rows have been worked, working increases into
pattern – 90 (96) sts. Work 18 (18) more rows
in pattern.
Shape top for padded shoulder: Decrease one
st at the beginning of the next 40 rows, leaving
50 (56) sts. Work 20 (31) rows straight in pattern. Bind off 17 (18) sts at the beginning of the
   next 2 rows. Work 18 rows on the center 16
   (20) sts then bind off.

Shape top for rounded shoulder: Decrease one
st at the beginning of the next 56 (67) rows – 34
(29) sts. Work 4 rows straight in pattern, omitting the bobbles. Bind off.

BODY

NB When knitting on a circular needle in the
round, one is always working with right side
facing.
With no 1 circular needles cast on 200 (240)
sts. Work in k1, p1 rib for 35 rows working the
first row into the back of the cast-on sts for a
neater edge. Place a marker after the first 100
(120) sts to mark where the seam would be.
Increase row: P10 (30), *inc 1, p2; rep from *
to last 10 (30) sts, p10 (30) – 260 (300) sts.
Change to no 3 circular needle. (Since the
sleeves, up to the beginning of the armhole
shaping are one complete 40 row pattern
longer than the body, to match the stripes
around the entire sweater, match the body
yarns to the sleeve yarns from the 41st row of
the sleeve.)
Round 1 P2; (k1, p4) 9 (11) times, k1, p2, k30,
   p2, (k1, p4) 35 (41) times, k1, p2.
Round 2 As round 1.
Round 3 P2, *mb, p4, k1, p4; rep from * 3 (4)
   more times, mb, p4, k1, p2; **yfwd, k2tog;
   rep from ** 14 more times, p2; ***mb, p4,
   k1, p4; rep from *** to last 8 sts, mb, p4,
   k1, p2.
Round 4 P2, *k1, p4; rep from * 34 (40) more
   times, k1, p2, k30 – for center panel – p2,
   **k1, p4; rep from ** to last 3 sts, k1, p2.
Round 5 P2, *k1, p4; rep from * 8 (10) more
   times, k1, p2, k2tog through back of sts,
   yfwd, k26, yfwd, k2tog, p2; **k1, p4; rep from
   ** to last 3 sts, k1, p2.
Round 6 As round 4.
Round 7 P2, *mb, p4, k1, p4; rep from * 3 (4)
   more times, mb, p4, k1, p2, k2tog through
   back of sts, yfwd, k26, yfwd, k2tog, p2; **mb,
   p4, k1, p4; rep from ** to last 8 sts, mb, p4,
   k1, p2.
Round 8 As round 4.
Repeat rounds 5–8 another 3 times.
Round 21 As round 5.
Round 22 As round 4.
Round 23 P2, *k1, p4, mb, p4; rep from * 3 (4)
   more times, k1, p4, mb, p2, k2tog through
   back of sts, yfwd, k26, yfwd, k2tog, p2; **k1,
   p4, mb, p4; rep from ** to last 8 sts, k1, p4,
   mb, k1, p2.
Round 24 As round 4.
Rounds 24–40 Repeat the last 4 rounds
   another four times.
These 40 rounds complete the pattern. Work
one complete pattern more and 8 (20) rounds
of the next, but instead of the first 4 pattern
rounds, begin at the 5th round and repeat
rounds 5–8 another 4 times instead of 3.

FRONT

Change to ordinary no 3 needles and follow
the pattern as for the sleeves.
Shape armholes: Bind off 3 (6) sts, work the
next 127 (144) sts, and turn. Leave the remaining 130 (150) sts on a stitch holder. Bind off 3
(6) sts at the beginning of the next row. Bind off
3 sts at the beginning of the next 4 rows, then
decrease one st at both ends of the next 11
rows – 90 (104) sts. Note that the st st panel
with a row of holes either side, formed by the
sts yfwd, k2tog, is continued throughout the 17
armhole rows on the front piece. Work 15 (23)
rows straight in pattern. There should now be

3 (3½) complete patterns from the beginning.
Shape yoke: K2 (1), *yfwd, k2tog; rep from * 14
(18) more times, k26 panel sts, **m1, k2tog;
rep from ** 14 (18) more times; k2 (1). Work 3
rows in st st beginning with a purl row. Then
continue in st st shaping the neck as follows:
Shape neck: K40 (45) sts for the left front
shoulder and leave these sts on a stitch holder.
Bind off 10 (14) sts, k40 (45). Working on the
right side only, decrease one st at the neck
edge on the next 13 (13) rows – 27 (32) sts.
Work 24 (31) more rows. Bind off. Work left side
to match, reversing shaping.

BACK

Return to the 130 (150) sts left on stitch holder.
Bind off 3 (6) sts at the beginning of the next 2
rows, 3 sts at the beginning of the next 4 rows,
then decrease one st at both ends of the next
11 rows – 90 (104) sts. Work 40 (55) rows
straight in pattern, bind off straight across.
Note that the front is longer than the back.

NECKBAND

Join left shoulder seam. With no 1 needles
and right side facing pick up 37 (41) sts from
back of neck, 38 (39) sts down the left side of
the front, 10 (14) bound-off sts from the center
front, 38 (39) sts up the right side of the front –
123 (133) sts. Work 7 rows in k1, p1 rib. Bind off.

PUTTING TOGETHER

Sew all seams, matching stripes and ensuring
all ends are sewn in firmly.
For padded shoulders: Sew a light washable
square-ended shoulder pad inside the top of
the sleeve.
For rounded shoulders: Ease in fullness at
the top.

MEASUREMENTS

To fit chest 34, 36in (86, 91cm)

47(54)cm
18½(21½)"
51(56)cm
20(22)"
42(47)cm
16½(18½)"

51cm
20"

63cm
25"

46cm
18"

designed by *JOHN AND CLARE*

Pom-Poms

Loopy mohair yarn is shot through with multi-colored knitting worsted bands. Attach matching lengths of marabou, made up into pom-poms, adding beads on the sleeves.

MATERIALS

Yarn
Main yarn M *9oz* knitting worsted bouclé (black)
Yarn A *2oz* knitting worsted (bright pink)
Yarn B *2oz* knitting worsted (bright blue)

Yarn C *2oz* knitting worsted (bright yellow)
Yarn D *2oz* knitting worsted (bright green)
Yarn E *1oz* random dyed knitting worsted (yellow, green, blue, pink) or *1oz* each of medium-weight yarn in two of the above colors run together.

Needles
1 pair no 4
1 pair no 7

Notions
4 × 10in strips of maribou in the same shades as yarns A, B, C and D
30 beads

Stitch gauge
18 sts and 22 rows to 4in over st st on no 7 needles (or size needed to obtain given tension).

BACK

With no 4 needles and yarn M cast on 87 sts. Work in k1, p1 rib for 2in, increasing to 88 sts on the last row. Change to no 7 needles and work in st st from now on.
Rows 1 to 4 Yarn M.
Row 5 *K4 M, k4 E; rep from * to the end of the row.
Rows 6 to 9 Yarn M.
Row 10 Yarn B.
Repeat this yarn sequence, substituting yarns C, D and A for yarn B (row 10) in turn. Work 75 rows of st st.
Shape armholes: Work in st st in the following yarn sequence: 4 rows M; 1 row A; 4 rows M; 1 row B; 4 rows M; 1 row C; 4 rows M; 1 row D. At the same time, bind off 4 sts at the beginning of the next 2 rows, 3 sts at the beginning of the next 2 rows, and 2 sts at the beginning of the next 2 rows. K2tog at each end of the next row. Continue straight until work measures 23½in (should be 55 rows after the start of the armhole shaping). Work 6 rows yarn M. Bind off.

FRONT

Knit the same as the back.

SLEEVES

With no 4 needles and yarn M cast on 39 sts. Work in k1, p1 rib for 2in, increasing to 40 sts on the last row. Change to no 7 needles and st st and work in the same yarn and color sequence as on the body, except that the first solid color row should be yarn A, not E, and at the same time increase one st at each end of the next and every following 7th row until there are 64 sts. Continue straight until 85 rows of st st have been worked altogether (stripes should match body at armhole shaping).

Shape top: (Work in yarn sequence to match the body.) Bind off 4 sts at the beginning of the next 2 rows and 3 sts at the beginning of the following 2 rows. Decrease one st at each end of every other row until the sleeve head measures 8¼in (44 rows from the beginning of the armhole shaping). Bind off.

PUTTING TOGETHER

Join 4in of each side for shoulders. Sew in sleeves. Join side and sleeve seams, being careful to match stripes.

EXTRA DETAILS

Pom Poms
Cut 20 short lengths of marabou and sew the ends together, to form pom poms. Thread 3 beads on to the 10 to be used on sleeves. Sew 5 on each sleeve, 5 on the front top edge of the sweater and 5 along the back.

Boa

Fanciful mohair top incorporates a lurex snakeskin body
culminating in a free-standing headed collar. Looks just as
effective in knitting worsted yarns.

MATERIALS

Yarn
Main yarn M *15 (15, 16)oz* mohair (lilac)
Yarn A *2 (2, 2)oz* medium-weight lurex, or
fine lurex used double (silver)
Yarn B *2 (2, 2)oz* medium-weight lurex, or
fine lurex used double (gold)

Needles
1 pair no 4
1 pair no 7

Notions
Dacron wadding for snake
2 beads or small buttons for eyes
Scrap of narrow red ribbon for tongue
1 press stud

Stitch gauge
17 sts and 24 rows to 4in over st st on no 7
needles (or size needed to obtain tension).

BACK

With no 4 needles and yarn M cast on 61 (65,
69) sts. Work in k1, p1 rib for 3in ending with
a wrong side row. Change to no 7 needles.
Increase row: Knit, increasing 19 sts evenly
across the row – 80 (84, 88) sts. Next row K1,
purl to last st, k1. (Always knit the first and last
sts of purl row in st st.) *
Continue in st st, beginning with a knit row, for
a further 90 rows, ending with a purl row.
Shape armholes: Bind off 10 sts at the beginning of the next 2 rows. Increase one st at each
end of the 3rd and every following 4th row
until there are 80 (84, 88) sts. Work a further 9
rows in st st ending with a purl row.
Shape shoulders: Bind off 28 (30, 32) sts at the
beginning of the next 2 rows. Leave remaining
24 sts on a stitch holder.

FRONT

Work as back to *. Work in
st st following the

designed by **BETTY BARNDEN**

chart for front, commencing on row 1 and working within outline of chosen size. Use separate balls of yarn M and twist yarns where they join on every row. Work to row 90.

Shape armholes: Work increases as for back to row 128 of chart (purl row).

Shape neck: (left side) K31 (33, 35) sts from chart, turn. Decrease one st at neck edge on the next row. Increase one st at armhole edge and decrease one st at neck edge on the next row. Decrease one st at neck edge on next 2 rows. Work a further 7 rows from chart, ending with row 140 of chart (purl row). Bind off 16 (18, 20) sts at the beginning of the next row and

leave remaining 12 sts of "Snake" on a stitch holder.

Shape neck: (right side) With right side of front facing, slip 16 sts at center front onto a spare needle. Rejoin yarn M at right of remaining sts and complete to match first side, reversing shaping, as shown on chart, using yarn M and binding off all sts at shoulder edge.

Make snake: With no 7 needles and yarn B cast on 6 sts. Knit these sts, then knit across 12 sts from stitch holder on left shoulder according to first row of snake's head chart, then cast on a further 6 sts in yarn A. Work to row 20 of chart. Repeat these 20 rows 6 more times (7 times in all). Continue to follow chart from row 21, increasing one st at each end of the next and every alternate row 6 times as shown – 36 sts. Purl one row (row 32 of chart). Continue to follow chart: decrease one st at each end of every row as shown until 10 sts remain. Purl one row (row 46 of chart). Bind off.

SLEEVES

With no 4 needles and yarn M cast on 33 (35, 37) sts and work in k1, p1 rib for 3in ending with a wrong side row. Change to no 7 needles. Increase row: Knit, increase 9 sts evenly across the row – 42 (44, 46) sts. Next row K1, purl to last st, k1. Continue in st st, increasing one st at each end of the next and every following 4th row until there are 72 sts. Work without shaping until sleeve measures 17¾ (18, 18½)in in all ending with a purl row. Inserting a marking thread at each end of the next row, work a further 14 rows of st st. Bind off loosely.

NECKBAND

Join right shoulder seam. Using no 4 needles and yarn M, with right side of work facing, pick up and knit 13 sts from left front neck, knit 16 sts from stitch holder at center front, pick up and knit 12 sts from right front neck, knit 24 sts from back of neck – 65 sts. Work in k1, p1 rib for 1in ending with a wrong side row. Change to no 7 needles and bind off in rib.

PUTTING TOGETHER

Join left shoulder seam, joining last 12 sts to wrong side of snake and joining neckband seam. Sew top edges of sleeves to armhole edges and backstitch in position, joining 14 rows above marking threads to 10 bound-off sts at each side on armhole shapings. Join side and sleeve seams. Cut wadding to length of snake with extra to fold in to fill head. Fold the snake's head in half lengthwise over the wadding and join the side edges together right up to its nose. Sew one half of press stud under its chin and the other half to snake's body just below left shoulder, on a level with the beginning of neck shaping. Sew on glass buttons or beads for eyes. Cut a V in one end of the ribbon for tongue and sew in position.

MEASUREMENTS

To fit chest 33 (35, 37)in (84, 89, 94cm)
Back width 19 (20, 21)in (48, 51, 53cm)
Length 21in (66cm)
Sleeve seam 17¾ (18, 18½)in (45, 46, 47cm)

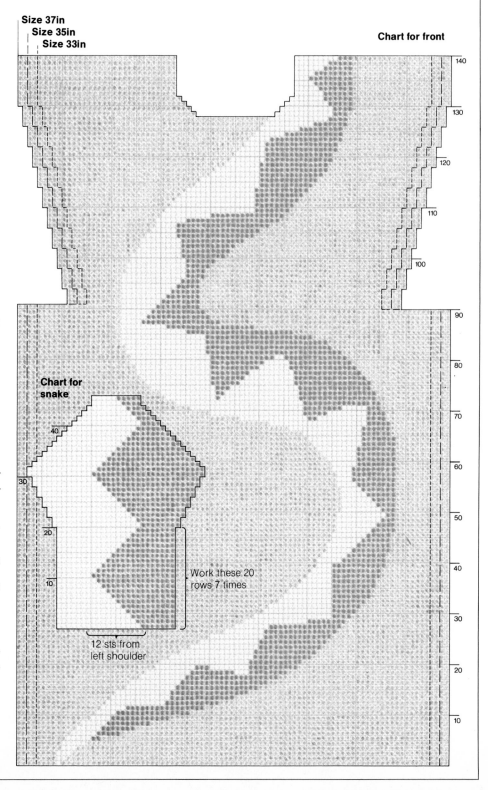

Size 37in
Size 35in
Size 33in

Chart for front

Chart for snake

Work these 20 rows 7 times

12 sts from left shoulder

Country Cousin

Small child's or toddler's heavy-weight cardigan is knitted up in a variety of stitch patterns with scenic trim embroidered in duplicate stitch using yarn leftovers.

MATERIALS

Yarn
13oz bulky (cream)
Scraps of bulky in approximately 10 shades for embroidery
Needles
1 pair no 7
1 size E crochet hook
Notions
4 buttons
Stitch gauge
14 sts and 21 rows to 4in over st st on no 7 needles (or size needed to obtain given tension).

BODY

The body of the jacket is knitted all in one. Cast on 87 sts.
Row 1 (Wrong side of work) K1, *p1, k1, rep from * to the end of the row.
Row 2 K to the end of the row.
Repeat rows 1 and 2 until the work measures

SLEEVES

Cast on 25 sts. Work in rib as for body for 11 rows, increasing 9 sts in the last row – 34 sts. Work pattern as on body. Continue in st st until the work measures 8in. Then continue in Moss stitch until the work measures 10¾in. Bind off.

BUTTON BANDS

Button border (left front for girls, right front for boys)
Work 4 rows of single crochet along the front edge.

Buttonhole border (right front for girls, left front for boys)
Work 2 rows of single crochet along the front edge. In the 3rd row make 4 evenly spaced buttonholes to fit buttons (see p. 130). Crochet one more row.

COLLAR

Sew shoulder seams. Pick up 32 sts round neck omitting the button and buttonhole bands. Work 22 rows in Moss stitch. Break off yarn. With another needle and starting from the neck edge pick up 11 sts on the right side of the collar. Work across 32 sts on needle then pick up 11 sts on the left side. Work a further 4 rows in Moss stitch, then 3 rows in Garter stitch. Bind off. Attach edges of collar to button borders.

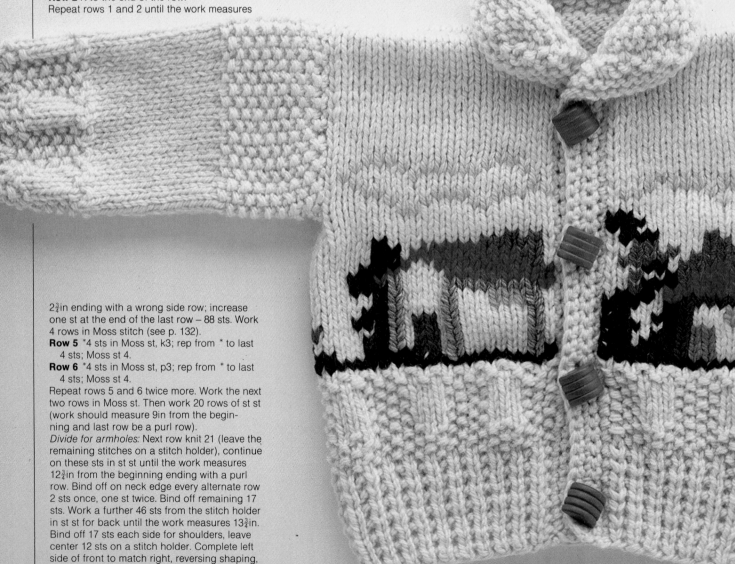

2¾in ending with a wrong side row; increase one st at the end of the last row – 88 sts. Work 4 rows in Moss stitch (see p. 132).
Row 5 *4 sts in Moss st, k3; rep from * to last 4 sts; Moss st 4.
Row 6 *4 sts in Moss st, p3; rep from * to last 4 sts; Moss st 4.
Repeat rows 5 and 6 twice more. Work the next two rows in Moss st. Then work 20 rows of st st (work should measure 9in from the beginning and last row be a purl row).
Divide for armholes: Next row knit 21 (leave the remaining stitches on a stitch holder), continue on these sts in st st until the work measures 12¼in from the beginning ending with a purl row. Bind off on neck edge every alternate row 2 sts once, one st twice. Bind off remaining 17 sts. Work a further 46 sts from the stitch holder in st st for back until the work measures 13¾in. Bind off 17 sts each side for shoulders, leave center 12 sts on a stitch holder. Complete left side of front to match right, reversing shaping, knitting the last 21 sts from the stitch holder.

PUTTING TOGETHER

Sew in sleeves. Join sleeve seams. Sew on buttons.

EXTRA DETAILS

Work embroidery in duplicate stitch (see p. 128) following chart.

MEASUREMENTS

To fit chest 24–26in (61–66cm)

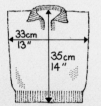

designed by **NURIT KAYE**

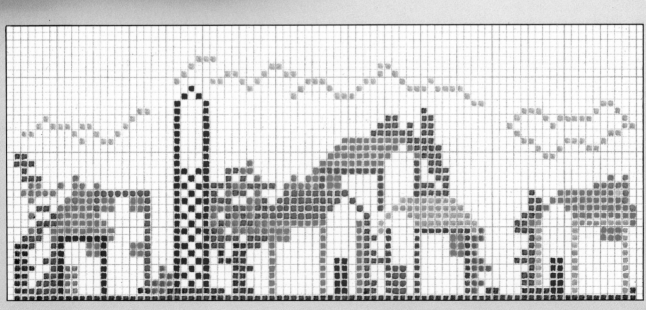

| Left front | Back | Right front |

Chunky Cardies

These two children's sweaters with matching caps knit up quickly using bulky yarn and large needles. The stockinette stitch panel on the rust version can be decorated with embroidery, if desired.

MATERIALS for blue cardigan and hat

Yarn
Main yarn M 7oz bulky (blue)
Yarn A 1oz bulky (rust)
Yarn B 1oz bulky (dark blue)
Yarn C 1oz bulky (green)
Yarn D 1oz bulky (fawn)
Yarn E 1oz bulky (natural)

Needles
1 pair no 10
1 size E crochet hook
1 cable needle

Notions
5 buttons

Stitch gauge
13 sts and 24 rows to 4in over Moss stitch on no 10 needles (or size needed to obtain given tension).

Special note:
Abbreviation c4 means slip next 2 sts onto a cable needle and leave at front of work; k2, k2 from cable needle.

BODY

The body of the cardigan is knitted all in one. Cast on 80 sts in yarn M.
Row 1 (Wrong side of work) K2, p4, k2, *p1, k2, p4, k2, rep from * to the end of the row.
Row 2 P2, k4, p2, *k1, p2, k4, p2, rep from * to the end of the row.
Row 3 As row 1.
Row 4 As row 2.
Row 5 As row 1.
Row 6 P2, c4, p2, *k1, p2, c4, p2, rep from * to end.
Repeat rows 3–6 once more.
Row 11 As row 1.
This completes the ribbing. With right side of garment facing, work as follows: Knit 2 rows E; knit one row C; Moss st 3 rows C; knit one row D; Moss st 3 rows D; knit 2 rows B; knit one row A; Moss st 3 rows A; knit 2 rows E; knit 8 rows M; knit 2 rows A; knit one row B; Moss st 3 rows B; knit 2 rows D.
Divide for armholes: With right side of work facing and using yarn M, knit the first 19 sts (leave the remainder on a stitch holder). Continue in Moss stitch for 28 rows for front. Bind off 2 sts on the neck side every alternate row twice, one st once. On the next row bind off remaining 14 sts. Knit a further 42 sts for back from stitch holder. Continue in Moss stitch for 32 rows. Bind off 13 sts from each side for shoulders, leaving the center 16 sts on a stitch holder. Complete the left side of front to match, reversing shaping, knitting the last 19 sts from the stitch holder.

SLEEVES

Cast on 25 sts in yarn M. Work in k1, p1 rib for 11 rows. Then continue as follows: knit one row A; Moss st 3 rows A; knit 2 rows B; knit one row D; Moss st 3 rows D. Continue in Moss stitch, using yarn M and increasing one st 3 times on each side of work – 31 sts altogether. Work 34 rows in all in yarn M. Bind off.

BUTTON BANDS

Button border (left front for girls, right front for boys)
Using yarn M work 3 rows of single crochet along the front edge.

Buttonhole border (right front for girls, left front for boys)
Using yarn M work one row of single crochet along the front edge. In the 2nd row make 5 evenly spaced buttonholes to fit buttons (see p. 130). Crochet one more row.

COLLAR

Join shoulder seams. Using yarn M pick up 37 sts round the neck (from back, fronts and button bands) and work in Garter stitch for 24 rows. Bind off.

PUTTING TOGETHER

Sew sleeves in place. Sew sleeve seams. Sew on 5 buttons.

HAT

Cast on 56 sts in yarn M. Work in Garter stitch throughout, in the following yarn sequence: 30 rows M; 2 rows A; 2 rows D; 2 rows M; 2 rows B; 2 rows M; 2 rows E; 2 rows M; 2 rows A. With yarn B *k6, k2tog; rep from * to end;

one row B. With yarn M *k5, k2tog; rep from * to end; one row M. With yarn E *k4, k2tog; rep from * to end; one row E. With yarn M *k3, k2tog; rep from * to end; one row M; *k2, k2tog; rep from * to end; one row M. With yarn B *k1, k2tog; rep from * to end; one row B. With yarn M k2tog to end. Pull the wool through the loops.
Stitch the seam so it does not show when the brim is folded back about 2½in.

MEASUREMENTS

To fit chest 22–24in (56–61cm)
Back width 12½in (32cm)
Length 12in (31cm)
Sleeve seam 9½in (24cm)

MATERIALS for rust cardigan and hat

Yarn
Main yarn M *7oz* bulky (rust)
Yarn A *6oz* bulky (natural)
Yarn B *2oz* bulky (blue)
Yarn C *2oz* bulky (fawn)
Yarn D *2oz* bulky (green)

Needles
1 pair no 10
1 size E crochet hook
1 cable needle

Notions
5 buttons

Stitch gauge
13 sts and 24 rows to 4in over Moss stitch on no 10 needles (or size needed to obtain given tension).

designed by **NURIT KAYE**

Special note:
Abbreviation c4 means slip next 2 sts onto a cable needle and hold at front of work; k2, k2 from cable needle.

EXTRA DETAILS

Using yarn M and starting on the 2nd st from the border embroider 12 evenly-spaced motifs in the st st panel.

BODY

The body of the cardigan is knitted all in one. Cast on 86 (95) sts in yarn M.
Row 1 (Wrong side of work) *k2, p1, k2, p4; rep from * to last 5 sts, k2, p1, k2.
Row 2 *P2, k1, p2, k4; rep from * to last 5 sts, p2, k1, p2.
Row 3 As row 1.
Row 4 As row 2.
Row 5 As row 1.
Row 6 *P2, k1, p2, c4; rep from * to last 5 sts; p2, k1, p2.
Repeat rows 3–6 twice more.
Row 15 As row 1.
This completes the ribbing. Now work as follows; knit 2 rows A; knit one row B; Moss st 3 rows B; knit one row C; Moss st 3 rows C; knit 4 rows D; knit 4 rows A; st st 6 rows A; Moss st 4 rows A; knit 4 rows B; knit 2 rows A; knit 4 rows D. For larger size only: knit 2 rows A.
Divide for armholes: With right side of work facing and using yarn M knit first 21 (23) sts (leave the remainder on a stitch holder). Continue in Moss stitch for 30 (32) rows for front. Bind off 2 sts on the neck side every alternate row twice, one st once. On the next row bind off remaining 16 (18) sts. Knit a further 44 (49) sts for back from stitch holder. Continue in Moss stitch for 34 (36) rows. Bind off 16 (18) sts from each side for shoulders, leaving the center 12 (13) sts on a stitch holder. Complete the left side of front to match reversing shaping, knitting the last 21 (23) sts from the stitch holder.

SLEEVES

Cast on 27 (29) sts in yarn M. Work in k1, p1 rib for 11 (13) rows. Then continue as follows: knit one row A; Moss st 3 rows A; knit 2 rows B; knit one row D; Moss st 3 rows D. Continue in Moss stitch in yarn A increasing one st on each side 3 (4) times – 34 (37) sts. Continue until 40 (42) rows in A have been worked. Bind off.

BUTTON BANDS

Button border (left front for girls, right front for boys)
Using yarn M work 3 rows of single crochet along the front edge.

Buttonhole border (right front for girls, left front for boys)
Using yarn M work one row of single crochet along the front edge. In the 2nd row make 5 evenly spaced buttonholes to fit buttons (see p. 130). Crochet one more row.

COLLAR

Join shoulder seams. With yarn A pick up 36 (40) sts around neck (from back, fronts and button bands). Work in Garter stitch for 26 rows. Bind off.

PUTTING TOGETHER

Stitch sleeves into place. Join sleeve seams. Sew on buttons.

HAT

Cast on 64 sts in yarn M. Work in Garter stitch throughout in the following yarn sequence: 28 rows M; 2 rows B; 2 rows A; 2 rows M; 2 rows D; 2 rows C; 2 rows M; 2 rows A; 2 rows B; 2 rows C. With yarn A *k6, k2tog; rep from * to end; one row A. With yarn M *k5, k2tog; rep from * to end; one row M; *k4, k2tog; rep from * to end; one row M. With yarn B *k3, k2tog; rep from * to end; one row B; *k2, k2tog; rep from * to end; one row B. With yarn D *k1, k2tog; rep from * to end; one row D. With yarn M k2tog to end. Pull wool through loops. Stitch the seam so it does not show when the brim is folded back about 2½in.

MEASUREMENTS

To fit chest 24–26 (26–28)in (61–66, 66–71cm)
Back width 13½ (15)in (34, 38cm)
Length 15 (16)in (38, 40cm)
Sleeve seam 11 (12)in (28, 30cm)

My Big Pocket

A child's – up to 8 years – pullover in dark knitting worsted has contrasting neck and sleeve trim and large knitted pocket, sewn on afterwards. The back is reserved for messages embroidered in duplicate stitch.

designed by **NURIT KAYE**

MATERIALS

Yarn
Main yarn M *7oz* knitting worsted (dark blue)
Yarn A *2oz* knitting worsted (yellow)
Yarn B *2oz* knitting worsted (red)

Needles
1 pair no 2
1 pair no 4
1 set no 2 double-pointed (optional)

Notions
3 buttons

Stitch gauge
25 sts and 30 rows to 4in over st st on no 4 needles (or size needed to obtain given tension).

BACK

With no 2 needles and yarn A cast on 91 sts. Work in k1, p1 rib for 6 rows; change to yarn M and continue until the rib measures 2¾in from the beginning. Change to no 4 needles and continue in st st until the work measures 14in from the beginning. Bind off one st at the beginning of the next 2 rows (to mark armholes). Continue straight until the work measures 18½in from the beginning. Bind off the center 27 sts, continue on one side only, binding off 6 sts at the beginning of the next row. Bind off remaining 25 sts. Complete the other side to match, reversing shaping.

FRONT

Work as for back until the work measures 16in. Bind off center 17 sts. Continue on one side only, binding off 4 sts at the neck edge on the next row, 3 sts on the following alternate row then one st on the following 4 alternate rows. Bind off remaining 25 sts when work measures 19in.

SLEEVES

With no 2 needles and yarn M cast on 55 sts. Work in k1, p1 rib for 2½in. Change to no 4 needles and yarn A and st st. Increase 4 sts in the first row and work 6 rows. Continue in yarn M increasing one st at each end of every 10th row until there are 75 sts. When work measures 15½in from the beginning bind off.

NECKBAND

Either sew both shoulder seams and use set of no 2 double-pointed needles, or sew only one shoulder seam and use ordinary no 2 needles. With yarn A pick up 104 sts (103 sts using ordinary needles) round the neck edge. Work in k1, p1 rib for 2¾in. Bind off.

POCKET

With no 2 needles and yarn B cast on 72 sts. Work 3 rows in k1, p1 rib. Buttonhole row: Rib 13 sts, bind off 2 sts, rib 20 sts, bind off 2 sts, rib 20 sts, bind off 2 sts, rib 13 sts. Next row rib 13 sts, cast on 2 sts, rib 20 sts, cast on 2 sts, rib 20 sts, cast on 2 sts, rib 13 sts. Rib 3 more rows, change to no 4 needles and continue in st st until the work measures 7in. Bind off.

PUTTING TOGETHER

Sew shoulder seam, if necessary. Sew in sleeves. Stitch side seams and sleeve seams. Fold the neckband in half to the inside and slip stitch down ensuring an easy fit over the head. Stitch pocket to the front of the sweater, sew on 3 buttons to correspond with buttonholes.

EXTRA DETAILS

Embroider child's name on the back of the sweater using duplicate stitch (see p. 128) following chart.

MEASUREMENTS

To fit chest 28–30in (71–76cm)

38cm
15"

47cm
18½"

39cm
15½"

Using duplicate stitch (see p. 128) and the alphabet chart below you can embroider any name, or message, onto the back of this pullover. It is a good idea to scale up the name first (see p. 74), so that you can be certain it fits in properly across the width. You can, if you wish, write the letters in chalk on the sweater and use this as a guide for your embroidery.

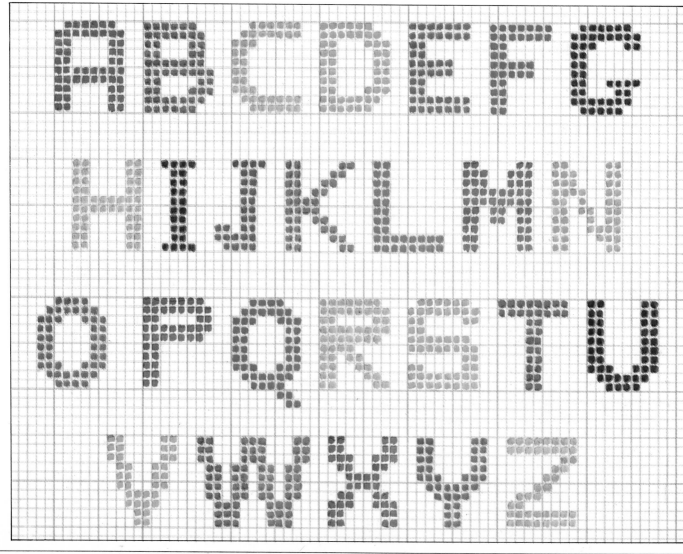

Knitting know-how

Knitting Aids

Straight needles and yarn are all you need for plain knitting but some additional accessories come in handy from time to time. For knitting in the round you will need either a set of double-pointed needles or a circular needle, while for cable work a special cable needle is quite useful. Stitch holders and yarn bobbins keep unworked stitches and yarns separate; needle guards prevent dropped stitches. A counter keeps track of rows and stitches while small rings are used to mark rounds. A crochet hook, scissors, blunt-ended needle and pins can be used for finishing off and making up; a tape measure is necessary for keeping track of vital measurements during both the construction and blocking of a garment.

2mm
No 0
No 1
No 2
No 3
No 4
No 5
No 6
No 7
No 8
No 9
No 10
No 10½
No 11
No 13
No 15
10mm

1
2
3
4
5

Key
1 Cable needles
2 Stitch holder
3 Yarn bobbins
4 Circular needle
5 Tape measure
6 Needle guards
7 Pins
8 Double-pointed needles
9 Crochet hook
10 Marker rings
11 Scissors
12 Wool needle
13 Stitch and row counter

BEGINNING TO KNIT

To start knitting all you need are two needles and some yarn. The information on the following pages will tell you all you need to know to make the patterns in the book as well as helping to design your own knitting. An illustrated glossary of available yarns on pages 134–9 will enable you to be more inventive in choosing colors and textures for your designs.

The instructions are written and illustrated for right-hand knitters. If you are left-handed, reverse any instructions for left and right, or prop the book up in front of a mirror and follow the diagrams in reverse.

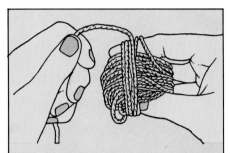

To form a ball with the working end on top, unwrap yarn from a hank tightly over 3 fingers. Remove the coils, change the position and continue winding.

Casting on

When you begin to work on a pattern placing the first row of stitches on the needle is known as "casting on". All further rows are worked into these initial loops.

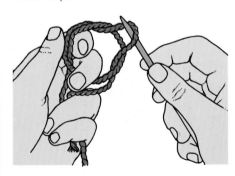

1 Make a slip loop by wrapping your yarn twice around two fingers and pulling a loop through the twisted yarn with a knitting needle.

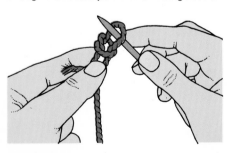

2 Pull both ends of the yarn to tighten the slip loop.

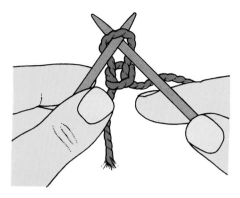

3 With the slip loop on your left-hand needle, insert your right-hand needle through the loop from front to back.

4 Bring the yarn under and over your right-hand needle.

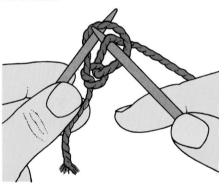

5 Draw up the yarn through the slip loop to make a stitch.

6 Place the stitch on your left-hand needle. Continue to make stitches drawing the yarn through the last stitch on your left-hand needle.

Binding off

When you end a piece of knitting, such as a sleeve, or part of a piece of knitting, such as up to the neck, you must secure all the stitches by "binding off". This is preferably done on a knit row but you can employ the same technique on a purl row. The stitches, whether knit or purl, should be made loosely. With ribbing, you must follow the pattern, and cast off in both knit and purl.

In knit stitch

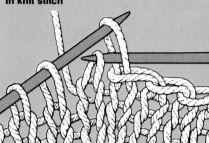

1 Knit the first two stitches and insert the tip of your left-hand needle through the first stitch.

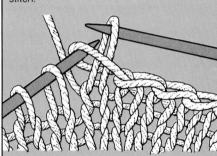

2 Lift the first stitch over the second stitch and discard it. Knit the next stitch and continue to lift the first stitch over the second stitch to the end of the row. Be careful not to knit too tightly. For the last stitch, cut your yarn, slip the end through the stitch and pull the yarn tight to fasten off securely.

In purl stitch

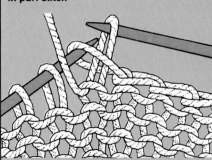

Purl the first two (and all subsequent) stitches and continue as for knit stitch above.

Holding needle and yarn

The way in which you hold your knitting will affect the tension and evenness of the fabric. Threading the working end of the yarn through the fingers not only makes knitting faster but it does produce a firm, even result.

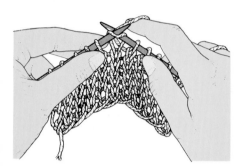

Holding yarn in the right hand
With the working yarn in your right hand, use the right forefinger to wrap the yarn over the needles.

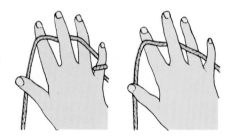

Threading the yarn
Place the working yarn through the fingers of your left hand either way.

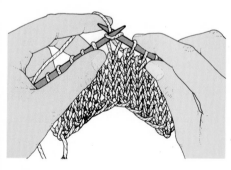

Holding yarn in the left hand
With the working yarn in your left hand, use the left forefinger to position the yarn while you move the right needle to encircle the yarn to form a new loop.

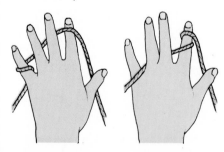

Threading the yarn
Place the working yarn through the fingers of your right hand either way.

BASIC STITCHES

Knit stitch and purl stitch are the two basic knitting stitches. Either one knit continuously in rows forms Garter stitch pattern and knit alternately forms Stockinette stitch pattern.

Knit stitch (k)

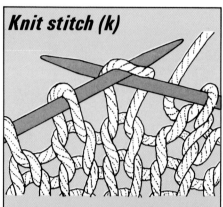

1 With the yarn at the back, insert your right-hand needle from front to back into the first stitch on your left-hand needle.

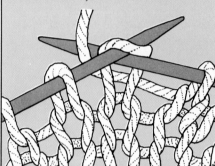

2 Bring your working yarn under and over the point of your right-hand needle.

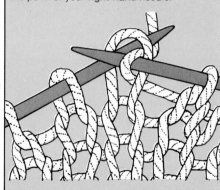

3 Draw a loop through and slide the first stitch off your left-hand needle while the new stitch is retained on your right-hand needle. Continue in this way to the end of the row.

4 To knit the next row, turn the work around so that the back is facing you and the worked stitches are held on the needle in your left hand. Proceed to make stitches as above, with the initially empty needle held in your right hand.

Purl stitch (p)

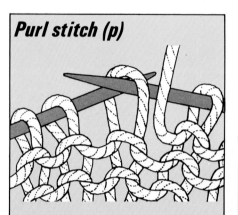

1 With the yarn at the front, insert your right-hand needle from back to front into the first stitch on your left-hand needle.

2 Bring your working yarn over and around the point of your right-hand needle.

3 Draw a loop through and slide the first stitch off your left-hand needle while the new stitch is retained on your right-hand needle. Continue in this way to the end of the row.

4 To purl the next row, turn the work around so that the back is facing you and the worked stitches are held on the needle in your left hand. Proceed to make stitches as above, with the initially empty needle held in your right hand.

Garter stitch

Knitting or purling every row back and forth on two needles produces Garter stitch.

Stockinette stitch (st st)

Knitting the first and every odd row and purling the second and every even row produces Stockinette stitch when made on two needles. When working in the round (see p. 118) the work does not have to be turned around because the knit stitch will always be on the outside and the ridged purl will be on the inside.

Ribbing

A combination of knit and purl stitches, usually one or two knit stitches and then one or two purl stitches, in the same row is known as ribbing. Ribbing is used on sleeve and body edges to form a neat, stretchable finish. It is usually worked on smaller needles than the body of the garment.

Changing from a knit stitch to a purl stitch (on a three by three rib)
Knit three in the usual way and bring the yarn to the front. Purl three in the usual way.

Changing from a purl stitch to a knit stitch (on a three by three rib)
Having purled three in the usual way, bring the yarn to the back and knit three in the usual way.

Stitch gauge

Before starting to make any garment, you must make a tension sample in order to measure stitch gauge. You should do this in order to check your individual control of the yarn against the pattern you are following – so that the desired measurements are the same as in the pattern. It is also imperative to do this when you are planning a design of your own, or adapting one (see p. 132).

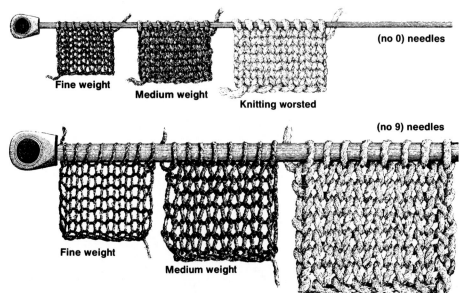

(no 0) needles

Fine weight   Medium weight   Knitting worsted

(no 9) needles

Fine weight   Medium weight   Knitting worsted

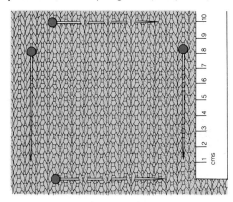

The stitch gauge, or tension, is always given at the beginning of a pattern. It is written as the number of stitches, and the number of rows in a particular pattern, e.g., stockinette stitch, to a specified size such as 4in using the yarn and needles called for in the pattern. An example is 22 sts and 30 rows to 4in over st st on no 5 needles.

A variation in tension within a garment will result in an uneven appearance. By knitting the required number of stitches and rows, your sample will reveal whether the yarn and needles you are using will make up into the size and shape you require.

The ball band provides important information regarding stitch gauge. The one shown right gives metric and US crochet hook and needle sizes and the ideal tension sample.

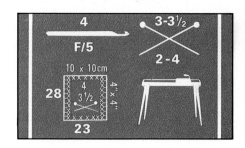

Making a tension sample

Using the same yarn, needles and stitch pattern called for in the pattern, knit a sample slightly larger than 4in square. Smooth out the finished sample on a flat surface being careful not to stretch it. Using pins, mark out the tension measurement given in the chosen pattern.

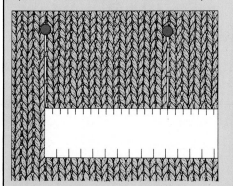

Measuring the number of stitches
To determine the width of the knitting, place a steel ruler or tape measure across the sample and count the number of stitches between the pins. Remember to include any half stitches over the width of a garment; a half stitch which is left uncalculated may amount to several inches in the final width.

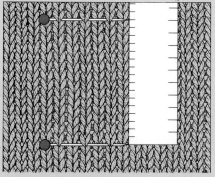

Measuring the number of rows
To determine the length of the knitting, place a steel ruler or tape measure vertically along the fabric and count the number of rows to the inch.

Adjusting the stitch gauge

If the number of stitches given in the pattern knit up to too wide a measure your knitting is too loose and you should change your knitting needles to a smaller size. If they knit up to too small a measure, then your knitting is too tight and you should change your knitting needles to a larger size.

Changing to needles one size larger or one size smaller makes a difference of one stitch usually every two inches. Changing your needle size will normally be sufficient to adjust the dimensions. Sometimes, however, the width will match but not the length. If there are too many vertical rows to that called for in the pattern, you must calculate the length of the garment from your tension sample and adjust the increasing and decreasing rows accordingly. However, in certain patterns such as raglan or set-in sleeves, the shaping is dependent on a specific number of vertical rows. If your vertical tension matches but not your horizontal then in this case it is better to lose some stitches across the width.

Dropped stitches

Occasionally, a stitch may fall off your needle. This is especially likely if you stop working in the middle of a row.

Picking up a dropped knit stitch

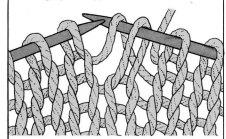

1 Pick up both the stitch and strand on your right-hand needle, inserting the needle from front to back.

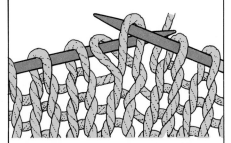

2 Insert your left-hand needle through the stitch only, from back to front. With your right-hand needle only, pull the strand through the stitch to make the extra stitch. (Drop the stitch from your left-hand needle.)

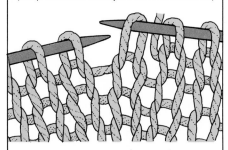

3 Transfer the re-formed stitch back to your left-hand needle, so that it untwists and faces the correct way. It is now ready for knitting again.

Picking up a dropped purl stitch

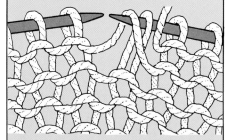

1 Pick up both the stitch and strand on your right-hand needle, inserting the needle from back to front.

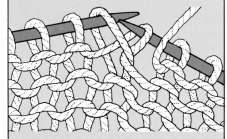

2 Insert your left-hand needle through the stitch only, from front to back. With your right-hand needle only, pull the strand through the stitch to make the extra stitch. (Drop the stitch from your left-hand needle.)

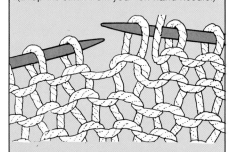

3 Transfer the re-formed stitch back to your left-hand needle, so that it untwists and faces the correct way. It is now ready for purling again.

Unpicking mistakes

Holding the stitch on your right-hand needle insert your left-hand needle into the row below and undo the stitch. Transfer the stitch back to your right-hand needle and repeat undoing until the error has been reached. Correct stitch as if it had been a ladder, see above.

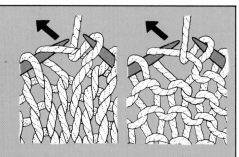

Ladders

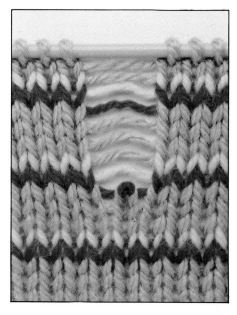

If a dropped stitch is left, it can unravel downwards and form a "ladder". In such a case it is easiest to use a crochet hook to pick up the stitches in pattern although you can try it with your needles. If you make a mistake in your knitting, you may have to "unpick" a stitch, in which case a ladder may result. Pick up one dropped stitch at a time, securing any others with a safety pin to prevent further unraveling.

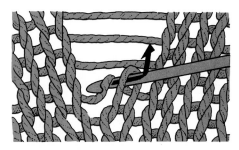

Correcting a "knit" ladder
Insert a crochet hook through the front of the dropped stitch. Hook up one strand and pull it through the stitch to form a new stitch one row up. Continue in this way to the top of the ladder then continue in pattern.

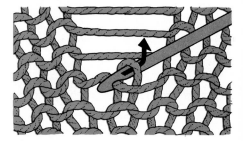

Correcting a "purl" ladder
Insert a crochet hook through the back of the dropped stitch. Hook up one strand and pull it through the stitch to form a new stitch one row up. Continue to re-insert hook to make stitches until you reach the top of the ladder.

INCREASING STITCHES (INC)

When shaping garments it is usually necessary to add additional stitches. If they are made "invisibly", there will be no hole or gap left in the fabric. The three "invisible" methods shown below all use part of an existing stitch to create a new one. Use the "inc 1" (making two stitches from one) method for shaping your side edges, and "M1" (raised increase) and "up 1" (lifted increase) for shaping within the body of the garment. The visible increase (see p. 116), variously written as "yrn" (yarn round needle), "yfwd" (yarn forward), and "yo" (yarn over) is used for decorative stitch patterns.

"Inc 1"

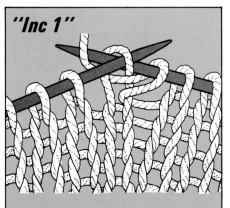

In a knit row
Knit into the front of the stitch in the usual way. Without discarding the stitch on your left-hand needle, knit into the back of it, making two stitches.

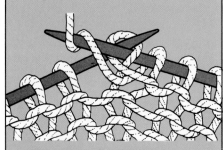

In a purl row
Purl into the front of the stitch in the usual way. Without discarding the stitch on your left-hand needle, purl into the back of it, making two stitches.

"Up 1"

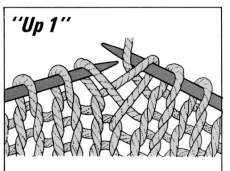

In a knit row
1 Insert your right-hand needle from front to back into the top of the stitch below the next one to be knitted. Knit the stitch in the usual way.

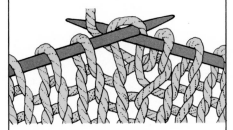

2 Then, knit the next stitch on your left-hand needle.

In a purl row
1 Insert your right-hand needle from back to front into the top of the stitch below the next one to be purled. Purl the stitch in the usual way.

2 Then purl the next stitch on your left-hand needle.

"M1"

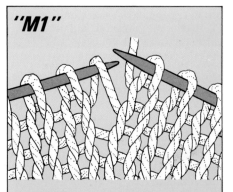

In a knit row
1 Insert your left-hand needle from front to back under the running thread between your left- and right-hand needles.

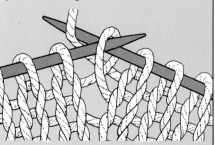

2 Then, knit into the back of the raised running thread.

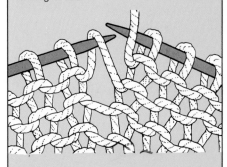

In a purl row
1 Insert your left-hand needle from front to back under the running thread between your left- and right-hand needles.

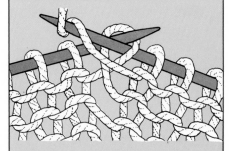

2 Then, purl into the back of the raised running thread.

"Yrn", "Yfwd" or "Yo"

This visible increase is usually used when making fancy patterns as in bobble stitches. Any number of stitches may be increased by the yarn-over method. Depending on the number of increases required in the pattern (and the position, see below), take your yarn forward, around or over your needle one, two, three, four or more times. On the subsequent row, knit the stitches in pattern order.

Patterns are usually written with "yfwd" when the increase occurs between two knit stitches, as "yrn" when the increase occurs between two purl stitches or between a knit and purl, and as "yo" when the increase occurs between a purl and knit; "yo" is also used to represent all three situations.

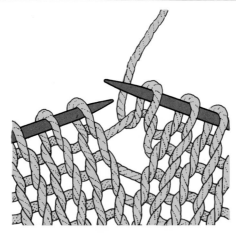

A visible increase can be seen clearly as a hole after the loop has been knitted into on the following row.

In a knit row

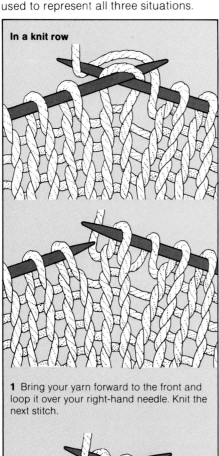

1 Bring your yarn forward to the front and loop it over your right-hand needle. Knit the next stitch.

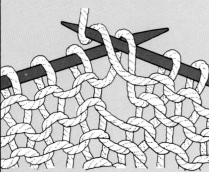

2 On the subsequent row, purl (or knit) the yarn-over loop in the usual way.

In a purl row

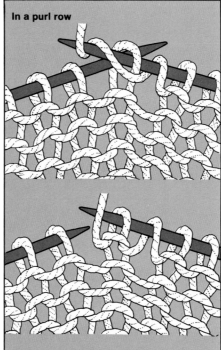

1 Take your yarn back around your right-hand needle and then under to the front. Purl the next stitch.

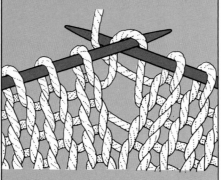

2 On the subsequent row, knit (or purl) the yarn-over loop in the usual way.

Taking measurements

Before you knit up any garment make sure the measurements given in the pattern are suitable for you. You will also need to know where to take measurements if you decide to alter an existing pattern or design a new one altogether.

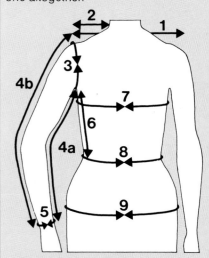

1 Shoulders – Measure across back from one shoulder tip to the other.

2 Top of shoulder – Measure from shoulder point to neck edge. From this you calculate neck shaping.

3 Armhole – Measure loosely from the highest point of the shoulders.

4a & b Sleeve – Measure with elbow bent from armpit to wrist, and outside arm from shoulder to wrist.

5 Wrist – Measure around the wristbone.

6 Waist to underarm – Measure with the arm raised.

7 Chest – Measure around the fullest part.

8 Waist – For easy movement, measure with a finger between waist and tape measure.

9 Hip – Measure around the broadest part.

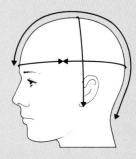

To calculate the size for a hat or cap: measure around the head at the widest part to obtain the circumference. Measure across the top of the head from ear tip to ear tip and from mid-forehead to the base of the skull to obtain the diameter.

DECREASING (DEC)

There are two ways to lose stitches for shaping and these are to knit or purl two stitches together (k2tog or p2tog) at the beginning, end or at any given point in a row – or to use the slip stitch method (sl 1). Knitting stitches together is the simpler method, but slipping stitches produces a more decorative effect on a garment.

Decreases are always visible and have a definite angled slant. It is important to pair your decreases so that the direction of slant for the various decreases are balanced, i.e. one side of a raglan sleeve slants to the right, and one side slants to the left.

Knitting two stitches together

Abbreviated as *k2tog* or *p2tog*, the decrease forms a slant to the right if the stitches are knitted together through the front, and a slant to the left if knitted together through the back.

In a knit row
Insert your right-hand needle through the front of the first two stitches on your left-hand needle. Knit them together as a single stitch.

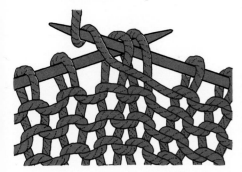

In a purl row
Insert your right-hand needle through the front of the first two stitches on your left-hand needle. Purl them together as a single stitch.

Slip stitch decrease

Abbreviated as *sl 1, k1, psso* (slip one, knit one, pass slip stitch over), the decrease forms a slant to the left on the front of the knitting. A slant to the right is formed on the front if it is made on the purl row – *sl 1, p1, psso* (slip one, purl one, pass slip stitch over).

In a knit row

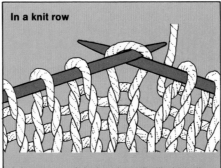

1 Insert your right-hand needle "knitwise" and lift off the first stitch from your left-hand needle.

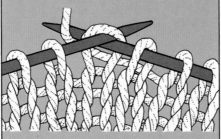

2 Leave the stitch on the needle and knit the next stitch on your left-hand needle in the usual way.

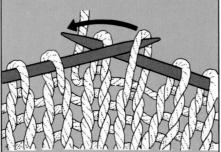

3 Using the point of your left-hand needle bring the slipped stitch off your right-hand needle, over the knitted stitch.

In a purl row

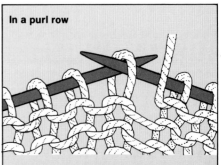

1 Insert your right-hand needle "purlwise" and lift off the first stitch from your left-hand needle.

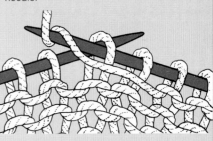

2 Leave the stitch on the needle and purl into the next stitch on your left-hand needle in the usual way.

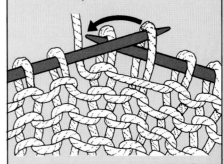

3 Using the point of your left-hand needle, bring the slipped stitch off your right-hand needle, over the purled stitch.

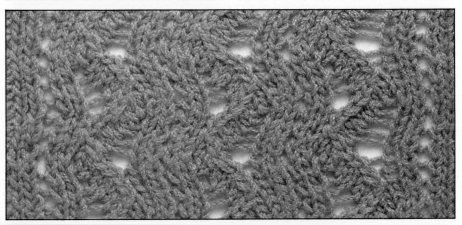

Fancy openwork patterns such as Ric Rac depend on slip stitch decreases.

KNITTING IN THE ROUND

It is sometimes easier to make garments working with circular or double-pointed needles. Such needles produce a seamless garment, and the front of the work always faces you making patterns somewhat easier to follow. Circular needles are used from the beginning when knitting a garment, but a set of double-pointed needles are more useful when picking up stitches such as when knitting necklines and fingers for gloves. Two circular needles can also be used for flat knitting on very large-sized items.

Using a circular needle

This is a flexible nylon tube which has two pointed metal ends which are traditionally sized. You cast on stitches in the usual way and then knit into the first stitch to make a continuous round. You should always mark the beginning of a new row. Remember, the outside of the work will always face you, so that when knitting stockinette stitch, you simply knit every row.

Using three or more needles

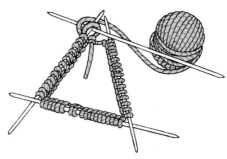

Sets of double-pointed needles are sold in the traditional sizes. As many as six needles can be used if the area is large. When knitting with double-pointed needles, the stitches are divided among all but one of the needles which is used to knit off, so that each needle in turn holds stitches and then is used to knit off.

To knit, divide your stitches among the needles and knit a round. To close the circle, knit the first stitch with the working yarn from the last stitch. Keep your last and first needle as close together as possible. Make sure your first knitted stitch (you should mark this) is close to the last needle so that no gap forms in the knitting.

Continue to work around in this way, using your empty needles to knit off and keeping the stitches evenly divided. Hold the two working needles as usual, and drop the others to the back of the work when not in use.

Cables

Special, small, double-pointed needles of varying shapes are used to produce the individual patterns called "cables". These are created when stitches are moved out of position so that plaited rope-like twists form in the knitting. Such a needle is necessary to hold stitches to the front or back of the work as required in a pattern.

Use the cable needle to form twists in the knitting. Stitches held at the front will twist the cable from right to left when knitted off; stitches held at the back will twist the cable from left to right when knitted off.

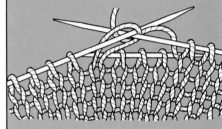

Cabling
In the illustration of a six stitch cable, the first three stitches are slipped onto a cable needle and held at the back of the work. The next three stitches are knitted from the left-hand needle followed by knitting the three stitches from the cable needle. This produced a cable twist from left to right.

A simple cable pattern with a central panel of 12 sts is worked as follows:
Rows 1, 3, 5 and 7 K2, p8, k2.
Row 2 P2, sl next 2 sts to cn and hold at front, k2, then k2 from cn; sl next 2 sts to cn and hold at back, k2, then k2 from cn; p2.
Rows 4, 6 and 8 P2, k8, p2.
Repeat rows 1 to 8.

Bobbles

These patterns involve repeatedly increasing into a single stitch to form a cluster. Different patterns produce different effects ranging from fat bobbles to a slightly raised embossed look. After the increasing has been worked, the cluster is decreased and all but one stitch discarded.

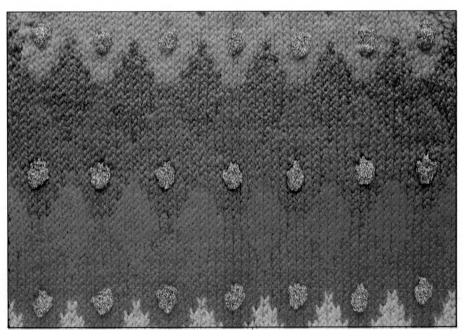

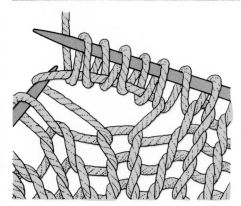

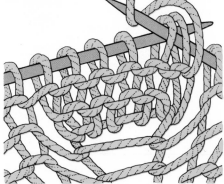

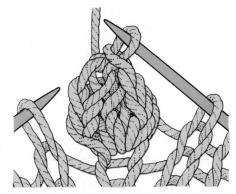

You can make a simple bobble over five rows by following the accompanying instructions.

Row 1 Knit two, take the yarn forward to the front of the work and over the needle. Knit one but do not discard the stitch. Instead, continue working into the stitch twice more. In a knitting pattern this would read:
*K2, yfwd, k1; rep from * twice more.

Row 2 Turn the work. Slip the first stitch purlwise onto your right-hand needle and purl five stitches.
Turn. Sl 1 pwise, p5.

Row 3 Turn the work. Slip the first stitch knitwise onto your right-hand needle and knit five stitches.
Turn. Sl 1 kwise, k5.

Row 4 Turn. Purl two stitches together three times.
Turn. P2tog 3 times.

Row 5 Turn. Slip one stitch knitwise, knit two stitches together, pass the slipped stitch over. One stitch remains on the needle.
Turn. Sl 1 kwise, k2tog, psso. 1 st rem.

ADDING NEW YARNS OR COLORS

Adding yarn in the middle of a row

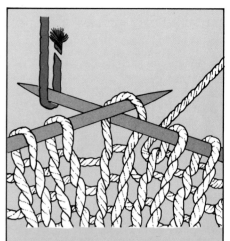

1 Insert your right-hand needle through the first stitch on your left-hand needle. Wrap the new yarn over, and knit (or purl) the stitch with the new yarn. Leave the old yarn at the back of the work.

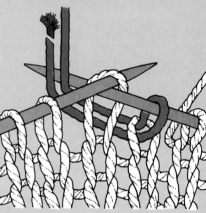

2 Knit (or purl) the next two stitches using the double length of the new yarn.

3 Discard the short end of the new yarn and continue to knit as usual. On the following row, treat the two double stitches as single stitches.

Join in a new ball of yarn or another color at the beginning of a row, if possible. With a new ball of yarn, the ends of both the old and new yarn are darned in neatly into the edge or the back of the work.

When working with additional colors, the yarn can either be broken off and darned in, or carried up the side of the work until it is needed.

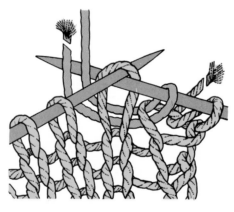

2 Leaving the old yarn at the back, knit (or purl) the next two stitches using the double length of the new yarn.

Adding yarn at the beginning of a row

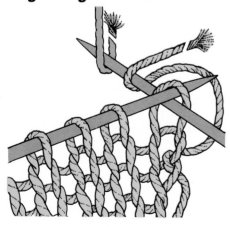

1 Insert your right-hand needle through the first stitch on your left-hand needle and wrap the old, and then the new yarn over it. Knit (or purl) the stitch using both yarns.

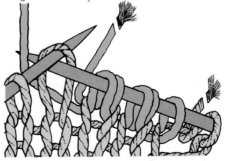

3 Discard the short end of the new yarn and continue to knit as usual. On the following row, treat the three double stitches as single stitches.

WORKING WITH MORE THAN ONE YARN

When knitting with more than one yarn, you will find it necessary to adopt various techniques to keep the back of the work neat and to prevent holes from appearing. There are three basic methods: stranding, weaving and crossing. Stranding and weaving yarns produces a thicker fabric.

Stranding yarn

Use this method for working narrow stripes, small repeats of color, and Fair-Isle and other patterns requiring only two colors in a row. Strand yarn over two to five stitches only.

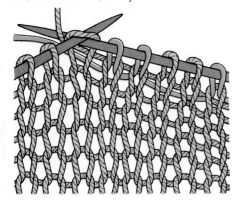

In a knit row
With both yarns at the back of the work, knit the required number of stitches with yarn A (in this case two), and then drop it to the back. Pick up yarn B and knit the required number of stitches and then drop it to the back. Both yarns should be stranded loosely along the back of the work.

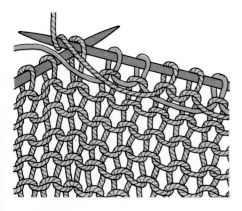

In a purl row
With both yarns at the front of the work, purl the required number of stitches with yarn A (in this case two), and then drop it. Pick up yarn B and purl the required number of stitches and then drop it. Both yarns should be stranded loosely along the front (side facing you).

Weaving yarn

Use this method for working large pattern repeats, for patterns requiring three or more colors, and when yarn has to be carried over more than five stitches.

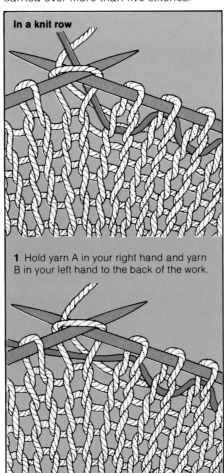

In a knit row

1 Hold yarn A in your right hand and yarn B in your left hand to the back of the work.

2 Knit one stitch with yarn A and, at the same time, bring yarn B below yarn A. When yarn B is being used, weave yarn A as above.

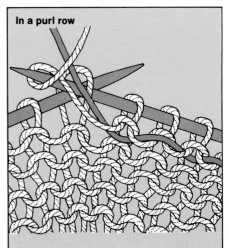

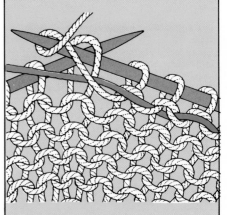

In a purl row

1 Hold yarn A in your right hand and yarn B in your left hand to the front of the work.

2 Purl one stitch with yarn A but this time bring yarn B below yarn A. When yarn B is being used, weave yarn A as above.

Checking your technique

To prevent the different yarns getting tangled, the strands must be caught up in the back of the work, but not so as they interfere with the pattern or produce undesired effects.

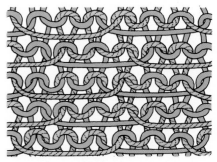

If you have worked weaving correctly, the yarns will cross evenly and remain at the same depth. A "smocking" effect means that you have pulled the yarns too tightly. It is better for the yarns to be woven too loosely than too tightly.

If you have worked stranding correctly, the yarns will be running evenly across the back of the work at the same tension as the knitting. Puckering indicates that you have pulled the yarns too tightly.

Crossing colors

Use this method for working large blocks of color, e.g., diagonal or wide vertical stripes or jacquard motifs. Each color is kept as a separate ball or on a bobbin and is not taken across the work. Rather, the yarns are crossed at a join. Follow the method below for vertical color patterns, but cross the colors on every row.

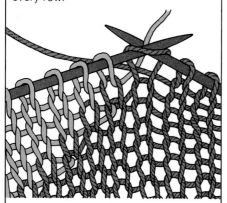

In a knit row for a diagonal stripe to the right
Cross yarn A in front of yarn B and drop it to the back. Knit the first stitch on your left-hand needle using yarn B. On the return row the yarns will automatically loop together.

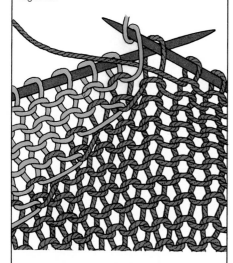

In a purl row for a diagonal stripe to the left
Pick up yarn B in front of yarn A and use it to purl the next stitch on your left-hand needle. On the return row, the yarns will automatically loop together.

Winding bobbins

To help keep different yarns separate when working complicated color patterns, wind manageable lengths onto bobbins, yarn holders or spools. Replenish as necessary. Or, keep yarns in individual plastic bags secured at the "neck" with an elastic band.

PATTERN CHARTS

While most patterns are written out, those that involve complicated shaping, and almost all color patterns are reproduced in chart form. Charts are extremely effective in conveying the shape and coloration of a garment.

Colorwork charts

In these charts each square represents an individual stitch and each line a row or round of knitting. Each color has its own symbol or shading which is contained within the individual squares. The chart will be accompanied by a key that explains the symbols or colors used.

It is essential that you adhere to the correct multiple of stitches in a color pattern. This will usually be delineated by additional lines on the grid. It is often possible to adjust the edges without affecting the pattern repeat if you must change the size.

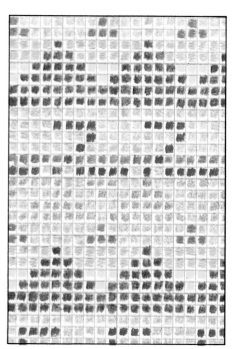

Stitch charts

In these charts, each square represents an individual stitch and each line a row or round of knitting. Each pattern instruction has a different symbol which is contained within the individual squares. The pattern will be accompanied by a key that explains the symbols used.

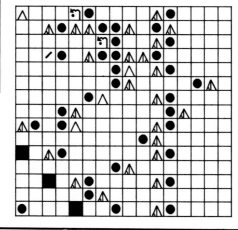

☐	**Knit stitch**
■	**Purl stitch**
◁	**K2tog**
●	**Yarn over**
●●	**YO2**
╱	**K1-b**
⌐	**Sl 1, k1, psso**
◮	**P2tog**
◭	**P3tog**

Stitch and colorwork charts

Modern designers today tend to chart out both stitch and color patterns on grids, as they are extremely easy to follow. In such a case each square would be colored and contain a stitch instruction.

Reading charts

All charts, whether of color or stitch pattern or both, are read from the bottom of the chart upwards and from right to left on the first and all odd-numbered rows and from left to right on the second and all even-numbered rows. Therefore, the bottom right-hand corner indicates the first stitch.

When knitting in the round, however, the front of the fabric always faces you so the work is always read from right to left.

EDGES

The sides of a piece of knitting are also known as the selvages. Special care must be taken to ensure that these are kept straight.

Stockinette stitch edge

This is the most common edge and the first and last stitches must be firmly made. All knit row stitches are knitted and all purl row stitches are purled.

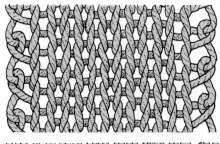

Open edge

To produce this more decorative edge slip the first and last stitches of every knit row knitwise. Purl all the edge stitches in the purl row.

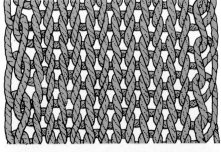

Slip stitch edge

This is especially useful as a neat edge on cardigans. "Pips" are formed in a regular sequence which look neat and make row counting easier – each "pip" counts for two rows. Slip the first stitch of each row knitwise then knit the last stitch of each row.

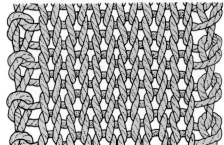

To make buttons out of yarn

Wrap your main yarn around your forefinger approximately six times. Slip the loops off and hold them firmly. Wrap the yarn around the center three times making a bow shape. Fold in half and continue wrapping yarn around to make a small ball – it should fit neatly in the buttonhole. Test for size. To hold the button together, snap off the end of the yarn, leaving about 40cm. Thread this into a darning needle and sew into the button securing the wrapped-around yarn. Sew the button onto the garment.

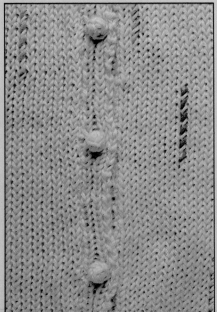

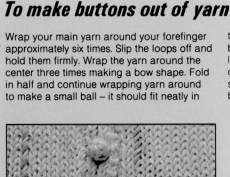

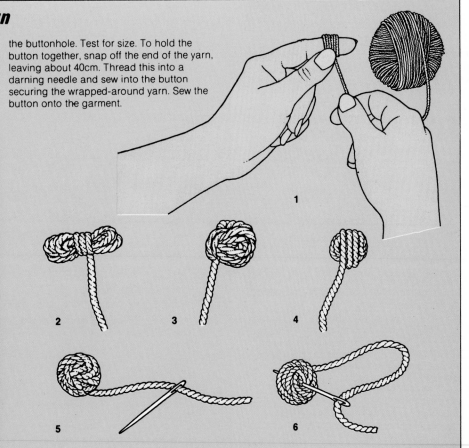

BUTTONHOLES

Horizontal buttonhole

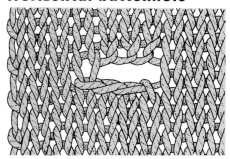

A horizontal buttonhole is the most useful for sweaters, cardigans and jackets. Calculate the position of all the buttonholes before beginning to knit. It is a good idea to knit up a sample buttonhole in order to check it for fit with your chosen buttons.

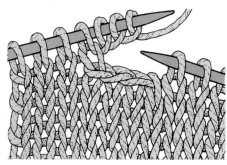

To make the buttonhole, knit up to the marked position (about three to four stitches in from the main fabric or buttonband), and bind off two or more stitches according to the size of the button. Continue in pattern to the end of the row.

On the following row work up to the bound-off stitches and replace them by casting on the same number of new stitches. Complete the row in pattern.

Eyelet buttonholes

If you are using small buttons or are making fastenings for baby clothes, an eyelet buttonhole is preferable. Eyelets can also be used as slotting for ribbons. An open eyelet is useful for tiny buttons while the bold eyelet can take bigger ones.

Open eyelet

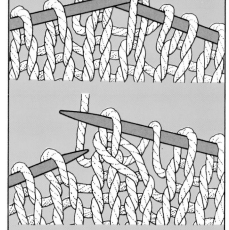

K2, yfwd, sl the next kwise onto your right-hand needle, k1, psso. The yfwd increase replaces the stitch which was decreased by slipping.

Bold eyelet

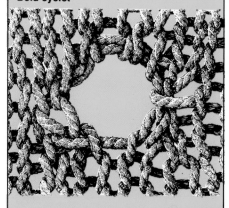

Row 1 K3, k2tog, yfwd2, sl 1, k1, psso, k3.
Row 2 P3, p2tog (one st is first yo), k2tog (one st is second yo), p3.
Row 3 K4, yfwd2, k to end.
Row 4 P3, p2tog (one st is first yo) and at the same time through the strand below, k1, p1 into second yo and at the same time knit and purl through strand below. Purl to the end of the row.

Buttonstand

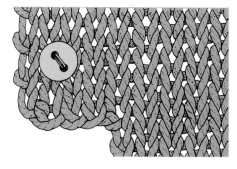

Sometimes when the knitting divides to form the opening of a garment, you will have to knit in an extra piece of fabric, a buttonstand, in order to hold a button.

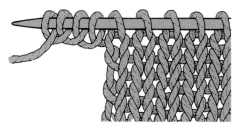

To do this, cast on an extra number of stitches at the end of a row (in this case four), and work these stitches until the fabric is large enough to support your button. Bind off the extra stitches.

Buttonbands

Patterns often call for buttonbands which can either be knitted in two separate pieces or in one long piece which goes right around the front openings and neck. They can be knitted to match the garment's color or in contrasting shades and should be worked in either Garter or Moss stitch which give a flatter surface.

If you are knitting your buttonbands in two parts (one to hold the buttons and one in which to place the buttonholes), knit them together using separate balls of yarn as this will ensure an equal length. When you work the buttonhole on one band, you can mark the button's position on the other.

You will have to sew the buttonband onto the finished garment when making up at the end.

DECORATING KNITTING

In addition to fancy stitch and color patterns, garments can be decorated by the addition of beads and sequins and/or embroidery. Usually, beads are knitted into the garment while it is being produced, but occasionally you may wish to sew them on afterwards, as you do with embroidery.

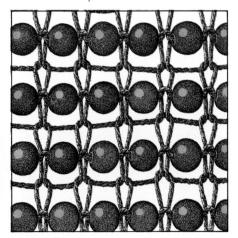

Beading

If you so wish, you can make an entire fabric of beading, or you can add beads to form motifs. A beaded fabric is naturally more solid. Beaded motifs should be charted out as part of the pattern; the beads are introduced when the appropriate pattern place is reached.

Beads are usually added on the second and every alternate row, but not on the first or last stitch. If you add them every row or at the ends, the knitting is likely to curl. Beads should be introduced from the back of the fabric.

If you are making an all-over pattern, use Garter stitch throughout. For a neater edge, start adding the beads about two or three stitches in.

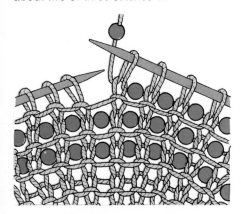

Slip a bead up to the front of the work, close to the stitch just knitted. Knit the next stitch then add another bead. The beads should sit firmly to the front of the work.

When working beaded motifs, add the beads on alternate rows as before, and before and after a stitch. Work all other stitches in pattern.

Choosing beads

You can knit with many different types of beads and sequins but bear in mind that they can put substantial strain on the fabric of the knitting and weigh it down considerably. Make sure your knitting yarn is strong enough to carry the weight of the beads, but thin enough so that you can thread it through the beads. Sequins must have a hole in the side, not in the center. As a guideline, use knitting yarn with wooden beads and large sequins and thinner cotton with small beads. Use small knitting needles to prevent large loops forming; the beads can slip through these to the back.

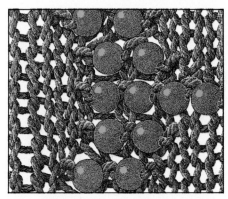

Threading beads

Beads and sequins have to be added to your yarn before you begin knitting. They occasionally come strung on lengths of string and you can thread them onto your knitting yarn using the simple method shown below. Where beads and sequins come separately, you must pick up and thread each one individually.

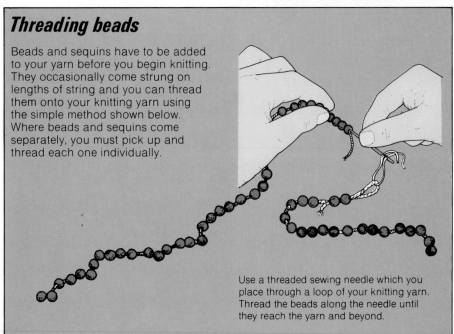

Use a threaded sewing needle which you place through a loop of your knitting yarn. Thread the beads along the needle until they reach the yarn and beyond.

Buttons and Trimmings

A strong decorative element can be added to handknits by the careful choice of buttons and trimmings. Metal, bone, wood and plastic buttons look best on day-time sweaters while evening tops are complemented by pearlized, glass, silvered or sparkling fastenings. Buttons can also be used along with beads, sequins and spangles in figurative or abstract motifs with or without embroidery, and threaded ribbon can accentuate openwork patterns or be used as ties. Feathers look best lightly stitched on to knitting and anchored with colored beads.

EMBROIDERY

Embroidery is used to enrich a knitting design and add not only color, but texture to a garment. Make sure you always use a blunt-ended wool or tapestry needle to avoid splitting the yarn and keep your tension the same as the knitting. The most common techniques are duplicate stitch and Cross stitch, but individual stitches can also be worked to create motifs.

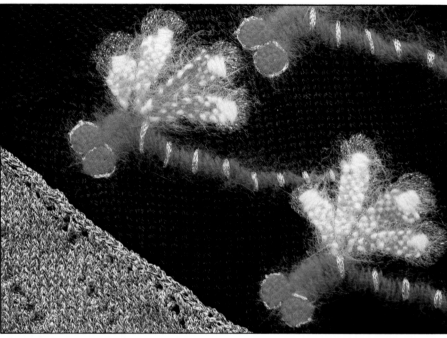

Duplicate stitch

This technique imitates knitting. It works up quickly and produces a slightly raised design as it covers, or duplicates, the knitted stitch. It can be used to add stripes and motifs as well as letters.

Working horizontally

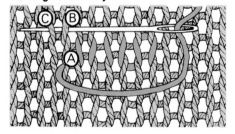

1 Secure the embroidery yarn at the back of the work and bring your needle out to the front of the work at A. Insert the needle at B, under the base of the stitch above, and bring it out at C.

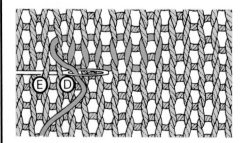

2 Insert the needle at D and emerge at E ready to embroider the next stitch.

Working vertically

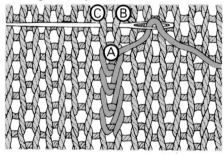

1 Secure the embroidery yarn at the back of the work and bring your needle out to the front of the work at A. Insert the needle at B, bringing it out at C.

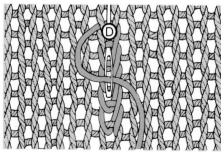

2 Take the needle under the head of the stitch below and emerge above it at D, ready to form the next stitch.

Cross stitch

This is worked in a similar way as with any woven fabric but care must be taken not to draw the stitches too tightly or the garment will be pulled out of shape.

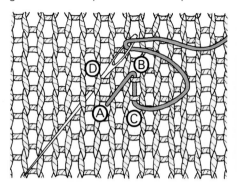

1 Secure the yarn at the back of the work and bring your needle out at A. Make a diagonal from A to B and bring your needle out at C. Insert at D.

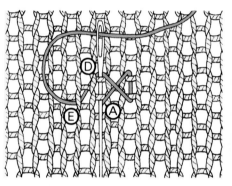

2 For the second cross, bring your needle out at E, insert again at D and re-insert at A.

Working in rows

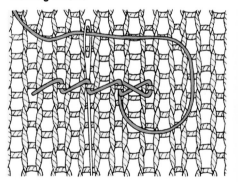

Work one row of diagonals. On the return journey, cross these with a second row.

Filling-in stitch

1 Work satin stitches to and fro across the area to be filled in and pick up a small amount of the surface yarn to anchor the stitches.

2 Then work backwards and fill in any remaining spaces.

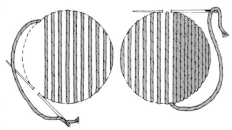

Chain stitch

Loop the working thread under the tip of your needle and hold it down with your left thumb while you pick up some of the ground fabric in each stitch. The needle is inserted into the same hole from which it has emerged.

To make a leaf shape, bring out your needle and insert it into the same spot bringing it out with a loop under the needle. Take it over the loop so that you make a small tying stitch to anchor it.

Back stitch

Work in small, even stitches by first making a stitch forwards and then a stitch backwards.

French knot

Twist the yarn two or three times around your needle and insert the needle back into the hole where it first emerged.

Stem stitch

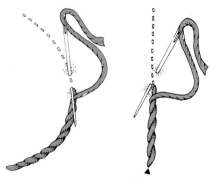

Work the stitch with the thread kept on the same side of the needle. For a wider effect, insert the needle into the ground fabric at a slight angle. The greater the angle, the wider the effect.

Attaching beads and sequins

Thread your beads onto the yarn and insert your needle through the same hole from which it just emerged. Make a stitch slightly longer than the bead. Pull the yarn firmly and repeat over the motif.

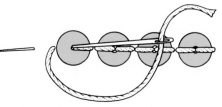

For sequins, bring your needle through the middle of the sequin. Work a back stitch over the right side, bring your needle out to the far left, ready to thread on another sequin.

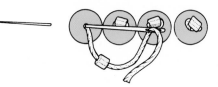

If you want to top a sequin with a bead, thread both onto your yarn then insert the needle through the middle of the sequin and draw through a short distance from the hole. Pull firmly and repeat for the next sequin.

SEAMS

Your pattern will usually set out the order of seaming; normally the shoulder seams are joined first if you have to pick up stitches to make the neckband. There is a choice of two methods, the edge-to-edge seam and the backstitch seam.

Edge-to-edge seam

Useful on lightweight knits, this seam is almost invisible and forms no ridge.

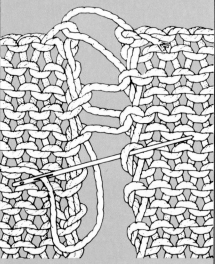

Place the pieces to be joined edge-to-edge with the "heads" of the knit stitches locking together. Match the pattern pieces carefully row for row and stitch for stitch. Using the main yarn, sew into the head of each stitch alternately.

Backstitch seam

A stronger and firmer seam, this is suitable for all garments but forms a ridge.

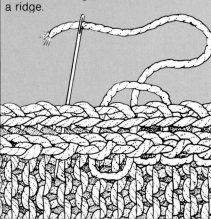

Place the pieces to be joined together with their right sides facing. Carefully match pattern to pattern, row to row and stitch to stitch. Work a back stitch (as in sewing) along the seam, sewing into the center of each stitch to correspond with the stitch on the opposite piece. Sew $\frac{1}{4}$in from the edge of the knitting.

CROCHET

Occasionally, the finishing of some garments calls for the use of crochet stitches, as in collars, for instance. The stitches illustrated below are the most useful.

Chains (ch)

1 Make a slip loop (see p. 110). Thread your yarn in your left hand and hold the crochet hook with the slip loop in the right hand. Twist the hook first under and then over the yarn to make a loop.

2 Draw the hook with the yarn on it through the slip loop to form a chain.

Making a crochet buttonhole

Work from the side edge to the buttonhole position (about 3 or 4 stitches in). Make two or more chains, depending on the size of your button. Miss the same number of stitches in the row below.

Re-insert your hook and work in pattern to the end of the row. On the following row, work in pattern over the chains.

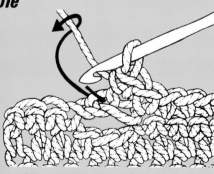

Single crochet (sc)

1 Make a chain row. Insert your hook into the second chain from the hook. Bring your yarn round and draw one loop through (two loops on hook).

2 Bring your yarn round again and draw yarn through both loops on your hook.

3 Continue to end, working single crochets into the next and following chains to end.

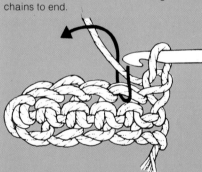

4 Make a chain and turn. Insert your hook through the first stitch in the row below.

Double crochet (dc)

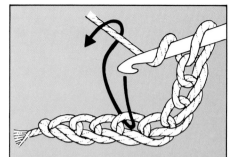

1 Make a chain row. Bring your yarn round and insert your hook into the fifth chain from the hook. Bring your yarn round again and draw one loop through (three loops on hook).

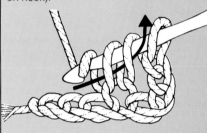

2 Bring your yarn round and draw through the first two loops on the hook (two loops on hook).

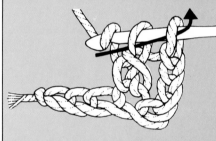

3 Bring your yarn round and draw through two loops making one double crochet.

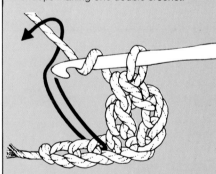

4 Continue to the end then make three chains; turn. Make first double crochet into the second stitch of the row below.

Finishing off

Complete your final stitch and cut your yarn about 6in from the end of the work. Pull the yarn through the last loop and tighten. Thread the yarn into a needle and darn the end into the back of the work.

FINISHING TECHNIQUES

Before pattern pieces are joined up, they are usually blocked and pressed to ensure a good fit. It's always a good idea to check the yarn band for any special instructions. The pieces are blocked when dry and are pressed with a damp cloth.

Blocking

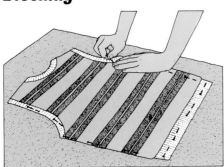

Garment pieces need blocking, or putting into shape, before they can be joined up. Cover a table with a folded blanket and a sheet. Using rustless pins, block the pieces wrong side out to the correct measurements. Be careful not to stretch or distort the fabric and make sure that any rows run in straight lines.

Pressing

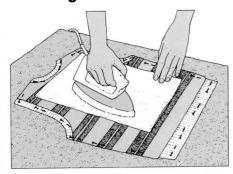

After blocking, the garment pieces are usually pressed in position. Use a warm iron and a damp cloth on wool. Lay the iron on the fabric and lift up, do not move it over the surface. Do not remove any of the pins until the piece has cooled and dried completely.

Raised and embossed patterns should be pressed under a damp cloth, but remove the pins and adjust the fabric while it is still hot to avoid the patterns being flattened.

Ribbing should be lightly stretched and pinned before ironing. Use a heavy cloth and remove the pins in order to adjust the fabric while it is still warm.

Washing knitwear

Always use a mild soap, preferably one especially designed for knitwear, and warm water. Before washing a brightly-colored garment, check that it is color-fast by dipping a small piece of it into the soapy water. Press it out in a white cloth. If it leaves a stain, wash in cold water.

1 Always squeeze the suds into the garment gently and do not rub or felting will occur. Don't leave the garment to soak, but rinse and remove quickly. Make certain the rinse water is clear before removing the garment. You can add fabric softener to the last rinse if you wish.

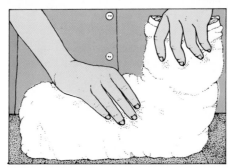

2 Place the garment in a thick turkish towel, white if possible, and roll both up. You can place extra towels on top of the garment for extra absorption if you like before rolling up. Press the roll with your hands or "hammer" it with your fists to remove as much water as possible. You can repeat this with another towel if the garment is still very wet, or to facilitate drying.

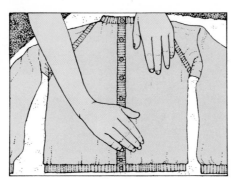

3 Finish drying the garment by laying it out flat on another clean towel, away from direct heat. Make sure the knitting is correctly shaped. Use a soft brush to restore the surface once the garment is dry. Store the garment in a drawer; never hang it up as it can be easily pulled out of shape.

Re-using yarn

If you are unpicking a made-up garment, undo the seams first and then locate the last bound-off stitch. Start here to unravel the knitting, winding it around the back of a chair to keep the yarn from getting tangled or stretched, and to facilitate washing. Fasten the hank at two ends; catch the end of the yarn in one of the ties. Hand wash then rewind yarn into loose balls when dry.

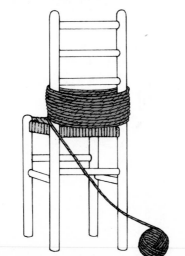

DESIGN POSSIBILITIES
Altering the pattern stitch

When you change from one stitch to another, say a lacy stitch from Seed stitch, you must make sure that the multiple of stitches called for in the patterns match. For instance, if your pattern calls for a multiple of 8 stitches you can use alternative patterns that consist of multiples of 8, 4 and 2. Therefore, you may be able to work with repeats over 8, 16, 24 or 32 stitches, depending on the width of your garment and the number of stitches required.

It is imperative that you make a new tension sample if you change a stitch, so that you end up with an identical size.

Altering the yarn

NEEDLE AND YARN TABLE	
Size	**Yarn type**
2mm no 0 no 1	Fine-weight yarn 2-ply, 3-ply, baby yarn
no 1 no 2 no 3	Medium-weight yarn 4-ply, baby quick-knits
no 3 no 4 no 5 no 6	knitting worsted
no 7 no 8 no 9	thick knitting worsted
no 8 no 9 no 10	bulky yarn, mohair
no 10½ no 11 no 13	heavyweight yarns

If you decide to change the type of yarn from the one specified, you should check that it falls into the same category (see pp. 133–40). Always knit up a tension sample before beginning work. The accompanying table will give you some idea of what needles work best with different weights of yarn.

Changing the size

While most printed patterns come in more than one size, you will occasionally find that you have to adapt a pattern to specific requirements. Here again, a tension sample is vital. Before you begin knitting make a note of the measurements that need changing and adjust the length, width and shaping to match.

If you have to add to the width and length of a sweater, calculate the number of extra stitches needed from your tension sample, add half to the front and half to the back and increase the number of rows until you get to the armhole shaping. Adjust the length and shaping of the sleeves to match. For instance, if you have to add 4in to the width and 6in to the length of a garment and the stitch gauge is 10 stitches and 8 rows to 1in, cast on 20 additional stitches to both front and back and work 48 rows more on both. Add additional stitches to the sleeves adjusting the shaping to match the added length and width.

Designing with a grid

Begin designing with a simple pattern in fairly straight shapes. Draw it out on a piece of paper, making sure you've allowed an excess to the body measurements for a comfortable fit. If possible, make the pattern lifesize. Then transform your pattern for knitting purposes using a grid which relates to your tension sample.

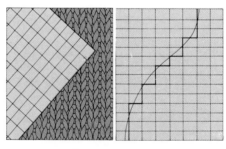

Knit up the sample first using the chosen stitch pattern and calculate the number of stitches and rows to a desired measurement. Draw on a large sheet of tracing paper a grid to match the size of your tension stitch (this is usually rectangular). Therefore, if you have 10 stitches and 8 rows to 1in, your grid will contain rectangular "boxes" 10 across and 8 deep.

Place your drawn pattern under the tracing grid and trace off the outline, stepping curves to match the grid lines. You will now be able to tell from the grid exactly how many stitches you will need to cast on and where you have to increase and decrease.

Abbreviations

alt	alternate
beg	beginning
dec	decrease
dc	double crochet
foll	following
Garter st	knit or purl every row
g	gram
inc	increase
inc 1	work into the front and back of stitch
k	knit
k2tog	knit two stitches together
kwise	knitwise
m1	make one (by picking up the loop between the needles and working into the back of it)
Moss st	k1, p1 to end; next row p1, k1 to end
( )	repeat all the material between parentheses as many times as indicated
oz	ounce
psso	pass slip stitch over
patt	pattern
p	purl
pwise	purlwise
rem	remaining
rep	repeat
rep from *	repeat all the instructions that follow *
sc	single crochet
sl	slip
ssk	slip, slip, knit. Slip the first and second stitches knitwise one at a time, then insert the tip of the left-hand needle into the fronts of these two sts from the left and knit them together from this position
st st	stockinette stitch
tbl	through back of loop
tog	together
turn	turn the work around at the point indicated, before the end of a row
up 1	pick up top of stitch below the next one to be worked and work into it to increase
yfwd	yarn forward
yo	yarn over needle
yrn	yarn round needle

Yarn fibers

A variety of materials is available to the hand knitter. The natural yarns, especially wool and cotton tend to be more expensive than synthetic yarns but many designers prefer their wearability. The tendency today is for yarns to contain more than one fiber: synthetics are added for their strength, elasticity and shape-retention properties; silk and rayon add sheen.

Natural fibers

Wool is a pure animal fiber, most commonly available from sheep. It is the classic knitting yarn and most manufacturers produce a wide array of different yarns in it, both in blends of individual breeds and from animals of one breed such as Shetland. Other animals also supply us with wool: *mohair*, an extremely warm, fluffy yarn is made from the long silky wool of the Anatolian goat (pure mohair); cashmere comes from the Kashmir goat; *angora* comes from Angora rabbits; luxury yarns such as camel hair, vicuña and alpaca are also available in limited quantities.

All wool is a very good insulator, keeping you warm when it is wet, due to its curling, twisted fibers. It is extremely elastic and supple and crease resistant. "Superwash" wool can be washed in a machine; otherwise dry cleaning or hand-washing is required to keep it from felting and shrinking.

Silk, produced from certain worms, has a shiny, lustrous finish and is often combined with wool to produce a luxury look.

Cotton, harvested from a plant, is a fresh, cool, comfortable and hardwearing fiber which is highly absorbent. It is sometimes mixed with **linen,** a product of the flax family.

Synthetic fibers

Manufacturers offer many chemically-produced yarns which are easy care and non-allergic. They are made in the same weights as wool and are easily substituted. Usually a yarn is made up of more than one synthetic fiber. **Acrylic** is the most widely-used synthetic due to its lightness and excellent washing properties. It gives strength to wool and by itself is a good insulator and is easy to dye. It never shrinks or felts. **Nylon/polyamide** is an extremely hard-wearing and crease-resisting fiber which is very easy to care for and dries quickly. **Viscose** is a slightly shiny yarn which is rather heavy and helps garments hold their shape. It is non-felting.

Yarn construction

Fibers are spun in different ways to produce varying textures. They are first made into single threads, called *plys*, and then the plys are evenly combined to form classic textured yarns. A *4-ply* yarn contains four separate strands; a 3-ply yarn contains three. Ply does not indicate thickness since individual plied yarns can vary quite a bit, depending on the thickness of the separate strands.

Special ways of combining strands result in novelty finishes such as *crepe*, where the yarns are "locked" together, resulting in a firm elastic twist; *boucle*, where one or more of the strands is wound loosely about the others to produce a loopy, raised texture, and *chenille*, where tightly wrapped strands are cut to produce a velvet-like finish. Some yarns, *meche* or *roving*, are not plied but are spun and pulled together.

Calculating yarn quantities

Yarns are sold according to weight, not length. How much you get out of a ball depends upon a great many factors including the fiber content: synthetics normally go further than wool; the fiber texture: fluffy, finer yarns go further than heavy-weight ones; the fiber construction: looser twist yarns go further than tightly twisted ones; your tension: a loose tension can mean a saving of up to two balls; and the stitch pattern you are using: any variation from stockinette stitch will mean a change in the manufacturer's given length. As a rough guide, the chart below sets out approximate amounts of yarn for a long-sleeved pullover using different weight yarns, and the same weight yarn of differing fiber content.

Yarn weight	number of 2oz balls
Medium-weight	6–7
Knitting worsted	8–10
Thick knitting worsted	10–12
Aran	12
Bulky	14

Yarn fiber	number of 2oz balls
Acrylic 80%; nylon 20%	7
Acrylic 75%; wool 25%	8
Wool 70%; mohair 30%	8
Wool 50%; Aran 50%	9
Shetland 100%	9
(Tight twist)	11
Cotton	12

The best way to determine how much you need of a certain type of yarn is to knit up a ball in a medium color, in the chosen stitch pattern. Compare the size of the sample to your pattern. Say a 10oz ball knits up to a swatch 8×8in (the area is 64in). You then have to calculate the approximate area of each garment section, add these figures together and divide by the area of the swatch. The resulting figure is the number of balls of the chosen weight that you require.

Substituting yarns

The sweater patterns in this book are non-specific as to brand of yarn. This is, in part, because individual yarns have short life-spans, but also because the designers believe that knitters should be able to use and experiment with different yarns. In all cases, you should compare your chosen yarns with the table on page 140 which sets out the tension for different weight yarns with specific needle sizes. Compare the information on your yarn band with the chart, and with the pattern. Remember, the proper tension can often be achieved if you alter the needle size (see page 113). It is a good idea, in any event, to knit up a swatch beforehand to see if tension and texture are satisfactory.

When substituting cotton, linen or metallics for wool, you will have to add additional stitches for proper fit as these yarns have less elasticity. Yarns that are "interchangeable" may be of the same or different textures, but it's always safest to knit up a sample first.

Knitting tips

* Always buy sufficient quantity of the same dye lot. If you run out, don't continue a piece (i.e. a sleeve) with the new dye lot but knit it *from the beginning* with the new yarn. A change in the dye lot on Fair-Isles and 2-color patterns is less noticeable.

* Knit to the recommended tension. If you knit too loosely the stitches will rub against each other causing pilling; if you knit too tightly the garment will be stiff and unpleasant to wear.

* To keep your knitting even when using several yarns, make certain the yarns are of the same weight (i.e. two or more bulkys, Shetlands, or mohairs, etc.). If necessary, use double or triple amounts of thin yarns.

* Occasionally, if you're winding lurex around another yarn, you may have to change the needle size to preserve tension (the extra strand affects the number of plys).

* When buying a lurex or glitter-type yarn, make sure it has a polyester base as other materials will tarnish or the shine will wear off.

* Cotton has a tendency to "shift" while it is being knitted. To correct this when working stockinette stitch, change the needle size on the purl row.

Classic Yarns

Classic yarns are the most enduring and popular yarns as their simple construction and wide color range make them the most versatile. Previously most often found as wool, price and convenience considerations account for the growing numbers of synthetic yarns being marketed today. Generally of a single shade and 4-ply construction, they are also found as tweeds and variegated mixes sometimes of more than one fiber.

For the purposes of the patterns in this book, as well as for more general knitting, the yarns are classified as fine-weight, medium-weight, knitting worsted, thick knitting worsted and bulky. Not all the yarns listed as bulky on these pages are "classic" ones, but they serve to highlight the differences in weight found in this range. A list of manufacturers who produce classic yarns similar to the ones shown is on page 141.

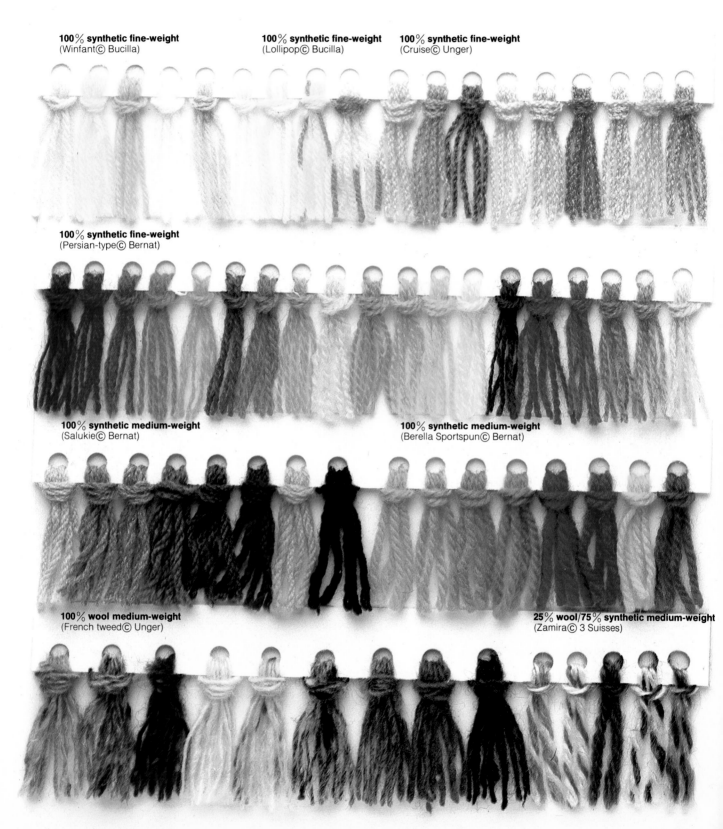

100% synthetic fine-weight
(Winfant© Bucilla)

100% synthetic fine-weight
(Lollipop© Bucilla)

100% synthetic fine-weight
(Cruise© Unger)

100% synthetic fine-weight
(Persian-type© Bernat)

100% synthetic medium-weight
(Salukie© Bernat)

100% synthetic medium-weight
(Berella Sportspun© Bernat)

100% wool medium-weight
(French tweed© Unger)

25% wool/75% synthetic medium-weight
(Zamira© 3 Suisses)

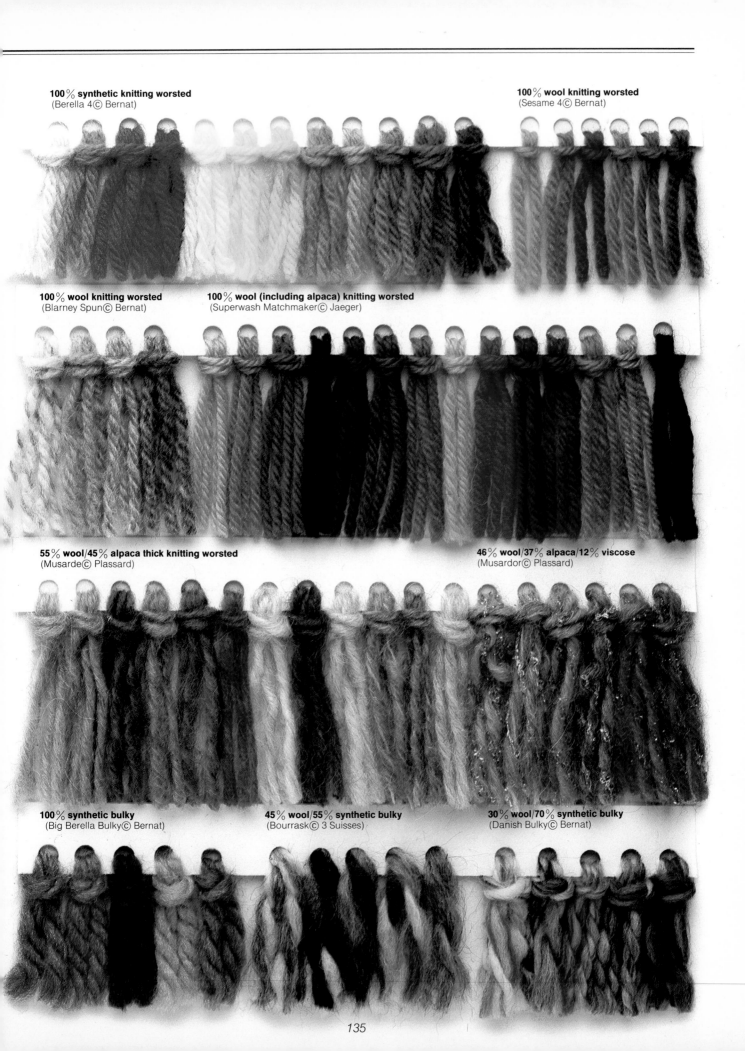

100% synthetic knitting worsted
(Berella 4© Bernat)

100% wool knitting worsted
(Sesame 4© Bernat)

100% wool knitting worsted
(Blarney Spun© Bernat)

100% wool (including alpaca) knitting worsted
(Superwash Matchmaker© Jaeger)

55% wool/45% alpaca thick knitting worsted
(Musarde© Plassard)

46% wool/37% alpaca/12% viscose
(Musardor© Plassard)

100% synthetic bulky
(Big Berella Bulky© Bernat)

45% wool/55% synthetic bulky
(Bourrask© 3 Suisses)

30% wool/70% synthetic bulky
(Danish Bulky© Bernat)

Cottons

Increased demand by handknitters for the cooler cotton yarns has encouraged manufacturers to produce a wide range. Today, cottons and cotton mixes are found in weights ranging from fine to "dish cloth".

Cotton is a practical fabric in that it is washable, and when silk is added it becomes a luxurious one as well. Often synthetics are added to improve the decorative effect or to make it more easy-care.

In addition to the "classic" types, cotton comes in various finishes including boucles, raggy-texture, uneven plys and chenille. More and more deep-dyed colors are being added to the soft pastel shades commonly found.

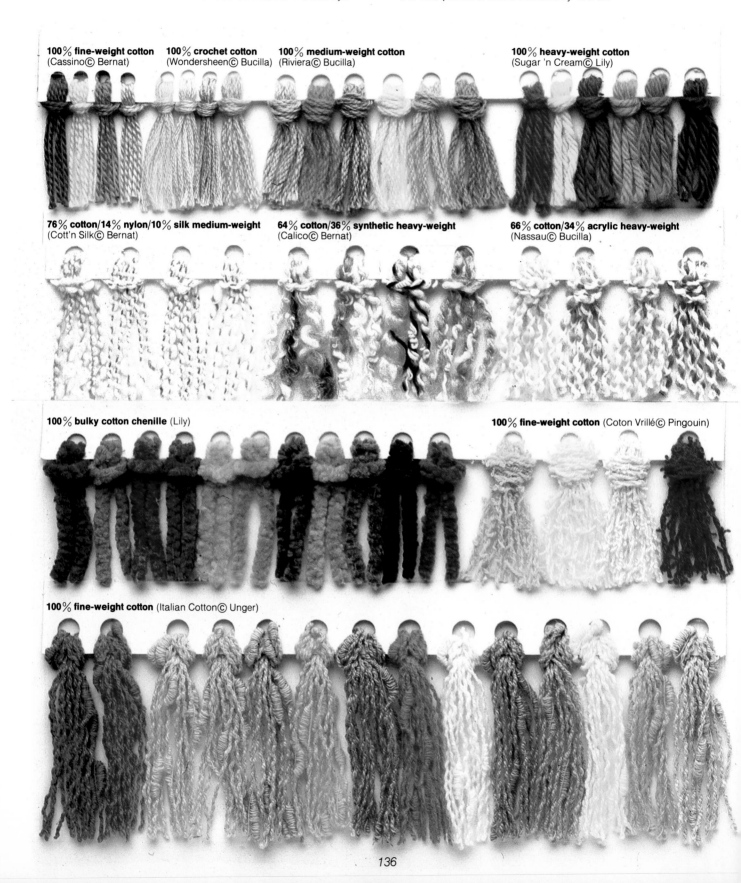

100% fine-weight cotton (Cassino© Bernat)

100% crochet cotton (Wondersheen© Bucilla)

100% medium-weight cotton (Riviera© Bucilla)

100% heavy-weight cotton (Sugar 'n Cream© Lily)

76% cotton/14% nylon/10% silk medium-weight (Cott'n Silk© Bernat)

64% cotton/36% synthetic heavy-weight (Calico© Bernat)

66% cotton/34% acrylic heavy-weight (Nassau© Bucilla)

100% bulky cotton chenille (Lily)

100% fine-weight cotton (Coton Vrillé© Pingouin)

100% fine-weight cotton (Italian Cotton© Unger)

Mohairs

Because they are very expensive, few 100% mohair yarns are produced but mohair types are among the most popular yarns so manufacturers produce yarns with the required fluffy effect but which contain very little mohair, and sometimes none at all.

Most mohair-type yarns fall within the same tension range (see p. 140) but some fine and chunky ones are available.

Extra textural interest can be achieved with boucle or mohair loop types as well as with lurex or wool-wrapped yarns.

Mohair normally improves with wear and can be brushed up to make it even more fluffy. Its qualities are best served if it is knitted in Reverse stockinette stitch or Garter stitch rather than regular stockinette stitch.

43% mohair/50% acrylic/7% wool
(Foliole© 3 Suisses)

21% mohair/79% synthetic
(Angelspun© Unger.)

15% mohair/15% wool/70% synthetic
(Cloudspun© Bernat)

14% mohair/14% wool/72% synthetic
(Cloudspun Sparkle© Bernat)

15% mohair/15% wool/70% synthetic
(Cloudspun Fleck© Bernat)

66% mohair/17% wool/17% nylon boucle
(Fifi© Bernat)

40% mohair/60% wool
(Harmonieuse© Plassard)

Novelty Yarns

Growing interest in novelty yarns, both in natural and synthetic fibers, has resulted in a plethora of usually non-interchangeable types, all producing unusual textural effects. As well as being the most varied in terms of fiber content, they also differ widely in their textural effects and can be rough, smooth, soft, hairy, nubby, looped or slubbed.

Most popular are the shiny lurex yarns, good for more dressy garments, which are also found in combination with other synthetic fibers or wool. It is important that the lurex has a polyester base otherwise it will tarnish or wear off. Previously found in gold and silver only, manufacturers now produce lurex and lurex-wrapped yarns in all the colors of the rainbow. Other sought-after knitting yarns include those of uneven plys,

raggy-textured ones and fur-type yarns which knit up quickly on large-sized needles. Also available are unplied yarns and ones incorporating boucle, chenille, crepe and tubular finishes.

Most novelty yarns pass rapidly in and out of a manufacturer's range and it can be very difficult to get hold of a particular type once a season is over. Because they are the most reliant on popular taste, they go out of date the quickest.

However, most of the patterns in this book rely on leftovers, at least, of novelty yarns and used in small amounts they can add contrast and interest to essentially simple garments made in more classic yarns. Of all the yarn types, they need the most experimentation and checking of tension since their properties are so individual.

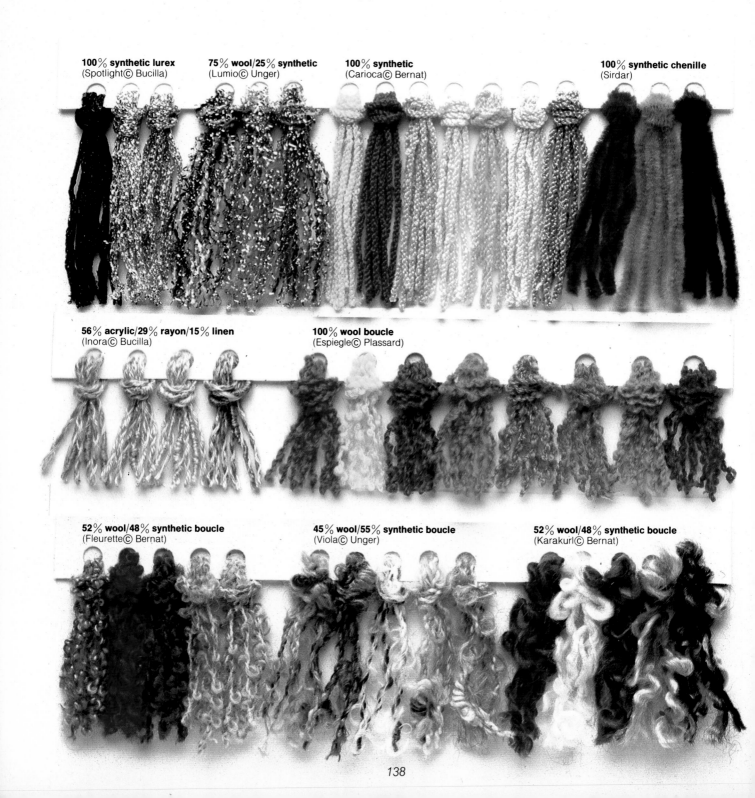

100% synthetic lurex
(Spotlight© Bucilla)

75% wool/25% synthetic
(Lumio© Unger)

100% synthetic
(Carioca© Bernat)

100% synthetic chenille
(Sirdar)

56% acrylic/29% rayon/15% linen
(Inora© Bucilla)

100% wool boucle
(Espiegle© Plassard)

52% wool/48% synthetic boucle
(Fleurette© Bernat)

45% wool/55% synthetic boucle
(Viola© Unger)

52% wool/48% synthetic boucle
(Karakurl© Bernat)

100% wool uneven spun
(Quenouille© Plassard)

100% wool uneven spun
(Prelude© Plassard)

60% alpaca/32% synthetic/8% cotton (Furriere© Bernat)

100% synthetic
(Aurora© Bucilla)

78% wool/22% acrylic
(Olympia© Unger)

66% wool/34% acrylic
(Spectrum© Unger)

37% wool/63% synthetic
(Derby© Unger)

100% wool
(Corde de Moine© Plassard)

100% wool
(Mèches Cocktail©
Plassard)

TENSIONS FOR CLASSIC YARNS

Needle size	Very fine-weight (2-ply) sts	rows	Fine-weight (3-ply) sts	rows	Medium-weight (4-ply) sts	rows	Knitting worsted sts	rows	Thick knitting worsted sts	rows
no 1	36	44	34	42						
no 2	34	42	32	40	30	38				
no 3	32	40	30	38	28	36				
no 4	30	38	28	36	26	34	23	31		
no 5	28	36	26	34	24	32	22	30		
no 6			24	32	22	30	21	28	19	25
no 7					20	28	20	26	18	23
no 8							19	24	17	21
no 9							18	22	16	19

TENSIONS FOR NOVELTY YARNS

Needle size	Mohair types sts	rows	Bulky sts	rows
no 7	17	22	16	20
no 8	15	20	14	18
no 9	13	18	12	16

Non-classic yarns, such as mohair, bulky and other novelty yarns have variable tensions which can't be standardized and must be ascertained from information on the ball band, or by knitting up a tension sample. As a guide for using mohair and bulky yarns for the patterns in this book, the above tensions are acceptable.

Above, you will find the recommended tensions for the principal classic handknitting yarns for a 4 inch square of stockinette stitch.

KNITTING NEEDLES CONVERSION CHART

U.S.	0	1	2	3	4	5	6	7	8	9	10	10½	11	13	15
Continental – mm	2¼	2¾	3	3¼	3¾	4	4½	5	5½	6	6½	7	7½	8½	9
English	13	12	11	10	9	8	7	6	5	4	3	2	1	00	000

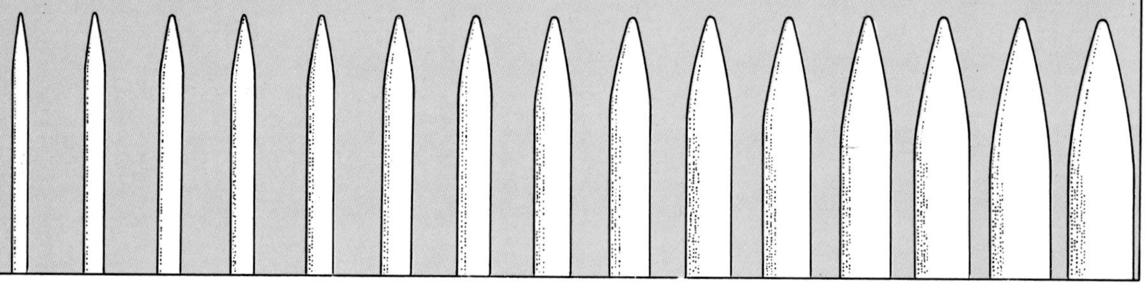

METRIC/IMPERIAL CONVERSION CHART

Please note that these conversions are approximate to the nearest ¼ inch.

cm	in	cm	in	cm	in	cm	in
1	½	11	4¼	21	8¼	31	12¼
2	¾	12	4¾	22	8¾	32	12½
3	1¼	13	5	23	9	33	13
4	1½	14	5½	24	9½	34	13½
5	2	15	6	25	9¾	35	13¾
6	2¼	16	6¼	26	10¼	36	14¼
7	2¾	17	6¾	27	10¾	37	14½
8	3¼	18	7	28	11	38	15
9	3½	19	7½	29	11½	39	15¼
10	4	20	7¾	30	11¾	40	15¾

GRAM/OUNCE CONVERSION CHART

Please note that these conversions are approximate. One ounce = approximately 28.35 grams.

grams	ounces	grams	ounces
25	1	250	8¾
50	1¾	275	9¾
75	2¾	300	10½
100	3½	325	11½
125	4½	350	12¼
150	5¼	375	13¼
175	6¼	400	14
200	7	425	15
225	8	450	15¾

Yarn Suppliers

The following manufacturers all bring out a
wide range of natural and synthetic yarns.

ANNY BLATT
24770 Crestview Ct.
Farmington Hills, Michigan
48010

AUNT LYDIA'S
Talon American
PO Box 3823
Stamford, Connecticut
06905

SUSAN BATES INC.
212 Middlesex Avenue
Chester, Connecticut
06412

BRUNSWICK YARNS
PO Box 276
off Sangamo Road
Pickens, South Carolina
29671

BUCILLA
Sales Service Dept.
150 Meadowlands Pkwy.
Secaucus, New Jersey
07094

CARON INTERNATIONAL
Handknitting yarns and crafts
Box 300
Rochelle, Illinois
61068

CASCADE TEXTILE CORP.
325 East Grand Avenue
South San Francisco, California
94080

CHAT BOTTÉ YARNS
Armen Corporation
1400 Brevard Road
Asheville, North Carolina
28806

COATS & CLARK INC.
Attn: CEAD
72 Cummings Point Road
Stamford, Connecticut
06904

COLUMBIA MINERVA YARNS
Handknitting yarns and crafts
Box 300
Rochelle, Illinois
61068

**CONSHOHOKEN
COTTON COMPANY**
Ford Bridge Road
Conshohoken, Pennsylvania
19428

DAWN
Talon American
PO Box 3823
Stamford, Connecticut
06905

DOROTHEE BIS YARNS
Knitting Fever Inc.
180 Babylon Turnpike
Roosevelt, New York
11575

EMU
Merino Wool Company
230 Fifth Avenue
New York, New York
10001

FANTACIA, INC.
415 East Beach Avenue
Inglewood, California
90302

JOSEPH GALLER, INC.
27 West 20th St.
New York, New York
10010

GEORGES PICAUD
Merino Wool Company
230 Fifth Avenue
New York, New York
10001

JAEGER
Susan Bates Inc.
212 Middlesex Avenue
Chester, Connecticut
06412

LANE BORGOSESIA YARNS
128 Radio Circle
Mt. Kisco, New York
10549

LILY CRAFT PRODUCTS
B. Blumenthal & Co. Inc.
Carlstadt, New Jersey
07072

**LION BRAND
YARN COMPANY**
1270 Broadway
New York, New York
10001

**MELROSE
YARN COMPANY, INC.**
1305 Utica Avenue
Brooklyn, New York
11203

MERINO WOOL COMPANY
230 Fifth Avenue
New York, New York
10001

NEVADA YARN COMPANY, INC.
230 Fifth Avenue
New York, New York
10001
Attn: Consumer Inquiries –
Dept. ASB

NOMIS YARN COMPANY
146 Tosca Drive
Stoughton, Massachusetts
02072

PATONS
Susan Bates Inc.
212 Middlesex Avenue
Chester, Connecticut
06412

PHILDAR KNITTING YARNS
6438 Dawson Blvd.
Norcross, Georgia
30093

PINGOUIN CORPORATION
PO Box 100
Jamestown, South Carolina
29453

PLYMOUTH YARN COMPANY
PO Box 28
Bristol, Pennsylvania
19007

REYNOLDS YARNS, INC.
Box 1776
Hauppauge, New York
11788

SCHEEPJES
Ulltex Yarns Inc.
21 Adley Road
Cambridge, Massachusetts
02138

STUDIO YARN FARMS, INC.
Dept. L
PO Box 46017
Seattle, Washington
98146

3 SUISSES
Bucilla
Sales Service Dept.
150 Meadowlands Pkwy.
Secaucus, New Jersey
07094

TAHKI YARNS
92 Kennedy St.
Hackensack, New Jersey
07601

TALON AMERICAN
PO Box 3823
Stamford, Connecticut
06905

ULTEX YARNS, INC.
21 Adley Road
Cambridge, Massachusetts
02138

WELCOMME PERNELLE
Mark Distributors Inc.
20825 Prairie St.
Chatsworth, California
91311

The following foreign yarn companies supplied
samples for the yarn glossaries.

BELDING LILY COMPANY
Shelby, North Carolina
28150

EMILE BERNAT YARN AND CRAFT CORP.
Depot & Mendon Sts.
Uxbridge, Massachusetts
01569

BUCILLA YARNS
Armour Handcrafts
150 Meadowlands Pkwy.
Secaucus, New Jersey
07094

FILATURES JEAN ET PAUL PLASSARD
Varennes-Sous-Dun
F. 71800 La Clayette
France

available from

Joseph Galler Inc.
149 Fifth Avenue
New York, New York
10010

UNGER YARNS
230 Fifth Avenue
New York, New York
10001

Maggie White has branched out from machine knitting to the creation of handknits from her design workshop in Oxford.

Betty Barnden hopes to revive an interest in making three-dimensional shapes with knitting, both as garments and as furnishings.

Joan Chatterley works with oddments of many types of yarn to create her multi-colored and textured designs.

Sara Kotch specializes in knitting-in-the-round designs which enable her to achieve very structured sweater shapes.

Zoë Hunt finds inspiration for her knitting in things that are very rich in color and "feel" such as oriental carpets, patchwork quilts and Arabian dresses.

Acknowledgments

The Sweater Book was designed by *Denise Brown* with the assistance of *Derek Coombes* and *Stephanie Todd* and art directed by *Debbie MacKinnon*

Photography
Ian O'Leary

Illustrators
David Ashby
David Baird
Russell Barnet
Kuo Kang Chen
Lucy Su

Typesetting Chambers Wallace

Reproduction F. E. Burman Ltd.

Dorling Kindersley would like to thank:
Melanie Miller for assisting with the editorial work; Jean Litchfield for her careful checking of the patterns; Sue Conn of French Wools Ltd., Rebecca Elliott of Laines Couture, Eleanor Bernat of Bernat Yarns, Seymour Simon of Bucilla and Miriam Greenfield of Unger Yarns for their help with yarn information; The Button Box, Covent Garden, for lending us a selection of buttons; Geoff Dann for additional photography; and all the designers for their assistance and enthusiasm.